Fred – The

The Alderman of BBC Radio's *Test Match Special*, Don Mosey is a former BBC Cricket Correspondent and has been a personal friend of Freddie Trueman for more than thirty years. He has written about Trueman as a newspaper correspondent, talked about him as a broadcaster, and the two of them have collaborated on four books about cricket and their native Yorkshire. It was Mosey who introduced Trueman to radio broadcasting when he retired as a Yorkshire player in 1968, and both of them became members of the *TMS* team on Radio 3 in 1974.

Fred
Then and Now

Don Mosey

Mandarin

A Mandarin Paperback
FRED - THEN AND NOW

First published in Great Britain 1991
by The Kingswood Press
This edition published 1992
by Mandarin Paperbacks
Michelin House, 81 Fulham Road, London SW3 6RB

Mandarin is an imprint of the Octopus Publishing Group,
a division of Reed International Books Limited

Copyright © Don Mosey 1991
The author has asserted his moral rights

A CIP catalogue record for this title
is available from the British Library
ISBN 0 7493 0900 8

Printed and bound in Great Britain by
BPCC Hazell Books
Aylesbury, Bucks, England
Member of BPCC Ltd.

Contents

Contents

Illustrations

The photographs in this book are reproduced by kind permission of the following: *Lincolnshire Echo*: la; The Hulton-Deutsch Collection: 1b, 3b, 4a, 4b, 5a, 6b; S & G Press Agency: 2a, 2b, 3a; Patrick Eagar: 6a; Veronica Trueman: 6c, 7a, 7b, 8b; Solo Syndication: 8a.

Author's Note

Let me at once declare an interest: I regard Freddie Trueman as the greatest fast bowler England has ever produced. There are a number of ways of substantiating the claim both in words and in figures, and they will be detailed in the following pages, but at this stage I content myself with a general observation: for twenty seasons he bowled faster, and with more sustained hostility and success, than anyone else in the world. *Twenty seasons* – seasons in which there were no three-day or sometimes week-long 'rests' in the first-class fixture list, but between 28 and 32 county championship games with others against the universities, touring sides, MCC and champion counties.

On top of these matches came the Tests, not as many as Fred might have played in, but 67 of them nevertheless, and they brought him 307 wickets at 21.57 along with 981 runs and 64 catches. In his first-class career he bowled a total of 16,470 overs, which means that he sprinted more than 2 million yards (or well over 1,200 miles) – and that does not include the more leisurely walk back to his bowling mark, which effectively doubles those figures of distance travelled. And yet in those twenty seasons the number of matches Fred missed through injury was absolutely minimal. It amounts to an astonishing testimony of strength and physical fitness.

Over and above his playing achievements he was the most colourful and best-known personality in the game, and in many ways he has remained so in the twenty-two years since retirement. He was the player everyone knew, the man spectators came particularly to see, and rarely if ever did he disappoint any of them. Since then, as newspaper critic, radio broad-caster, television personality and professional entertainer he has remained just as consistently in the public eye. At the age of fifty-eight he was subjected to the muck-raking scrutiny of one of Britain's seedier tabloid newspapers in much the same way as modern players, thirty years his junior, have suffered. Very few fifty-eight-year-olds have been accorded three whole pages of attention by a mass-circulation rag; it only happens to the truly famous.

This is in no way an attempt to whitewash a character who has often been tempestuous and frequently controversial. Fiery Fred would not have been the bowler (or personality) he was and is without an aggressive and competitive temperament. He has offended and alienated many people in his time. He made powerful enemies on the way to the top with the result that an honour, the OBE, was delayed for twenty-five years after his then unique achievement of more than 300 Test wickets and for twenty-one years after his retirement. Even then it came only after vigorous and prolonged lobbying by his admirers.

Fred does not claim to be a perfect human being but he does feel that he has often been more sinned-against than sinning. After more than thirty years of close friendship I am as aware of his faults as most people but do not (I hope) allow it to cloud a judgment of the man's greatness. I have considered his shortcomings as conscientiously as I have admired his achievements – and he may not thank me for that – but this book has been written entirely without Fred's knowledge. Thus he has exercised no influence whatsoever over its contents. It is by no means slavishly uncritical. I have even seen Fred bowl badly (and that he will *not* like!). But in the course of watching a fair percentage of his 2,304 wickets taken I have shared with so many others the tingle of excitement when he took the new ball; marked out that smooth, accelerating run; dashed the flopping shock of black hair from his eyes; cast one final, menacing glance at the batsman and started to move in. In those moments it was possible to feel the air of expectancy amongst the crowd, the apprehension in the batsman, the tension of the close catchers. Few have generated such an atmosphere; few have made such an impact upon the game. And even fewer have remained at such a high point of public recognition more than twenty years later. Fred, his deeds and his sayings, is still the subject of something like 50 or 60 per cent of the folklore of the game.

D.M.

The Player

I

The Beginning

The house where Fred Trueman was born has long since been reduced to a heap of bricks and rubble and buried under colliery waste on the edge of the South Yorkshire coalfield. The house where he now lives is a delightful detached bungalow in one of the loveliest (but quietest) corners of the Dales in the north-west of the county. The boy who walked down the lane near his first home to note the registration numbers of passing cars on the main road has had two Rolls Royce saloons of his own and is contemplating his third.

From the age of twelve until he was into his twenties Fred lived in the mining town of Maltby, deep in the heart of Arthur Scargill (whom he loathes) country. For the past twenty years he has looked out over a superb walled garden, rich in bird-life, resplendent with flowering shrubs -- and even a wishing well! - to the pine and bracken of Pennine hills where hawks swirl and dive. On long summer evenings he may be found sitting on his patio with a glass of wine, or occasionally Scotch, always with one of his prized selection of pipes and a couple of dogs frolicking on the lawn. These are the moments when F. S. Trueman, one of cricket's most prominent stormy petrels, is relatively at peace with a troubled world.

Life has been good to Fred, though it has not always been kind, and nothing he has achieved has come to him without an enormous amount of sweat and toil. His playing days were marked by storm and tempest, fire and fury, argument and controversy; the twenty-two years since he retired from the first-class game have not been noticeably more tranquil. Whether embroiled in the furore of Yorkshire cricket politics or splashed across the front pages of newspapers for other reasons, Fred has always been, and remains to this day, very definitely NEWS. Fame and notoriety, hand in hand, have brought material comfort together with much spiritual torment. Only on rare and transient occasions have his friends been able to look at Fred and feel, 'There is a completely happy man.' He has courted dispute as often as it has descended, unbidden, upon him by an attitude to life and to people as uncompromising as his fast bowling was over those twenty seasons of incandescent competitiveness. Paradoxically, it all began in a snowstorm.

The night of 6 February 1931 was inclement enough to prevent the doctor from fighting his way through to No.5 Scotch Springs, a terrace of twelve colliery-owned houses near the village of Stainton, where Alan Trueman and his wife were expecting their fourth child. Fred thus arrived in the world via the experienced hands of his maternal grandmother and was given her maiden name, Sewards, as his second forename. He weighed in at a massive 14 lbs 1 oz.

Popular legend dubs him 'a miner', or 'from a mining family,' which is not strictly accurate. Derbyshire, and to some extent Nottinghamshire, may have found it helpful from time to time to whistle down the nearest colliery shaft when in need of a fast bowler, but the industry has never been liberal in its gifts to Yorkshire County Cricket Club. Fred's grandfather was, in fact, a horse-trader and dealer, while his father spent much of his life in the employ of local landowners – first Earl Fitzwilliam, at Wentworth Woodhouse, then Captain Adcock, of Stainley Woodhouse – as a stud groom and steeplechase jockey. As a boy, FST spent much time, along with his elder brother Arthur, on Captain Adcock's estate and thus developed a love of animals and the countryside at an early age.

It was the severe economic recession of the 1920s and 1930s which forced his father off the land and into the mines, and while Alan Trueman retained a life-long respect for the men who undertook dangerous and dirty work far under the countryside he, too, loved he had no personal affection for the job. On his sixty-fifth birthday he finished his final shift at two p.m. (having started at six), walked home, took off his pit-clothes and burned them in the backyard, at the same time resolving that none of his sons would follow that occupation. It saddened him deeply when Arthur refused to follow the parental dictum; when Fred's turn came to work in mining it was for a reason his father had to accept – a means to a much more glorious end.

The boy's childhood was typical of life in West Riding working-class circles of the 1930s: regular visits to Sunday School and church; respect for parents; contributing to the family income with seasonal pea-picking and potato-lifting; eating the food that was provided for him, or eating it at the *next* meal if he left anything on his plate. In return, his parents gave him love and care and concern and guidance; he always had enough to eat, plain fare but wholesome and nourishing, clothing which was practical and warm and a best suit for Sundays. He would not have dreamed of 'being cheeky' or 'answering back' to his elders, which would have earned him an immediate clip round the ear.

I have often reflected that one of the reasons Fred and I have got along so well for so long was that his boyhood was in so many ways a mirror-reflection of my own. We understand each other. We think of our youngest days with warmth and affection and gratitude, not with bitterness or resentment or envy of others.

The two major influences on Freddie Trueman in his earliest days were first of all his father Alan, more usually known to his friends as 'Dick' Trueman, and his elder brother Arthur. With the one it was a matter of love and respect for father's kindly but firm concept of morality and discipline; with the other it was hero-worship for big brother. Their sister Florence remembers that wherever Arthur went, there the lively, and occasionally mischievous, Freddie was sure to be; together they sang in the church choir; together they went with 'Dick' (before he had gone into the mines) to Stainton Grange, and while father exercised the horses the two boys did little jobs about the yard. 'Dick' kept chickens and it was the boys' job to do the plucking when one was killed for an occasional 'treat'. Together the boys went to watch father play cricket on Saturdays, and it never occurred to young Freddie that he might occasionally have been a bit of a nuisance to his elder brother as the years went by and Arthur developed more mature interests . . . like GIRLS.

One revelation we have from Florence is that the young FS did not like water and it often took a not-too-serious cuff on the ear from father to persuade him it was time to have a wash! On the other hand he was in trouble after an unscheduled bath on one occasion. A rope attached to a branch of a tree in the woods near Roche Abbey provided an opportunity for the boys to play Tarzan (as most of us did after the Johnny Weissmuller series of films began in

1932) and the rope broke under the weight of Tarzan Trueman, pitching him into a stream. As he was wearing his Sunday best at the time there was a rather more serious clip round the ear when he got home. New suits were not too regularly available in the industrial West Riding of the 1930s.

The first recorded instance we have of Fred being wrongfully accused of a crime came in these earliest days. He was charged with cutting a neighbour's clotheslines. In vain he protested his innocence, but his reputation as a lively sort of lad damned him and he was actually fined. After a rigorous cross-examination by his father, however, his denial of guilt was accepted and there was no supplementary punishment. Freddie's earliest reading came from the pages of the *Dandy* or *Beano* comic papers; later it was to become *Wisden*, and I very much doubt if there is a record in the Cricketer's Almanack of which FST is unaware.

As for the development of his cricket, he went to watch his father play in the first place . . . but like all boys of his age in the Broad Acres he joined in the impromptu games which were organised throughout the summer, in the school playground or on any open piece of ground. The stumps were chalked on the wall of the school or improvised by the placing of a jacket on the ground. Whether a batsman was out or not was a matter of negotiation, and it was usually the majority vote which decreed whether the ball had bounced over the jacket at an acceptable height. It was in a spirit of sheer competitiveness that the Trueman interest now began to develop. It was a game between two sides; he wanted to be on the one which won.

His sister Florence remembers:

> We all played cricket, boys *and* girls, with the wickets chalked on a wall. If Freddie was playing we were always out quickly because he bowled as fast at us as he did at anyone. That meant as fast as he could. We never got a chance to bat properly and it made us cry. Then we would go for Dad to have a word with Freddie but it didn't do any good. He was stubborn. He argued that if the girls wanted to play they had to accept the same conditions as anyone else. No concessions. Oh, he always wanted to win. If he didn't he'd go away and try to work out where he had gone wrong.

The village school at Stainton consisted of one room divided by a partition: seniors on one side under the care of Miss Nelson, juniors on the other with Miss Robinson. The school team took a beating one day and an eight-year-old FST preened himself on the junior side of the screen as he overheard Miss Nelson tell his peers that they ought to go and watch Freddie Trueman play if they wanted to learn what determination was about. His maxim from the very first was quite simply to bowl as fast as he could and, somewhat to the surprise of his father (a left-arm spinner) and brother Arthur (an opening batsman), the young Freddie was able to generate a remarkable degree of pace, although his physical development had belied his 14-lb arrival in the world. He was now something of a lightweight but, incredibly it seemed, he could bowl fast.

When he was twelve the family moved to a bigger house in Tennyson Road, Maltby, and it was at the secondary-modern school that Fred took the first steps along the road to glory. The school cricket team was run by two enthusiasts, Dickie Harrison and Tommy Stubbs, who were the very stuff that Yorkshire cricket used to be made of. In every corner of the county fifty or sixty years ago (and it continued some time after the war before, sadly, virtually disappearing) there were schoolteachers with one burning desire – to find a boy good enough to recommend as a recruit for the county schoolboy nets. Messrs Harrison and Stubbs spotted the combative potential of young Trueman's fast bowling and included him at once in the school team. Now Fred could not only begin to learn what real cricket was all about; he could also supplement his pocket money, because Dickie Harrison imaginatively organised practice by placing a penny on the off-stump, a florin (10p) on the middle one. Any coin the bowlers dislodged with the teacher batting, they kept. Fred 'made a bob or two' in his first few weeks at Maltby Secondary Modern; this was cricket practice very much to his liking.

It was not until the 1960s and 1970s, when the seemingly endless pipeline of talent from the schools dried up, that the county club at last realised what a debt they owed to teachers like Dickie Harrison and Tommy Stubbs. There were still isolated pockets of enthusiasm, but nothing like the breadth and depth of interest shown by teachers in finding a budding Yorkshire player. School cricket meant devoting a great deal of personal leisure time to the boys, and fewer and fewer members of staff were willing to do it. Then came a phenomenon that was new to Yorkshire. Early in 1990 I heard of a thirteen-year-old of great promise in an area which rarely, if ever, produced a county player, or even a prospect. I addressed an inquiry to Headingley: 'Had the coaches heard of this boy and if so why had his father not been informed of their interest? The lad was in danger of being poached by another county.' Back came the reply: 'We don't know anything about him. There's nothing on the files.' My further inquiries revealed that the boy attended a school where the headmaster was one of those crackpots who believed competitive sport is not in the best interests of a developing youngster! Mercifully, that sort of chap was not around in F. S. Trueman's schooldays.

When Fred was still only twelve, however, disaster struck. Batting in a match against a Rotherham school, he was hit in the groin by an opposing fast bowler and very badly injured indeed. In fact, for a time the procreation of any future Truemans seemed unlikely. It is still possible to sense the feeling of terror in the family as Florence recalls the time when young Freddie was brought home after the accident: 'He was a healthy boy and didn't have many illnesses until he was brought back from that game. It kept him off school for twelve months and he had to have lessons at home. It was only the care of Dr Holdsworth which saved his leg and prevented him from being a cripple for life.'

Abdominal protection in those days and at that level of cricket was largely unheard of. Even in the higher echelons of league clubs no one possessed a personal 'box', and those who insisted on wearing one – usually the married men! – had to hope that the single communal guard was not already in use when their turn came to bat. No one had his own bat in junior league cricket, much less his own pads or gloves, and I have even heard scorn poured upon a dressing-room colleague who modestly turned his back on the rest of the team to strap on an antique contraption of webbing and buckles which invariably would start to slip after a couple of runs had been taken. So it was not to be expected that a school team would be generously equipped with protective gear. Fred paid a heavy price. He was out of cricket for nearly two years, and at the very age when most boys are making that difficult decison – whether to devote a major part of their energy and drive to sport, or to academic studies.

It is a sobering thought to those of us who derived so much pleasure and excitement from Fred's career that those couple of seasons spent mostly in reflection might have killed his interest in the game altogether or, perhaps even worse, chastened his need to bowl faster, and with more deadly intent, than anyone else. Many teenagers would not have given the game a second chance; others would at least have approached it with a certain diffidence. Not so with Fred. It gradually becomes pretty clear that F. S. Trueman was born to be a cricketer, even if it took him a long time to realise it. Following a logical course in the development of his personality, it becomes even clearer that he was born to be a fast bowler.

At fourteen he returned to the fray and to his disgust and chagrin was turned down by his father's club on the grounds that they were well enough equipped with bowlers of his type! So he turned to Roche Abbey, a smaller club taking its name from a ruined ecclesiastical foundation under the shadow of Maltby Crags. He prospered, with a certain amount of help from the topography of Roche Abbey's ground and the advice of the wicket-keeper, John Skelding: 'If tha can pitch it outside t'off stick it'll come back down t'ill.'

In the first four matches of 1947 FST took twenty-five wickets for 37 runs. The club played only friendly matches but the day arrived when the opposition was provided by men from a more exalted sphere of the game. They bowled out the Abbey for 42 (Arthur Trueman 20) and seven of their players changed out of their whites in preparation for an early return to Sheffield. Father Trueman, a spectator, cautioned them, 'You're not laikin' on a Sheffield League pitch today and there's a lad here who might surprise you.' The visitors were not impressed, at least not until the sixteen-year-old took six for 1 and they lost by 31 runs.

Now it is possible – unlikely, but just possible – that Freddie Trueman might have been destined to spend all his cricketing days in that remote quarter but for the fact that the visiting skipper, who had known better days, was acquainted with Cyril Turner, an all-rounder in Brian Sellers' pre-war Yorkshire side and at that time professional with Sheffield United (the cricket side which played at Bramall Lane, not the football team). A couple of weeks later Turner went to watch Fred playing at Herringthorpe Valley, just outside Rotherham, and the following Tuesday night Sheffield

United's membership list (closed, with a full complement of players) was specially re-opened to admit the sixteen-year-old fast bowling prospect from Roche Abbey. Within a fortnight he had taken six for 11 as a Second Eleven player and four days after that he was put on show before an audience of Norman Yardley, then the Yorkshire and England captain: Arthur Mitchell, the senior county coach; Ron Aspinall, who opened Yorkshire's bowling; and the man who had commended him, Cyril Turner. The captain whose club side had been 'lad-licked' (as Father Trueman put it) had been generous in defeat.

His father was not sure that a sudden translation to higher things was the best way of developing Fred's bowling. He protested to Cyril Turner: 'T'lad's too young. I'll not have him rushed.' But Cyril, a kindly and genial soul, was also a persuasive man and he had his way. Now, if this was a story in a boy's magazine, the way to the top would have been clear and it would have taken FST a matter of months to reach it. Anything more hard-headed or less romantically inclined than Yorkshire County Cricket Club in the immediate post-war years, however, would be difficult to visualise. No one, but no one, had ever streaked through the ranks of their professional cricket to instant stardom. Excitement at a potentially great talent might occasionally be expressed in such extravagant terms as, 'Aye, 'e's not so bad,' but no more than that. Privately, more advanced approval could be harboured but never openly expressed. Yorkshiremen find it infinitely easier to damn than to praise. When one of his close-catching colleagues in the 1930s brought off a brilliant catch which required a dive, hand fully outstretched, and a somersaulting landing, the taciturn Arthur Mitchell growled, 'Get up and stop makin' an exhibition o' thissen.' And he meant it. This was now the man who presided over county coaching, and no one ever heard 'Ticker' express anything other than the most modified rapture.

So there was destined to be no meteoric rise to stardom for the young man from Stainton, via Maltby. Even if he made it – and despite the gathering of such a distinguished band of cricketers to see him in the nets there was no immediate acclamation – he would have to go through the mill in the same way as all other Yorkshire hopefuls, whether they were batsmen or bowlers fast or slow. If he had known just how much hard work faced him in the future, would he still have taken the same course? Given the glory that was to be his and the relative affluence it was, in due course, to bring, the answer has to be 'Yes'. Fred's work-rate today is the clearest possible indication that graft and toil have never for one moment deterred him. Throughout his playing career and in the twenty-two years since it ended Fred Trueman has worked harder than any man I have ever known.

But this was 1947 and thoughts of actually making a living by playing cricket were far from Fred's mind. He knew he did not want to go into mining when he left school, and in this he had parental support, but a job of some sort had to be found, nevertheless. He had never seen a county match, let alone a Test; like most of us he read of the game's heroes in newspapers or heard of them, briefly, on the radio. Television had not reached the north of England. Our cricketing idols were remote images, men we would never meet. Fred was not a natural idolator and he did not see himself standing in line at Bramall Lane to collect autographs. He was content to pit his strength and skill as a bowler against anyone who appeared as an opponent and the contest, no matter at what level, excited him. But it was a hobby, a pastime to be undertaken at weekends when he had taken home his pay packet. Ever a pragmatist where money was concerned, Fred's thoughts turned to bricklaying as a career. Much of Sheffield and the surrounding area had been laid flat by German bombs and there was much rebuilding still to be done. Thousands of servicemen had returned to marry, have families and seek homes. New schools and hospitals had to be built. Millions of bricks needed to be laid. Ergo: bricklaying was a job which offered definite prospects of relative prosperity. First, however, Fred worked for a newsagent, delivering papers morning and evening, collecting payment at the weekend and looking forward to Christmas, when the newspaper boy was second only to the dustman when householders handed out their annual tips.

Then came the chance he had been waiting for – a bricklaying job. But it was short-lived. For the good and sufficient reason that he felt he was being overworked and put-upon, Fred told his foreman to 'bugger off' in one of his first recorded brushes with Authority, and was sacked. Next came a job in a wireworks, followed by another producing glass bottles, both providing a regular wage but proving monotonous and boring. It is scarcely surprising therefore that cricket began to have an enhanced appeal. It was something to look forward to all through the week. And his appetite was further whetted by his now regular attendance at the nets at Bramall Lane. It all provided an escape route from the dreariness of five-and-a-half days of labour to a world where he was beginning to be a little more sure of himself. On the cricket field there was no bullying foreman to chivvy him; only men with bats in their hands trying to withstand the impact of his natural talent plus the refinements which Cyril Turner's coaching was now adding. There was still a certain astonishment that the boy could generate such a pace because he weighed something under ten stones and was little over 5 ft 4 ins tall; he had not yet developed the shoulders, chest, hips and thighs of massive strength which future generations of spectators were to see. His remarkable pace came from a completely natural co-ordination of his approach and delivery; this was raw, God-given talent to which Cyril Turner sought to add control. The outswinger was, glory be, something which came naturally but at that age, in the cricket in which he had so far played, Fred neither understood it nor harnessed it. He was all about sheer pace. Cyril's task was to embellish it with subtlety, with variation, with direction. A whole new world began to open up for the boy. Nevertheless, he was not prepared for what came next.

In the summer of 1948 Yorkshire were in the process of drawing up their Federation party – effectively the county's third team – to play against other county fledgelings, largely from the southern end of the country. Cyril Turner had mentioned the name of Trueman at Headingley but felt that Fred was not yet ready for more advanced competition and urged the Committee to wait another year until he had time to polish up the youngster's performances. Yorkshire insisted on 'having a look' at the boy, who bowled just eleven deliveries in the nets at Headingley. Three of them hit the stumps and one of his victims was Brian Close, a boy of almost exactly the same age who was regarded as the hottest property in Bradford League cricket. The short spell was watched with more than passing interest by George Hirst, one of the county's immortals who had scored over 32,000 runs and taken more than 2,500 wickets for Yorkshire in an illustrious career spanning the first twenty years of the century. He was now very much a father figure, an ideal personality for helping and encouraging young players. Hirst took Alan Trueman on one side, leaving young Fred to wonder what he had done wrong to be 'spelled' after less than a couple of overs of bowling. He was not asked to do any more and father and son went home on a bus in thoughtful silence until, as they approached Doncaster, Alan, with unexpected vehemence, told his son, 'It's going to cost me six pounds but I don't care. You are going.'

'Going where?' asked the mystified Fred.

'On the Federation tour, that's where. They've picked you and you're going, whatever it costs.'

Now, it is pretty certain that until his visit to Headingley – his first glimpse of a regular Test ground – Fred had never heard of George Herbert Hirst. He had not at that time developed his interest in the history of the game, or its past heroes, or its records. Later he came to revere the Grand Old Man of Yorkshire cricket and to admire the benign and gentle way in which he helped to 'bring on' young players. Fred didn't know anything about Federation cricket, either, and apart from summer holidays with the family in Cleethorpes he had never been far away from Maltby. He knew Close and Illingworth, purely by sight of them at Headingley, and the rest of the party were strangers, many with a background of greater (if only in relative terms) affluence, almost all of them with the advantage of better formal education. And it was in this company that the young Trueman spent his first night away from home without his family in a dormitory at Harrow School!

It cannot be said that in the best traditions of schoolboy fiction young Trueman flattened all oppostion on that tour and returned as his county's hero. He did take four wickets in one match and on a rest day he went with the party to Eastbourne to see Sussex play Somerset – his first sight of county cricket. He saw Harold Gimblett make 310, and by this time he knew that cricket was not merely something to anticipate at weekends. It could be a way of life, one he was now determined to pursue. There is a strong streak of sentimentality in Fred which he has managed effectively to disguise through most of his life, but he has confessed to finding a lump in his throat when the Federation team coach dropped him at Maltby at the end of the tour. He had had one small peek at how different life could be for him and he now found himself wondering if this was all that would be vouchsafed to him. It is perhaps difficult for those whose acquaintance with Fred has been casual and unperceptive to think of him tormented by insecurity and doubts, but then there has always been more to the man than superficial observation has revealed.

He was promoted to Sheffield United's First Eleven for the last five matches of the season in the Yorkshire League, playing on grounds which accommodated the county's first or second teams and on pitches which gave considerably less help to the bowler than those he was generally accustomed to. He took fifteen wickets and was rewarded with a summons to the Yorkshire indoor nets during the winter.

It is interesting to note that at this stage Fred recalls himself as having 'the perfect physique for a fast bowler – strong, thick legs, big shoulders and hips'. His memory has, on occasions, been known to be fallible and Fred's mental picture of himself at seventeen contrasts quite strongly with Ray Illingworth's ('a thin, pasty-faced, narrow-chested waif with hair falling over his right eye and ear'), while Illingworth's is supported by that of Brian Close. Now, in the winter shed, Fred was tutored by Bill Bowes and Arthur Mitchell, both of whom were later to recall that the youngster from Maltby at that time of his life did in fact present an unlikely fast bowling figure.

He was still not regarded as much more than an 'interesting' prospect though the natural talent was undeniable. No one at Yorkshire's headquarters was given to extremes of emotional enthusiasm. No one said: 'This is our hope for the future.' The problem was that no one in the county had seen anything like Frederick Sewards Trueman. He was the first of his kind.

2

The Demons

When Freddie Trueman was called up by Yorkshire to play against Cambridge University in May 1949 there could have been no thought in the minds of the County Committee that they were 'blooding' a potentially record-breaking England fast bowler. Men of genuine pace played little or no part in the forward planning of Yorkshire CCC: there was no precedent for it. In the eighty-six years of the club's history there had been no bowler who could be described as 'fast' until the arrival of Bill Bowes in 1929. In modern terms, Bill would have been a medium-pacer but in the decade before the Second World War, when he took 100 wickets in a season nine times, he was as quick as almost anybody around; more importantly, he could move the ball in the air and off the seam and he got bounce. He was as renowned for trapping the fingers of the bottom hand against the bat-handle as for anything else in his repertoire. Bowes and the up-and-coming Ken Farnes, who sadly lost his life during the war, were England's only real answer to Australian fast bowling in the 1938 series (Larwood and Voce having gone over the hill) because it was Australia who invariably posed the threat in that department. From the earliest days of Test cricket, Spofforth had been the legendary 'Demon'; in 1921, Gregory and McDonald proved the outstanding bowling partnership in the history, at that time, of international cricket; in 1930 and 1934 it was Thomas Welbourn Wall who appealed to the imagination of English schoolboys, who saw nothing like him (Larwood apart) in domestic cricket; and I remember vividly the apprehension with which we awaited the arrival, in 1938, of the latest Antipodean demon, Ernie McCormick.

True, in the immediate post-war years England seemed to be developing her own pace bowlers at last but the most potent, in Test wicket-taking terms, was Alec Bedser, and his success owed more to the application of aerodynamic principles than to naked aggression. Sheer pace was still regarded as a relatively crude way of taking wickets, and nowhere more so than in Yorkshire where the great dynastic line of slow left-arm bowlers had been the main agency of attack since 1863. To take the shine off the ball in 1949, and perhaps to take a wicket or two in the early stages (or more if conditions were right), the county had Alec Coxon and Ron Aspinall.

Waiting in the wings in case of injury to the front-line bowlers, or to give them a rest, were the bespectacled schoolteacher, Bill Foord, and the blond University student, Johnny Whitehead, but both these were generally regarded as journeymen rather than match-winners, at least by the Committee. So that when FST joined the county party at Doncaster, for the trip down the A1 to play in Cambridge on 10 May 1949, he was regarded as the least significant, in the long-term, of the three 'prospects' who were to be given their first taste of top-class cricket at Fenners. The other two were Frank Lowson, the batsman regarded as the most likely to succeed Harry Halliday as Len Hutton's partner, and Brian Close, the prodigiously multi-talented youngster (eighteen days younger than Fred) whose exploits in, first, the Airedale and Wharfedale League, then the Bradford League, had been noted at county headquarters, conveniently less than ten miles away.

Fred's extra pace and his obvious determination to knock stumps down had made him difficult to ignore, certainly in South Yorkshire cricket, but it had taken a lot of talking by his mentor, Cyril Turner, to excite the interest of the men who ruled Yorkshire cricket with a certain oligarchical detachment. Weaponry such as Fred possessed was regarded in much the same way as the flower of French chivalry felt about English bowmen after Crécy. It was going to be hard for him to impress.

For a time – quite a long time – he did not help his own cause. It was customary for young professionals newly admitted through the portals of the Yorkshire dressing-room to keep a low profile. Two years later Ray Illingworth was to be told, with marvellously-offensive Yorkshire brusqueness, to 'keep his mouth shut until he was spoken to for at least a year in that dressing-room'. Fred could never be expected to do that because it was simply not in his nature. He was nervous and insecure in the presence of men of Hutton's stature, and his way of overcoming this was to manifest a strident and extrovert personality. It is a characteristic which has remained with him all his life. If he feels intellectually or socially intimidated he screens it by coming out fighting, often with intemperate and ill-judged punches. There have been many, over the years, who have not understood this or, if they have, have felt unable to make allowances for it. So his was scarcely an unobtrusive entry into first-class cricket.

It was unlikely, therefore, that many members of the Yorkshire Committee in 1949 expected to see much more of the teenager from Stainton. Even the coaches at Headingley. Arthur Mitchell and Bill Bowes, in their little-more-than-fleeting glimpses of him had felt his main requirement was to cut down on speed and concentrate on accuracy to achieve maximum value from his natural outswinger. Such was the lack of general interest in Trueman that *Wisden* recorded his entry into the first-class ranks as a left-arm spin bowler! Just how this mistake occurred is not clear, but it is possible that the author of the piece had seen Fred turning his arm over in that style in practice as he occasionally did – just to show he could do it. Bowling flat out, right arm, in non-competitive circumstances never seemed a profitable exercise to FST.

With his so-far brief career having taken shape primarily on league pitches Fred was totally unprepared for the perfection of the Fenners wicket. Not surprisingly, he lost his rhythm and with it his length and direction in trying vainly to extract some response from the turf, and his first figures for Yorkshire were three wickets for 94. Another aspect of his career, however, took off during the match: the instant epigram. Fielding at mid-on, the position Bill Bowes had occupied with time-honoured absence of athletic skill, he put down a catch which arrived earlier than anticipated and when his captain looked at him quizzically for the expected humility he was informed, emphatically that, 'That bugger is laikin' wi a steel bat.' And such was Fred's rough-and-readiness that the story also came back that during dinner at the University Arms he had ordered one course on the menu (pretentiously printed in French) by pointing to the date! It is probably no more than half-true and Fred, now the world traveller who has dined with potentates and princes, does not like to be reminded of such occasions. It is a needless sensitivity but his friends have difficulty in convincing him of this.

Against Oxford University Fred fared better as a bowler, taking four for 31, and in the two Varsity matches he had bowled both Hubert Doggart (later to skipper Sussex and play twice for England, apart from becoming President of MCC) and Clive van Rynefeld, who subsequently captained South Africa. The names meant nothing to Fred; the sight of their stumps sent sprawling did. He was bitterly disappointed that when Yorkshire turned their attention to the county championship there was no place for him, though there was for Close and Lowson.

He still did not figure importantly in the county's long-term plans, and with Coxon and Aspinall available this was natural enough, no matter how Fred chafed impatiently at the delayed, full-scale launching of what he clearly foresaw as a dazzling career. Yardley, the captain, was a useful purveyor of medium-paced swing bowling and Close could bowl briskly, *and* swing the ball, as well as being an off-spinner. There was no place for Fred – yet. Less than a month later, Fate took a hand. Aspinall, tall as durable fast bowlers go and well-built, ruptured an Achilles tendon after taking thirty wickets in three games and setting himself up for a Test trial. It was cruel luck for a big-hearted and likable cricketer and to all intents and purposes it ruined his career. He was forced to retire the following year and, though he played league cricket, and Minor Counties with Durham, he was never again the bowler he had looked in the late forties. In 1960 he became a first-class umpire and spent something like twenty years on the list.

His injury at the end of May 1949 left a vacancy for an opening bowler, and young Trueman awaited the call. Instead, the Committee turned to Frank McHugh, another big man in the Aspinall style, and this caused a few raised eyebrows because his swing was from off- to on-side, whereas Yorkshire traditionally looked to the man who could move the ball away from the right-handed bat, either at pace or with spin. McHugh was given a three-month run without making any noticeable impression and did not appear in Yorkshire's colours again, though he did have a new career with Gloucestershire from 1952.

Another chance presented itself for Fred who, against Minor Counties at Lord's put in a brilliant second-innings spell and Yardley, sensing that here at last was something rather different in a Yorkshire bowler, kept him going throughout the innings, with a break for luncheon, to take eight wickets for 70.

It was a game which has lingered in Fred's mind because it was, of course, his first visit to the world headquarters of cricket. All his life he has nursed a love–hate relationship with the game's Establishment, torn between his affection and regard for the game's traditions (which he respects) and the Yorkshireman's natural inferiority complex (oh yes – we all have it), which induces a feeling of being patronised and tolerated at Lord's. Fred's only previous experience of London, let alone Lord's, at that time was having passed through the capital the previous year in the Federation team, coach. He remembered seeing Parliament, and Big Ben, and that was all. Now he was actually playing on the most famous ground in the whole world. But he nearly didn't make it.

He travelled by train from Doncaster to King's Cross without one vital piece of information – where the Yorkshire team were staying! He had just over £5 in his pocket and a written instruction from Yorkshire's secretary to report to the captain the following morning. John Nash gave copious instructions about wearing the correct dress at all times but omitted to say what Fred should do about finding a bed for the night. An inquiry addressed to a London bobby failed to provide the required information; he didn't know where the Yorkshire cricket team were staying, which surprised Fred! A cabby proved more helpful. He took the young man to the Bonnington Hotel in Southampton Row and he certainly gets marks for effort because that was where Yorkshire *used to* stay – but no longer. However, with the meter ticking merrily away the taxi-driver was willing to drive from one hotel to another in WC2 (where there are quite literally dozens of them) inquiring if Yorkshire were in residence while Fred saw his fiver disappearing before his horrified gaze. He cut his losses, went back to the Bonnington and booked in for the night with just enough money left to pay for his room. At 10 a.m. the following morning he made his way to Lord's, reported to Norman Yardley – 'Oh, you've got here, have you?' – and changed into his cricketing battledress.

Fred was now in a completely new world, and one which excited him. While waiting to bat, or in the intervals for luncheon and tea, he embarked on wide-eyed exploration of the Pavilion. When he went out as a member of the fielding side he was walking some distance above the clouds. Players all over the world will tell you exactly the same thing – walking out at Lord's for the first time is a very special feeling indeed, and Fred was no less susceptible than anyone else. It is difficult, perhaps, to think of Fred as a modestly shrinking violet but he was all of that in this early period of his life. In fact, during that game he had gone out for an evening walk after dinner with Frank Lowson and Roy Booth, both of whom were five or six years older than FST. They were accosted by a lady of the night who addressed her business inquiries to the two older men: 'Ten bob apiece and I'll throw in a couple of lollipops for the kid.' The wide-eyed 'kid' was much relieved when his team-mates declined the offer. But it may be that the cheerfully contemptuous dismissal of him as being too young for that sort of thing inspired him when Minor Counties batted for the second time and he took the first five wickets for 30 runs.

After the luncheon break he took the next three, and suddenly the impossible became a distinct possibility: all ten wickets on his first appearance at Lord's. He was encouraged by Alan Mason, bowling slow left-arm at the other end: 'Keep going, Fred,' he urged. 'I'll bowl wide of the off-stump so you can give it all you've got.' (It is worth pausing for a moment to reflect on Mason's generosity of spirit. He had been competing with Johnny Wardle for the left-arm spin bowler's position in the side since the retirement of Arthur Booth. Wickets were important to him.) Sadly, they reckoned without a tail-ender's incompetence and the Counties' NO. 10 batsman dragged a wide ball on to his stumps. The chance was gone! Fred returned eight for 70, nevertheless, and Bill Edrich (strangely, because he nursed a lifelong and almost pathological detestation of Yorkshiremen) wrote in a newspaper column that England might now have a new fast-bowling prospect if young Trueman could build up a more formidable figure with a few helpings of roast beef and Yorkshire pudding.

Unfortunately for Fred's more immediate prospects, Yorkshire's Committeemen rarely ventured further afield than the county's home grounds and relied more for information about the players on the columns of the *Yorkshire Post* than on personal observation. Their general reaction to Trueman's Lord's début was to dwell longer on the 70 runs conceded than the eight wickets taken.

Those bowling figures revealed that the fiery youngster was going for something between 3.5 and 4 runs an over, even when he was taking wickets, and Don Brennan, the amateur wicket-keeper, ruefully acknowedged having to do 'more diving than a Third Division goalkeeper' – though he said it without being destructively critical of the bowler. In the Surrey match at Park Avenue Trueman took four wickets, but an experienced batting line-up scored at around 6 an over, and this was too much for the Yorkshire Committee. As John Arlott once put it so succinctly, 'it offended their sense of economy'. Bill Foord was given a special leave of absence by his headmaster before the summer holidays began and Trueman was dropped. And that offended his sense of fairplay; after all, he argued, he was there to take wickets, not to put together a string of maiden overs. And the move planted in Fred a deep-rooted mistrust of selectorial opinion which the England Selectors in later years did nothing to dispel. His naturally undisciplined temperament was fuelled by the set-back, and the flame of resentment burned ever brighter.

Trueman was restored to the side for the fixture at Bramall Lane, his spiritual home, against Walter Hadlee's touring New Zealanders, and with his whole family in the ground he set his stall out to show that he compared favourably with at least one of his rivals, Johnny Whitehead. Predictably, he overdid his effort, damaged a thigh-muscle and had to be helped from the field, never to re-appear in the 1949 season. There are those who claim that Fred *never* learned from his mistakes; they should check the records to see how many games he missed through injury in the next nineteen summers and see how well he learned that one. His stamina was phenomenal, his consistency unparalleled.

But as Yorkshire, with Coxon, Foord and Whitehead as their fast bowlers, won seven of the last eight matches to be joint champions with Middlesex, Fred languished at home in Maltby, his absence seemingly unmourned by the Committee forty miles away in Leeds. There was an impersonal coldness about Yorkshire's relationships with their players in those days. Indeed, it was not until the late 1970s and '80s, when things went disastrously wrong, that Yorkshire cricketers became the subject of close attention, and even then it was scarcely of a benevolent or paternal nature.

If any thought *was* spared in Leeds for the injured youngster it was not translated into any sort of action, either a 'get well' card, a written inquiry or even a telephone call. Yorkshire did not believe in mollycoddling their players. To a county with a proper headquarters and a ground staff, of course (i.e. any one of the other sixteen) this distancing would have been unthinkable. But Yorkshire, with their offices in Park Row, in the business centre of Leeds, and no ground staff, were very much the exception to the rule and they expected the unswerving loyalty of the men who played for the Club as a sort of divine right in return for the inestimable honour – as indeed it was – of playing for a club of such exclusivity, whether they wore the white rose, or merely the rosebud of a Colt, on their caps. It needed all his father's enthusiasm and encouragement to prevent Fred snarling, 'Bugger the lot of them,' and giving the Yorkshire Committee the same cold shoulder they had showed to him.

When one looks at the smouldering resentment of Authority which marked – disfigured, perhaps, to some extent – his playing career, it is necessary to return to this early part of Fred's life and consider the effect it had upon him. Yorkshire, for their part, were treating him no differently from any other fledgeling in the same category. There was something magnificently feudal about the attitude and it is a sobering thought that only when this iron grip was relaxed, or prised loose, did the Club go to pieces! It was in that summer of 1949 that I first met Fred, during a second eleven match at York. He was brash and raw, true, but there was an entirely engaging openness about him, a readiness to laugh and enjoy life, an appetite for cricket and a great willingness to communicate with his fellow creatures.

From 1950 onwards, he was not the same man again. He became a great bowler but in many ways a less lovable human being. It may well be that the one could not have been achieved without the other but his friends – and I could not at that time count myself in that number – found they had to adopt a quite different approach to win his confidence. Once we had become more closely associated I found an exterior of brooding suspicion. I was a journalist and therefore just as likely to damn him to hell in my writing as laud his God-given ability. His friendship, never easily given, had to be earned by convincing Fred that one could be trusted to give him an honest answer and a square deal. That may not seem a great deal to ask, perhaps, but it has to be remembered that in the course of a long and distinguished career within the game, and then in its peripheral regions, he has met an awful lot of people who were not prepared to give him either. It is much easier to shrug off double-dealing when one is quite simply a cricket-lover than when one is a Very Public Figure. The slights, the prevarications, the insults, the broken promises, the treacheries all become magnified in direct proportion to the stature of the man.

It had been an unsatisfactory first summer in 1949 for Fred Trueman, and it has to be said that the county coaches were less than enraptured with the progress he had made. Fred, who saw himself as a *fast* bowler above all other considerations, was irked by the heavy concentration of attention on the waywardness of his bowling, the efforts to get him to concentrate on the basics of line and length. The impression that these efforts left him with, however, is still apparent today, forty years later, when the one thing that drives him to despair in the commentary box is the inability of England bowlers to deliver on line and length! Mitchell and Bowes might have irritated him as a youngster but they left their mark on him. While following the instructions of the coaches in seeking to improve his accuracy during the long winter months in the indoor shed at Headingley, Fred sharpened his mental attitude to his trade. He built up a formidable, if impersonal, dislike of batsmen *per se* and throughout his bowling life he was able to maintain an attitude of outright hostility. It impressed some opponents more than others; he could not, of course, sustain an attitude of permanent malevolence towards all who played against him – cricket does not lend itself to that sort of relationship and, in any case, he was too fond of trotting out his latest string of risqué stories – but he could, and did, manage to convey just a hint of menace to even the most experienced of his foes.

It was this more than anything else which diminished him in opposition eyes as a likeable human being. While Brian Statham (known throughout the game as 'George') could sit down and converse comfortably with opponents in the dressing-room without losing one shred of their respect for his ability as a bowler which was accorded throughout the game, Trueman became a compulsive *threatener* of batsmen. 'George' was never a great initiator of conversations but was ever a companionable participant; Fred had to be the centre of attention on such occasions. The one enjoyed the role of interested by-stander while the other demanded an audience. Fred played the part for all it was worth and so, over many years, projected an image which is not really the essential Trueman – but it is extremely difficult to fault those who have been forced to take him at face value. In the course of his sixty years he has given countless thousands of people a false impression and they cannot be blamed for being misled. Only a small circle of really close friends know him as a wonderfully caring and generous father and step-father, a man who has done an immense amount of unsung charity work, one who has a deep love of the countryside, animals and wild-life generally.

How many people, one wonders idly, have ever seen Fred laugh with genuine mirth at someone else's joke or witticism? How many people saw, or considered, how deeply wounded he was to be voted off the Yorkshire Committee in the Boycott controversy of 1984? This was a more devastating blow to his pride and sensitivity than any savaging he took from a batsman on the field of play. This vulnerable Fred Trueman does exist, but few people have been allowed to see it as Fred, from those earliest days and in the face of what he saw as ruthless treatment by the Yorkshire Committee, has cloaked himself in phoney belligerence and – let's face up to it – protective rudeness.

The development of his public persona was not helped by the make-up of the Yorkshire side, when he finally established himself in it, of the 1950s. Man for man, that was, arguably, as great a team as any to represent the county in its more glorious days: Yardley, Hutton, Watson, Wilson, Lester, Close, Appleyard, Illingworth, Lowson, Brennan/Binks, Wardle. Great players, almost to a man. And yet the team never won a thing. It was, unfortunately, a team of strong-minded individualists and it lacked the necessary lead to fuse so many talents into corporate effort as Surrey, seven times champions in succession, had been drawn together by Stuart Surridge. Fred, then, found himself in a crowd of towering personalities who seemed largely determined to do their own thing. Hutton might have been able to do for Yorkshire what Surridge did for Surrey but Yorkshire were not yet ready to appoint a professional captain, even if England could do it.

Fred was not happy in this distinguished company and his colleagues, in all truth, were not inordinately fond of the noisy and often abrasive newcomer who had yet to prove himself a county championship match-winner. In modern parlance, they sought to 'put him down', often in cruel and derisive terms. They could argue, and convince themselves that it was justified, that they were doing him a service by curbing his youthful exuberance and self-confidence, but Fred did not see it that way at all.

In the early part of 1950 he was faced with a choice of lessening his unhappiness by choosing a new career or digging in his heels and saying to himself. 'I'll show the bastards.' But how to do this, with limited opportunities? A partial breakthrough came against Gloucestershire, at Bristol, where he took six good wickets but it was, paradoxically, the England Selectors (who were to cause him so much anguish in the future) who now gave him his first real encouragement. In this, they were more long-sighted than Yorkshire's selectors, or at any rate they sensed a feeling in the country that it was time to serve the Australians with a dose of their own medicine.

As we have seen, there was a long history of fast bowlers from Down Under wreaking havoc with English batting. Savaging by Lindwall and Miller, at home and abroad, in 1946, 1947 and 1948 provided a recent and painful memory, and England were due to go to Australia again in the winter of 1950–1. No doubt with that tour very much in mind, the nineteen-year-old was now chosen to play in a Test trial at Bradford. As things turned out, Jim Laker made a nonsense of the whole affair by taking eight wickets for 2 runs as The Rest, with a whole crop of brilliant young Oxbridge batsmen on parade, were bundled out for 27. Fred, however, did not come away from Park Avenue entirely dissatisfied. He scored one of the only two runs off Laker's bowling, he clean-bowled his hero, Len Hutton, and caught his county captain, Norman Yardley! On the debit side, he ground his teeth that he – the fastest bowler in England and with a superb natural outswinger – was not given the new ball.

Yorkshire's Committee were left pondering very much more on how they came to let Laker slip through their net than on whether the England Selectors had possibly spotted greater potential in F. S. Trueman than they themselves had yet to perceive. Their scepticism was enhanced by the fact the Fred, in his next four games for the county, was still conceding nearly 4 runs an over, and as soon as Whitehead was free from his studies at London University he was immediately called up to replace the younger man. When Fred was recalled to bowl at Chesterfield, where the pitch was tailor-made for Derbyshire's Les Jackson at that time, along with Coxon *and* Whitehead he was not given first use of the new ball and when he ultimately did get on he was once again wildly erratic.

After another poor peformance at Trent Bridge he was dropped for six long and miserable weeks and once again it was left to his father to convince Fred – no one else at that time could have done it – that all was not yet irretrievably lost. Yorkshire and England cricket owes a lot to the patience and faith of Alan Thomas Trueman. Other counties – notably Lancashire (!), Surrey and Sussex – seemed to be taking a keener interest in the young fast bowler than his own county and, left to his own devices, Fred might have tried his luck in territory where he felt he would be more welcome, but Yorkshire pride burned brightly in Trueman *père*. Gently, tactfully but firmly he persuaded Fred that neither Whitehead nor Foord would, in the long term, suit Yorkshire's requirements and that he would get the call once more. In the meantime, Fred frightened the wits out of several league batsman, and stretched a few wicket-keeping muscles, too. At the end of the season the Yorkshire averages showed the name of F. S. Trueman in eighth place and he was decisively warned by the coaches that his bowling must become less expensive, or else.

Two things happened during the following winter which changed the course of cricket history. First, Alec Coxon unexpectedly announced his retirement and went off to the north-east of England to play much good league cricket. He was thirty-four, true, but he had been bowling as well as ever, economical both in terms of runs conceded and wear-and-tear on his physical resources. He had taken 131 first-class wickets in the previous season and his disappearance from the county scene gave rise to the same cryptic comment as his solitary Test appearance in 1948. Newspapers did not, in those days, intrude into dressing-room politics or Committee deliberations, and anyone who ventured an indiscreet inquiry was brusquely informed, with embarrassed finality, that 'Coxon's face didn't fit'. That was quite simply to be interpreted as: 'He has upset somebody and mind your own bloody business.'

The second was that Fred spent a lot of time concentrating his mind firmly on achieving greater discipline in his bowling. Despite Coxon's departure, he was still in competition with Whitehead, due to come down from university that summer; Foord, when available from school duties; and now Bob Appleyard, the Bradford player who could swing the new ball and also bowl medium-paced off-breaks and who had first appeared on the scene during 1950. Fred did not need to convince himself that he had the raw ability – confidence was not lacking in that respect. But he had to feel assured that if he could achieve the economy demanded by the coaches he would then be competing at least an equal terms with the others as a 'prospect'.

He could be forgiven, therefore, for thinking that the Fates were indeed conspiring against him when 1951 turned out to be very much Appleyard's season as he took 200 wickets at only 14.14 in what was only his first full summer in first-class cricket! Nevertheless, Fred knew that Appleyard was a bowler of an entirely different type and he believed firmly that genuine pace was still going to be his trump card. The belief was strengthened by the fact that during the winter a young fast bowler from the other side of the Pennines, Brian Statham by name, had been flown out to join England on their Australia–New Zealand tour and had made his Test début in Christchurch. Trueman knew something about Statham (not realising how close their association was to become), knew he did not bowl the outswinger, and his Yorkshire pride was bruised when a Lancastrian was now called up by England for two of that summer's Tests against Dudley Nourse's touring South Africans while he (Fred) was still seeking to establish himself as a county player.

After all, *he* had scattered the Springboks when they met Yorkshire. And during the season he watched his team-mates Watson, Lowson and Brennan go off to win their first Test caps. By the end of June he felt his moment had come. A magnificent spell of really hostile bowling on a rain-affected pitch at Bramall Lane saw Fred take eight wickets for 68 to rout Notts before his 'home' crowd, and as the team joined the spectators in applauding him first into the pavilion he felt for the first time the heady delight of being a Yorkshire county cricketing hero. A wild, fleeting fantasy flickered across his mind – the thought that he might be called by England to play in the next Test at Old Trafford before (like Brian Close) he had won a Yorkshire cap.

There is nothing, absolutely nothing, to compare with a Yorkshireman's gift for cutting one down to size, for throwing a bucket of ice-cold water over the most burning ambition and fervent hope. Pinned to the wall of the dressing-room he now saw the names of the county team for the next match. He was not included in the party; instead, he was required to go to Grimsby with the Colts to play against Lincolnshire! (Even when he got there he was made twelfth man.) What had happened was that the teams had been picked earlier in the day, before his eight Notts wickets had been taken, but even if selection had taken place later in the day he would probably still have been omitted. Yorkshire were great believers in the right of seniority, and with Hutton, Watson and Wardle returning from the Lord's Test, Trueman would almost certainly have been one of those to be relegated to second-team cricket. One swallow (eight wickets or not) did not make a Yorkshire summer.

As Fred struggled, in the course of his third summer in first-class cricket, to establish himself with a foot in the door of the Yorkshire dressing-room it is worth taking a sidelong glance at the entirely different course taken by the career of the most renowned of his partners, Brian Statham, fifty miles away in Manchester. He joined the Lancashire CCC staff in May 1950, from local league cricket, went into the first team in June and was never out of it from that moment onwards. No one tried to change one detail of his action, his run-up or delivery and by the following winter Statham was flown out to Australia and New Zealand to join Freddie Brown's England tour party.

Lancashire had learned one lesson – and learned it well. Before Statham's arrival they had two fast bowlers of some promise, Don Stone and Eddie Highton, who were sent for extra coaching in winter and returned no better for the experience. Lancashire took no chances with their newest discovery; Statham was left strictly to develop in his natural style and within six months the county had found an England bowler.

There can be small wonder that Trueman has a very soft spot in his heart for Notts CCC and Trent Bridge in particular. Three of the four hat-tricks he performed in the course of his career were against that county, and it was at Trent Bridge in 1951 that he finally convinced the County Committee that he was ready to be accepted as a regular and recognised member of the side. Fred had left a distinct impression on the minds of Notts batsmen the previous month in Sheffield and been relegated to the Second Eleven for his pains. Now he was back in action against the same county, but on the featherbed of a wicket which Trent Bridge offered for several years in the late forties and early fifties they felt a little more secure. The morning, however, was hazy, the pitch just a touch moist and, on winning the toss, Yardley asked Notts to bat, handed the new ball to Trueman and, figuratively speaking, sat back to observe the results.

At that time I was working on the *Nottingham Journal and Evening News* and my wife was back home in Yorkshire for the birth, on hallowed ground, of our first son. I wandered down to Trent Bridge, sat at the Radcliffe Road end and watched Fiery Fred wreak havoc amongst the Notts batsmen and register the first hat-trick of his career: Reg Simpson and Alan Armitage bowled, Peter Harvey caught behind. It was the fastest and most ferocious bowling I had ever seen, reared as I was on the attack of Bill Bowes and a medium-pace partner in my impressionable schoolboy days before the war. Young Trueman in all his glory was a wonderful sight. The smoothness of the approach did not for one second belie the menace of his bowling; he was like some finely tuned machine of destruction.

Gone was the wildness I had read, and heard, so much about. Not *every* delivery was spot on the target, though distant memory and the thrill of the occasion tempts one to recall that that was the case. But one impression remains with crystal clarity: no batsman was ever confortable and it was not difficult to imagine the dressing-room comments as one batsman succeeded another. This was something quite different which had arrived on the county circuit. Fred bowled on and on; when he had taken four of the first six wickets while Notts were reaching a nervous total of 16, Yardley gave him full rein to complete the mopping up. As Fred tired – and he *had* to tire, hurtling in from twenty-five yards and putting every last ounce of effort into every delivery – the captain never seemed to consider 'spelling' him, either by a word or even a glance in his direction. Yardley afterwards confessed to enjoying that morning's cricket and sensing that Yorkshire players and supporters were witnessing something rather special. They were. They were watching the start of the Trueman Era. Eight for 53 were his final figures. At Harrogate, on a good pitch and a quick-scoring ground, he took six Derbyshire wickets for 59 and on 13 August, at Bradford, he and Appleyard were awarded their county caps.

Appleyard's was not unexpected because his season had been outstandingly successful. Fred's came in the nick of time; he was on the verge of accepting an offer to join another county. Journeying home by train and bus, it was ten o'clock when he reached Maltby to find his father (who should have been down the pit on night-shift) sitting in his chair by the fireside, waiting. Fred playfully pretended not to know that the news of his cap had preceded him via the wireless and the *Sheffield Star*, then handed the cap to his father. FS never wore that particular cap again; it belonged to the man to whom it meant even more than it did to his son. When Alan Trueman died, Fred's first Yorkshire cap went with him in his coffin. To his mother, who had burst into tears of joy at the scene involving her husband, Fred gave his first *England* cap.

Such emotional moments will seem strange and uncharacteristic in the modern, more commercial and less sentimental age. They will, however, surprise no one who was involved with cricket, and Yorkshire cricket in particular, in the first three post-war decades. Traditions, and pride in them, had a direct link with the previous eighty years. Players felt a kinship with George Ulyett and Tom Emmett, with Brown and Tunnicliffe, Rhodes and Hirst, Verity and Bowes, Sutcliffe and Hutton. No one had ever set it out in cold print – it was too personal a thing for that. It was something that one *felt*, rather than read about or even put into conversational words. It is the loss of that feeling which has affected Yorkshire most deeply in the past twenty years, more poignantly and – let us not fight shy of the word – more spiritually than results and championship placings. Today, players' attitudes are more materialistic than nostalgic, more commercial than sentimental. Happily, in the Trueman Era they were not.

That is not to say that men who wore the White Rose cap in the fifties and sixties were unconcerned with financial matters. In prewar days and for a time after the war, a Yorkshire cricketer was comparatively well-off, especially in the Depression days of the twenties and thirties, but as the cost of living went up this was no longer the case and there were frequent wrangles with the

Committee in the quest for better stipends. Yet they never touched the essential importance, which transcended all other considerations, of *playing for Yorkshire*.

Fred had finally gone into mining in 1948, as a haulage hand, to be more readily available for Yorkshire than if he had been doing National Service in the Armed Forces, which many youngsters regarded as, at best, a waste of time and, at worst, an intrusion upon personal freedom. He had no great affection for the life of a miner and had taken it up as a means to an end. Cricket, the county circuit, opened up a whole new world for him and he certainly liked that. So when Yorkshire decided to pay £5 a week to any of their capped players called upon to serve for two years in the Armed Forces – as Brian Close, and the promising young Raymond Illingworth were doing – Fred's business sense told him this might not be such a bad thing. He joined the RAF in 1951 and was posted to Hemswell, in Lincolnshire, not much more than thirty miles from home, and quickly established a good working relationship with the station commander: if Yorkshire required him for a championship match it was usually possible for leave to be granted. Aircraftman Trueman settled down to a not-very-exciting but not-very-taxing-either job looking after the unit's sports equipment. Fred has since claimed that he enjoyed 'square-bashing, spud-peeling, discipline – the lot'. I did not believe this when Fred first said it and I don't believe it now. It is no more possible to visualise Fred coming off the parade ground after an hour's foot-drill and proclaiming it enjoyable than it is to picture him performing with the Bolshoi Ballet, or playing King Lear. But distance does lend enchantment, and most of us tend to look back with feigned affection upon times which were not exactly the best of our lives. Perhaps it is because we *are* looking *back*. Whatever the reason, memory has played a few tricks with Fred.

What National Service did do for Fred was to make him, in relative terms, rather well off and it also speeded up his physical development. He had his £5 a week 'retainer' from Yorkshire, match fees when he was released to play for the county, professional fees when he played in a Yorkshire League match for Leeds and a few bob here and there for personal appearances of one sort and another. Fred learned quickly that as a celebrity of any kind there is money to be earned all over the place. He was rolling in it – for a 21-year-old in the year 1952. He soon gave up drawing his RAF pay. At his initial pay parade he responded to the shout of 'Trueman' with his 'last three', saluted (now there's a thought to savour!), picked up the 18 shillings (90 pence) pushed across the table to him and considered it doubtfully.

'What's the matter?' asked the young officer. 'Isn't it enough for you?'

'It'll have to be, sir,' was the reply. That would have meant seven days' jankers in my day, but at RAF Hemswell in 1952 that modest piece of insubordination passed without remark. Fred went off to the Pay Office and arranged to draw his entire RAF emoluments in a lump sum when he was demobilised. In due course this enabled him to rejoin civilian life £238 better off, which was enough to buy himself a decent little car at that time. In fact it took his bank balance to around £2,800, and not many pit lads of his age could contemplate savings of that magnitude. Our Fred was a pretty wealthy young man.

During those two years the frail, spindly youngster Ray Illingworth had noticed at the nets grew to his fighting height of 5 ft 10 ins, with a 46-in chest, hips to match and he measured 19 ins round the thighs. This gave him a figure which would not have qualified him as a St Laurent model but was ideally suited to his particular calling. As Fred once remarked to a startled television audience: 'To be a great fast bowler you have to have a big heart and a big arse.'

Despite my dismissal of Fred's claim to have enjoyed all aspects of his National Service, it is possible to see that it was not without its attractions. He was, naturally enough, in permanent demand to play for unit, Command, RAF and Combined Service sides; his CO looked favourably on most requests from Yorkshire for his services; he was paid by the county and by the Air Ministry while having to shell out virtually nothing for bed and board; and above all he experienced that sense of general well-being which comes from reaching the full flush of youthful physical fitness. It is probably fair to say that Fred was as happy during 1952 as at any other time in his life. There now seemed no other 'prospect' who presented a threat to his Yorkshire place. The future seemed set fair.

In the modern era, where the fashion is to build up our sporting heroes only (it seems) to gain greater satisfaction in knocking them off their pedestals, it is perhaps difficult to think of an age in which the public and media searched for idols of a more enduring quality. We *wanted* our stars to do well and to keep on doing well; there was no pleasure to be gained from slagging and ridiculing. Newspapers did not write headlines like 'Gatt the Prat' about England captains any more than photographers followed them in furtive pursuit of personal indiscretion. In 1952, when we looked in awed admiration at Hutton and Compton, we yearned for bowlers – particularly *fast* bowlers – to match their artistry. Lindwall and Miller had been – still were on the occasions when England met Australia – a scourge which nevertheless excited our admiration. They were devastating but we loved to see them bowl in the hope that they could be mastered. When they were, the heroic stature of Hutton and Compton was enhanced, for they had done it against THE BEST.

And so, on 5 June 1952, England's Young Lochinvar came, if not out of the West, like Scotland's, most assuredly out of the North. Trueman's arrival had to be seen in context. He had been seen around the circuit and legends about his ferocity as well as his brusqueness were beginning to form. Statham, another North Countryman, had already made his Test début in New Zealand and had toured in India but without achieving startling figures. England as yet had no answer to Lindwall and Miller. But by the afternoon of 7 June 1952 they had. The Indian tourists, a mere 41 behind on the first innings, surveyed a Headingley scoreboard which showed their second innings in ruins at 0 for four wickets. It is very much worth remembering that, while Indian batsmen had looked vulnerable to high-class pace bowling in Australia in 1947–8, they had not otherwise shown signs of timorousness. They might be short of fast bowling in their domestic cricket, where the mildest of pitches discouraged that form of attack, but the real strength of their cricket was the durability of the batting, the willingness to stay there for ever, or at least until the runs started to come. Of the first six batsmen in the order at Headingley, five of them – Mankad, Roy, Umrigar, Hazare and Manjrekar – were destined to total around 88,000 runs in their collective careers. So they were not 'mugs'. Nevertheless, on that Saturday afternoon in Leeds and two Tests later at Old Trafford, they were swept aside like chaff, intimidated by sheer pace and the open ferocity of a young fast bower who operated as though he literally hated every one of them. There have been many peaks and pinnacles in the career of F. S. Trueman. The first, and in terms of schoolboy delight at storybook success, the greatest, was at Headingley. If there had been any doubt in Fred's mind that he was going to be England's outstanding fast bowler (and one doubts if there had) they were dispelled in the few brief moments when he had Pankaj Roy caught at slip, then bowled Mantri and Manjrekar with consecutive deliveries. The jubilation of the crowd, and the sight of the scoreboard (Alec Bedser had also taken a wicket) gave Fred his first heady experience of success at the highest level of the game and in that moment his whole life became dedicated to the search for more of it.

And yet less than a week earlier nothing could have seemed less likely. Group Captain Jim Warfield had given Aircraftman Trueman leave to play in four of Yorkshire's early matches that season and he took thirty-two wickets at 14.2 against Somerset, Worcestershire, Derbyshire and Lancashire before returning to RAF duties. The phone rang and Fred heard an unfamiliar voice asking what he thought about being picked for England. The caller, John Bapty ('Little John' of the *Yorkshire Evening Post*) received a reply which many have known over the years: 'Bollocks.'

John tried again and this time received a more lengthy but no more encouraging response, so he roped in Bill Bowes, at that time cricket correspondent of the *Yorkshire Evening News*, as well as a county cricket coach, to intercede. As the news came this time from a man he knew and trusted, Fred was finally convinced and went off to ask for more leave, but it must have been a rare journalistic occurrence for a reporter to have to enlist the aid of his principal rival to get a quote.

The next worry was that he might be the man to be left out of the team when final selection was made on the first morning, and Fred had genuine cause for concern there. Test squads were usually chosen with a 'spare' bowler, who would be the man left out in those days, and the bowling fraternity resented the system. However, England now had a professional captain for the first time in modern cricket and Len Hutton, despite some personal misgivings about Trueman at that stage of inexperience, felt that genuine pace might well be the instrument of India's undoing. Even so, Fred's euphoria at stepping out in an England sweater for the first time at

Yorkshire's principal ground was curbed when Hutton gave Alec Bedser the Kirkstall Lane end, which meant that Fred, sharing the new ball, had to run up the considerable slope from the football end. He was a trifle piqued, but it was good psychology by the captain, who felt that the best of Trueman was yet to come – in five or six years' time, in fact.

In that, Hutton was right but neither Fred nor his admirers realised it. The 21-year-old was all about blazing pace and flat-out aggression and it seemed to him absurd to waste vital energy in toiling up a hill – a task he likened many times in the future to 'running up the cellar steps with a barrel of beer on your back'. His first-innings figures of three wickets for 89 runs represented unnecessary lack of economy to Hutton's eyes, but he also knew that he had lighted the fires of predatory fury in his young Turk. He gave Trueman the Kirkstall Lane end to start the Indian second innings, and the atmosphere inside Headingley was something like that in a circus as the arena is prepared for the grand finale. Ringmaster Hutton stationed his field of close-catchers while lion-tamer Trueman marked out his run, pausing to scowl at the emerging batsmen, Roy and Gaekwad.

Remember – in seventy years of Test cricket, an English crowd had never seen anything like this: an English fast bowler attacking, flat out, with an umbrella field. Roy allowed Trueman's first ball to go through to the wicket-keeper; Fred dropped the next one short, Roy got a top edge and the ball seemed to hover for minutes before it dropped into Compton's hands. Although it was nowhere near close of play, India sent in Mantri, the wicket-keeper, who was scheduled to bat at no. 8, but it was Bedser who struck the next blow, making a ball lift unexpectedly in his first over to take the shoulder of Gaekwad's bat and give a catch to Laker in the gulley. Fred, almost jumping about with impatience to get hold of the ball, ripped out Mantri's off-stump and his very next ball disposed of the talented Manjrekar in similar fashion.

It was the stuff to set the pulses racing in the most phlegmatic of watchers: India 0 for four wickets. Hazare survived the hat-trick by no skill of his own; the ball missed his outside edge, and the off-stump, by the merest whisker. The tension which had built up to an almost unbearable degree subsided just a little, and then massively as Trueman was rested after only four overs. A second spell after tea brought no further reward and then, ten minutes before the close, Hutton calculatedly brought him back for a last gallop and Fred demolished Hazare's stumps.

Like the great showman he was to become he had chosen the perfect moment to announce his arrival as a Test bowler. The Saturday of the Headingley Test is Yorkshire's great cricketing occasion, with the ground full; when the Sunday newspapers had had their fill of the day of triumph, the dailies took over with their follow-up stories on Monday morning. England had at last found an answer to the terrors of Lindwall and Miller and all their predecessors through the ages. Frederick Sewards Trueman was a one-off, the first of his kind. Was he destined to be a four-day wonder, never to perform so dramatically and colourfully again, or would he go on and find new worlds to conquer? Was this the dawning of a new age?

The Second Test at Lord's did not provide a complete answer to those questions, for while he took four wickets in each innings Fred conceded 182 runs which again offended Hutton's Yorkshire sense of economy. The fact was that on a good wicket Fred, largely through striving for extra pace, was hittable at some stage of most of the overs he bowled because he overpitched. The boyish delight (and in cricketing terms he was still only a boy) in seeing the stumps scattered demanded a fullish length, and class batsmen were not slow to identify a half-volley from a yorker. There was no striving to achieve late outswing at this stage of his career – the ball which became his main destructive weapon later – and indeed he could justifiably point to the way in which he quite literally terrorised the prolific batsman 'Polly' Umrigar by the fire and fury of his deliveries of full length. Umrigar scored 16,155 runs in the course of his career, with 49 centuries and a top score of 252 not out. In Tests he totalled 3,631 runs (avge 42.22) with a best of 223. On that 1952 tour he enjoyed himself round the counties to the extent of 1,688 runs at an average of 48.22 and a couple of double centuries. But in the Test series he was shattered and demoralised by F. S. Trueman, a point which Hutton emphasised by introducing the young man (if he was not already in action) whenever Umrigar appeared at the crease.

At Old Trafford (Third Test) Fred was given the Stretford end with the usual south-westerly wind blowing over his right shoulder and was equipped with a close-catching field to gladden any bowler's heart – four slips, two gullies, a silly point and two short legs. He was centre stage, the spotlight focused directly on him, in the greatest show on earth, and it was one of those days when everything went just right. Catches ranging from the incredible to the impossible were edged by the mesmerised Indians and all were held. In one particular case no catch was required, that of 'Polly' Umrigar. Fred swears – and on such a day, in such a moment of triumph, who would be churlish enough to deny him a possible touch of artistic verisimilitude? – that as he ran in to bowl to Umrigar the batsman backed away sufficiently for Fred to see the figure of Tony Lock, leg slip, framed by stumps on one side and retreating batsman on the other.

His figures of eight wickets for 31 runs were achieved in fifty-two deliveries of the most thrilling and exhilarating fast bowling I have ever seen. No doubt patriotism plays its part in inducing the belief that it was a greater performance than Lindwall's at The Oval in 1948, but it is very easy indeed for those present on the morning of Saturday, 19 July 1952 to conjure up a picture, nearly forty years later, of a truly memorable occasion.

At the end of the season Fred was voted by the Cricket Writers' Club the outstanding Young Cricketer of the Year and the following year's *Wisden* made him one of its Five Cricketers of the Year. And not only Fred felt that both honours were entirely appropriate.

In the 1980s, that sort of start to a career would have meant a permanent England place for the next decade. Not only was Trueman a wicket-taker capable of knocking over numbers one to five in the batting order, but he was a bowler of the most spectacular kind. They were not thick on the ground in the early fifties, with Lindwall and Miller approaching the end of brilliant careers, the West Indies not yet finding a wealth of fast-bowling talent, and India, Pakistan and New Zealand finding it difficult to produce men of real pace. It was South Africa who provided quick bowlers of a 'nasty' nature in McCarthy, Heine and Adcock, but only the latter proved to be a wicket-taker with a credible degree of durability.

There was, in short, a world shortage of really quick bowlers and as Trueman was the first of his kind (Larwood, briefly and mostly abroad, excepted) he was the subject of massive publicity. He was, from the very start, a cartoonist's delight with the mane of black hair, the aggressively jutting jaw, the pincer-toed trudge back to his mark, the scowls, the belligerence. Television was not, in 1952, a nationwide medium of communication and entertainment and so radio commentators with the linguistic brilliance of John Arlott could feast upon an over of heavy artillery from Fred, as could the newspaper writers of that time, unfettered by the need to explore the details of his private life.

The photographic cliché was made-to-measure, too. Fred, the horny-handed son of toil from the South Yorkshire coalfields, was regularly pictured with a pint of beer in his hand at the end of the day's labours, boots off and feet upon the pavilion rails. It was an image he did not discourage and he has lived to regret that. The fact is that when he first came upon the first-class cricket scene he drank nothing but orange juice, and when he graduated to heavier refreshment he rarely overdid it. When his picture appeared in the pages of newspapers with the now-inevitable pint in hand his team-mates smiled indulgently: they knew it was the pint someone else had bought him, probably an hour earlier. But the implications, for the public at large, were inescapable; after twenty rampaging destructive overs the miner from Stainton needed massive in-fusions of ale to replace the sweat of his brow which had been so liberally sprayed around Headingley or Park Avenue or Bramall Lane. Legends grew of a phenomenal capacity for beer and they still haunt him today.

In all the years I have known him, I have only seen Fred on one solitary occasion the worse for wear. That was at Taunton on Saturday, 21 July 1962. In all the years Brian Statham worked in harness with him, *he* can remember with equal clarity the only occasion he saw Fred smashed. And yet the reputation established by the image-builders of the 1950s lives on, and Fred hates it. There is one speaker on the after-dinner circuit (who ought to know better) with a routine which includes the preamble; 'Well, after Trueman had drunk his usual twenty pints . . . ' And it's all a great, hoary myth.

Yet it has to be said that he contributed to the growth of these stories, and that the public cannot really be blamed for obtaining a completely false impression. After the publicists of the 1950s had completed their rough sketch, the TV artists of the '60s and '70s fleshed out the portraits. When Yorkshire Television produced a series on pub sports, with Fred as the linkman, he was seen signing off by hoisting a pint in the direction of the cameras as he uttered his catch-phrase, 'Ah'll sithee.' At the beginning of 1990 the portrait had now become an old master with Fred, and the actor Robin Bailey, advertising St Bruno tobacco on TV in the setting of a Home Counties cricket field with a pint apiece in front of them.

John Hampshire (now a Test umpire) recalls his early playing days with Yorkshire when he used to drive up and down the country in Fred's company. Whenever they called at a pub for a break in the journey (no motorways in those days) the locals, complete strangers to a man, would automatically make way at the bar for the best-known figure in English cricket with the invitation, 'Your's will be a pint, Fred, but what's your friend having?' In July 1985, when Fred criticised Ian Botham's bowling in the Trent Bridge Test in his *Sunday People* column, Botham retaliated in his ghost-written column in the *Sun*, like this: 'Fred Trueman put down his pint and his pipe for long enough to . . .' The journalists of the mid-eighties were still feeding off the fables of the fifties.

But while the public enjoyed the picture of Fred, the hard-drinking miner, in the early days of his career, and while our hero himself was not desperately anxious to discard the image, the men who ran English cricket from Lord's were far from enthusiastic about it. There was no Test and County Cricket Board representing grass-roots opinion from the counties; the game was administered by MCC, many of whose senior members preferred a low-profile, modest and self-deprecating persona in their Test cricketers. When they thought of Trueman, F.S., the Yorkshire bowler, they considered not only the personality as they saw it through their newspapers but dwelled also on the brash, noisy, outspoken figure they were being urged to include in the ranks of the men who represented the country, at home and abroad, in a dignified and ambassadorial sport. They drew back.

Over the next thirteen years England were to play 121 Tests with Fred figuring in no more than 67 of them. In 1980–90 terms it is unbelievable, but not only was there competition around in greater abundance during the fifties and sixties, but a far closer scrutiny was directed at the character and personality of players when selection was carried out. This may well evoke cries of dissent from present-day voices: 'What about Dilley, who was fined for misbehaviour on the field in New Zealand? What about Broad, who was fined in Australia and dropped after Pakistan?' It's a fair point, but one has to suggest that neither Graham Dilley nor Chris Broad was a figure to be compared in stature to that of Fred in the 1950s. A fairer comparison would be with Ian Botham, the greatest personality – as well as one of the most gifted players – in the game from the late 1970s onwards who was involved in some of the most hair-rising episodes, on the field and off it, yet was consistently selected for one Test after another.

In terms of competition, Trueman (and Statham), throughout their careers, were up against an emerging group of quicks. Apart from Trevor Bailey – who, for his all-round ability as well as great qualities of 'character' was a regular selection, there were at one time or another Peter Loader, Frank Tyson, Alec Bedser, Les Jackson, Alan Moss, David Larter, Fred Rumsey, Jack Flavell, Len Coldwell, John Price, Harold Rhodes and Derek Shackleton challenging for the right to use the new ball. And in those days the Selectors very rarely indeed picked a side without two spinners, which meant that one place fewer was available for the quicks. So any fast bowler who appeared to be an abrasive character was going to be looked upon with at least a certain amount of disfavour in some quarters.

There will be those who say – Fred would be foremost amongst them – that many on that list could not *really* be regarded as logical claimants for *his* place but they most certainly were in the eyes of the Selectors, and that was what counted. There can be little wonder, therefore, that he has watched with some bitterness and not a little cynicism as one modern bowler after another has passed his record of 307 Test wickets – a record which at that time seemed unassailable. Very few people foresaw the day when Test series would come around in a non-stop continuation and very few visualised (with the experience of what had gone before) the day when a bowler might enjoy selection for fifty and sixty consecutive games. With that sort of continuity, there can be little doubt that Fred would have topped 400 Tests wickets. It is perhaps as well, therefore, for a relative peace of mind, that Richard Hadlee is one of the bowlers to have passed his total whom he respects. Dennis Lillee is another. It is worth noting that it was nearly ten years after Fred's 300th wicket at The Oval in 1964 before anyone else reached that target. It was a slow bowler, Lance Gibbs, and it had taken him fourteen Tests (and a lot more deliveries) more than Trueman, whose 300th came in his sixty-fifth Test.

3
First Tour

If there was one lesson Fred had to learn at a very early stage it was that you can be on the pinnacle of success one minute, enjoying the plaudits of the crowd and the press, and down in the dumps the next, with no one cheering. He had taken twenty-nine wickets for 386 runs against India in 1952; for the First Test against Lindsay Hassett's Australians in 1953 he was not picked. He was not in the Second, Third or Fourth Tests, either, as the Selectors relied for their opening attack on Bedser, partnered either by Bailey or Statham. It was a fearful blow to Fred, who had started the season in the highest hopes of consolidating his position as a Test fixture. But a wet spring did not help his bowling for Yorkshire, and with the Selectors going very much on current form rather than recent reputation it was not until August, and the Final Test at The Oval, that his next chance came. A tumult of cheering throughout the ground as he took the new ball indicated where the public's sympathy lay. He took four first-innings wickets for 86, bowled a token couple of overs in the second and then watched Laker and Lock bowl out Australia for 162. The Test was won by eight wickets, and with it the Ashes, so at least he had been involved in a historic occasion at the end of a summer when well over half a million people watched the series. Fred was picked for his first tour – to the West Indies.

Len Hutton, later to become Sir Leonard, had a rough ride in many ways on his first tour as England's first professional captain. Tony Lock was no-balled for throwing in Jamaica and Barbados, there was rioting by the crowds in Guiana and there was severe criticism of some of the umpiring – by West Indian spectators in Jamaica and Guiana and by many of the tourists all round the Caribbean. Fred was one of those who had to be rebuked by the captain for his strictures, and this was something Hutton could well have done without. Apart from the pressures of his position –

dealing with sensitive temperaments amongst home officials – he had to bat magnificently throughout the tour to play a major part in the drawn series. It was all a tremendous strain on him, believing as he did that he was only a temporary, stop-gap captain and that MCC would revert to amateur leadership at the first opportunity. Although he was, and later became even more so after long-term residence in the London area, always a more pragmatic character than either of the two Yorkshiremen who followed him in later years as England captains, Close and Illingworth, he could not completely escape the belief, shared by generations of his fellow Yorkies, that there was a natural prejudice at Lord's against men from the Broad Acres, that they would only be picked if there was no possible, even remotely credible alternative, and that they would be dropped as soon as this could be made to appear acceptable. It was important to him, in consequence, that there should be no tour problems which could be avoided, and above all he expected none from his three fellow-countrymen in the party: Willie Watson, Johnny Wardle and Freddie Trueman.

Fred was, by all the available evidence, guiltless on one count on which Len found it necessary to remonstrate with him as we shall see, but he was certainly demonstrative on the field on a number of occasions – with just cause, no doubt, but in such a volatile atmosphere as that on the West Indian grounds of that era it had to be something a touring captain wanted to avoid at all costs. On the jute matting wicket at Port-of-Spain, Trinidad, where the West Indies amassed 681 for eight declared, Everton Weekes was 'out' four times to Fred before he finally left, caught Bailey, b. Lock. As Weekes walked back, Fred relates that he complimented him: 'Not bad – 206 in four innings.' And the great batsman's smiling response was (and this is Fred's own story): 'Five. I gave a catch behind that no one appealed for.' So it was hard going in the field for the tourists, but still Hutton would have been happier without such exchanges which could only confuse, or alienate, the umpires more.

There was at least one lighter moment in this Test (the Fourth) which Jim Laker used to relate. West Indies had only one bowler of any real pace, Frank King, and even he had to be a trifle jaded when he took the third new ball with England's total approaching the 500 mark for seven wickets. Instead, to England's surprise he was still, in relative terms, quick. He was partnered by Frank Worrell, at that stage of the proceedings barely medium pace, and it was at this moment that young Trueman, Laker's partner, first revealed himself as a sage judge of a batting situation. After Laker had bobbed and weaved through an over from King and Fred had presented a straight bat to one from Worrell, a mid-pitch conference took place. 'I've had a look at both of 'em,' declared Fred, 'and I reckon I can deal wi' Worrell if you take King.'

'It was,' observed Jim, drily 'a pretty fair assessment of the situation. In the next over from King I was helped off with blood pouring from a cut over the eye.'

Such lighter moments (even if the humour is a touch masochistic) were, unfortunately, all too rare. In Trinidad one of Fred's bouncers caught the genial leg spinner Wilf Ferguson in the face when he mishooked, and all the MCC team save FST rushed to sympathise. If Fred had been more experienced, or even better-advised, he would have joined the throng but, basing his attitude on some semi-fictional tradition of fast-bowling ruthlessness, he remained aloof. Fred, however, maintains that his uncompromising attitude resulted from being called 'a white bastard'. His next ball when Ferguson recovered was very nearly a beamer, of considerable pace. It is significant that Hutton was not playing in that match, but it was the sort of thing which made Fred's initial impact upon West Indian cricket, at least at the higher official level, an unfortunate one. It also embarrassed his captain, his manager, and some of his team-mates. The fact that he did not play in one of Hutton's remaining eleven Tests before ill-health dictated an earlier retirement than he, or cricket, desired, was not entirely in accordance with Hutton's wishes. When Peter May succeeded Leonard, Trueman played in only three of his first fifteen Tests as captain. He waited a long time for forgiveness.

Fred finished the tour in fifth place amongst the bowlers, and although his twenty-seven wickets in all matches was only one behind Lock, the leading wicket-taker, his only outstanding set of figures was five for 45 against Jamaica in the opening first-class match of the trip. More to the point, the managerial report on him as a tourist was not entirely favourable, his bonus was withheld and this resulted in an enduringly ambivalent attitude by Trueman towards Hutton – not to Charles Palmer, the manager. Fred yields to no one in his admiration of Hutton the batsman; he would strangle anyone who sought to offer even a whisper of criticism and refers to Hutton, always, as 'the great Sir Leonard'. He is utterly unswerving in this loyalty. But he is absolutely convinced that Hutton was instrumental in Fred's missing out on the following winter's tour – the one prized above all others – to Australia. Hutton had said, publicly and frequently, 'This is untrue. The fact is that he had my vote for Australia but the majority were against him.'

Through the years, Fred has remained unconvinced but Hutton's case seems to me to be incontrovertible. His whole strategy in 1954–5 was based on a pace attack and, much as he regarded Fred as not yet at the peak of his possible attainments, there was no question about the speed of his bowling. Furthermore, Hutton was a realist with a sound knowledge of Australian character and temperament; he reasoned, logically, that the Aussie batsmen would not react to Fred's on-the-field chatter in the sensitive way in which some West Indians had done. And finally, no doubt with one eye on Yorkshire's long-term prospects, he felt that a typically blunt and colourful Australian response to Fred's verbal assaults might knock some of the rough edges off the youngster, which would be mutually beneficial.

Whatever the rights and wrongs of selection, no matter where the blame lay for Trueman's omission, he was inconsolable during that winter and his morale was in no way improved by reports coming back from Australia describing Frank Tyson as the fastest bowler ever to tour Down Under. This was a fearful affront to Fred's professional pride. First, however, he had to endure an English summer in which he was out of favour with the Test Selectors for the four-match series against Pakistan. He chafed and fretted as his candidature was ignored in favour of Statham–Bailey, Statham–Bedser and Statham–Tyson combinations and savaged a horde of county batsmen in frustrated recrimination. He took over 134 first-class wickets and was at his fastest and most venomous on three occasions – the two championship matches against Northants and the occasion when Tyson was called up for the Final Test. If Fred ever resented Statham being selected when he (Fred) was not I cannot recall that he ever expressed himself on the subject. But Tyson – that was another matter altogether. Statham, superb bowler that he was, was nevertheless a mild and easy-going character. He was perfectly happy to concede that Fred was fractionally faster than he was and saw absolutely no reason to claim otherwise. Tyson, however, was now being spoken of around the circuit as 'a bit faster than Trueman', and that simply could not be borne. It was all about speed – nothing more, nothing less. I doubt very much whether Fred would have turned a hair if someone reported Tyson as having taken fifty wickets more, but the merest suggestion that he was faster was a very large crimson banner waved before a very angry bull.

It was a rivalry which gave a certain amount of pleasure to this big, burly Lancastrian who opened the bowling for Northants, and he was not unhappy to fan the flames. It was on one of these Northants–Yorkshire occasions (which other players described as quite simply Tyson–Trueman occasions) that FST gave the folklore of cricket possibly its best *bon mot*, though it might not be regarded in that light in the drawing-rooms of Belgravia. Johnny Wardle was bowled by Tyson in somewhat undignified circumstances, a trifle distant from his own leg stump. Fred *en route* to succeed him at the crease and reluctant as ever to concede that anyone else could frighten a batsman into retreat, flung at Wardle the terse comment, 'A bloody fine shot that were.' There was no time for Johnny to respond so he seethed in the dressing-room until Trueman returned, bowled Tyson, o. "And a bloody fine shot *that* were, anall,' he greeted Fred, savouring a little victory. But no one – as we shall see in the course of our story – *no one* ever has the last word with Fred. Without a second's hesitation he retorted, 'Aye. I slipped on that pile o' shit you left in the crease.' One of the features of Fred's public life has always been the ease and spontaneity with which he trots out these epigrammatic gems. None, I think, has surpassed that one. But many have been close to it.

The pleasure of leaving Wardle speechless – not the easiest thing to achieve – was but a momentary triumph for Fred. When the tour party for Australia was announced at the end of July the bowlers were Statham, Tyson, Loader, Bailey, Bedser, Appleyard, Wardle and Jim McConnon, of Glamorgan. It left two Yorkshiremen consumed with rage – F. S. Trueman and J. C. Laker. It was, of course, a successful tour, with Hutton retaining the Ashes and Tyson performing prodigiously in Sydney and Melbourne particularly. It found Fred in no mood for patriotic rejoicing. He believed he had been unjustly treated by Hutton and by 'the big guns of MCC, like Freddie Brown and Gubby Allen'. He also believed that Brian Sellers, the Yorkshire chairman, did nothing to help his cause and he nurtured these resentments through the remainder of his playing career, adding others to them along the way.

The following summer of 1955 brought little consolation to Fred in terms of Test ambitions. He took 153 first-class wickets at an average of 16.03 but was still picked for only one match against Jack Cheetham's South Africans – a game in which Statham bowled quite magnificently. But there was no thought in the minds of the Selectors that perhaps a combination of two outstanding fast bowling talents had been unearthed. Fred and 'George' had not bowled together since the West Indies in the winter of 1953–4 and then only in two Tests, in one of which Statham had broken down after nine overs. Out went Fred after his 2–73, 0–39 figures at Lord's in the Second Test of 1955 and Alec Bedser was restored to the side for what proved to be the last of his fifty-one matches, at Old Trafford. Fred ground his teeth as the conviction steadily grew that 'Lord's' – a term now firmly fixed in his mind as a generic reference to all Establishment matters – had decided his face didn't fit. He bowled on and on for Yorkshire, mowing down batsmen of every county; if he had bowled just nineteen more deliveries he would have completed 1,000 first-class overs with rarely a sign of injury or unfitness of any sort, with unrelenting hostility and with burning resentment.

His outswinger, which was a natural delivery resulting from his classic close-to-the-wicket action and delivery, left elbow pointing at fine leg, left shoulder at the batsman, was now a very much more controlled and disciplined part of his repertoire. As Hutton had so accurately forecast three years earlier, the best of Trueman had yet to come and he was now a very fine bowler indeed. But still the Selectors were not convinced. Fred has always believed, and there is much statistical evidence to support him, that he was only picked grudgingly and quickly dropped at the first excuse. His championship form positively demanded selection but, short of a 1952 demolition of the opposition and without any regard for the conditions in his Test appearances, out he went again very quickly indeed. There was no tour that winter and the following summer, with Ian Johnson's Australians here, was a wet one – Laker's summer. Seven of the top ten bowlers in the first-class averages were spinners. England's attack in the First Test was opened by Bailey and Moss, leaving Fred choking with emotion. He was recalled for the Second Test, took two for 54 and five for 90 at Lord's and then bowled only nineteen overs in the two innings at Headingley (two for 40) as Laker and Lock claimed the other eighteen wickets.

The decision to leave him out of the Fourth Test was not only manifestly unfair; it defied all logic. But Fate came to the aid of the Selectors in the form of Jim Laker's nineteen for 90 performance at Old Trafford and their decision was forgotten by the public at large in the glory of Laker's historic bowling analysis. Fred was again omitted for the Final Test – and for the winter tour to South Africa. And that *really* hurt.

It is not easy to ignore injustice, especially when drastic interference with one's career is involved, and Fred reacted predictably. No one was left in any doubt about his feelings because he did not care how, or to whom, he expressed them. It is only fair to point out that 1956 had been Fred's worst season by a long way – in terms of injury. He was troubled by sciatica and blistered feet, and experienced a great deal of pain from a strained left side. His haul of first-class wickets dropped to fifty-nine in that spinners' summer, and on figures alone the Selectors could reasonably claim their right to leave him out of the tour party. Fred remained unconvinced. Nor was his opinion of 'Southern' prejudice dissipated by the action of Gubby Allen, Chairman of Selectors, in taking him to the nets before the Headingley Test, putting down a handkerchief and instructing Fred to bowl on that length. As a fair crowd of Yorkshiremen gathered to watch the session Fred felt diminished and humiliated.

When his claims of bias by the Selectors inevitably reached the ears of 'them buggers at Lord's' the MCC Secretary, Ronnie Aird, took the unprecedented step of making a public statement that the tour party had been picked on an assessment of current form and that there was no question of discrimination against Trueman. Just a little less resentfully than might otherwise have been the case Fred occupied himself temporarily by turning his attention to Indian batsmen in two matches which were played to celebrate the silver jubilee of the Bengal Cricket Association. The following summer saw a complete change of his fortunes.

He played in all five Tests against the West Indies, took twenty-two wickets – four more than anyone else – and, to his huge delight, finished the series with a batting average of 89, thanks to three 'not outs' in four innings. Nevertheless, there was one disappointment for him. Roy Gilchrist, the volatile and unpredictable fast bowler, had let Fred have a bouncer and, naturally enough, had been warned of dire retribution to follow. Sadly, this personal confrontation never took place as Peter Loader polished off the West Indies first innings with a hat-trick, and Laker and Lock performed the last rites in the second. Gilchrist did not play in the Final Test at The Oval, and Fred's promise to 'pin him to t'bloody sightscreen' remained unfulfilled.

It was a happier season for Trueman in international terms, somewhat less so as a Yorkshire player. The side was torn by internal feuding, and when a players' petition was drawn up calling for the replacement of Bill Sutcliffe as captain, Fred refused to sign it. This put him at loggerheads with some of Yorkshire's most experienced players but Fred had (still has) a strong friendship with Sutcliffe and, whatever his faults, lack of loyalty to his mates has never been one of them.

And when the Scarborough Festival came round to complete his season Fred found himself once again, as he saw it, the victim of unkind Fate. With a strong wind blowing off the sea he was asked to bowl into the wind while Tyson was to have it behind him. He flatly refused – until Godfrey Evans, captain of the Players (v. Gentlemen) threatened to take the whole team off the field. Then, and only then, did Fred agree to take the work-horse's end. He bowled well, but it was Tyson who took the wickets, leaving his rival to mutter darkly that if *he* had had the advantage of the near-gale the wickets would have been more plentiful, and cheaper. Nevertheless, Trueman was now reaching his peak as a bowler and he was to remain at it for nearly ten years, until he was well into his thirties. Hutton's prediction had been absolutely accurate. Throughout this period – certainly when he played for Yorkshire – there was an air of expectancy whenever Fred had the ball in his hand. The crowd somehow sensed that it was not a matter of *whether* he would take a wicket but simply a matter of time before he took the first, and after that it would be a case of how many. If he was not liked by many county batsmen he was respected by all of them.

At this stage of his career it has to be remembered that all counties played twenty-eight three-day games and unless he was in a Test (where the work was even harder) Fred played in all of them. There were no week-long breaks in a county's programme, no rest periods with an odd limited-overs match here and there; it was a four-month slog, with players driving up and down the country every Tuesday and Friday night to the next venue. It must be borne in mind, too, that there were no motorways in the 1950s, so journeys were often long and tedious, with Yorkshire having to travel to and from the furthest-flung outposts of the first-class game. Bradford to Swansea, Clacton to Scarborough, Taunton to Dover. It was commonplace to reach a town well after midnight and, if the toss was lost the following morning, to have to spend all day in the field. And this happened six days a week from the end of April to the beginning of September.

Yet Fred continued to mow down the wickets – 106 in 1958 (when he also played in all five Tests v. New Zealand), 175 in 1960 (five Tests v. South Africa), 155 in 1961 (four Tests v. Australia), 153 in 1962 (four Tests v. Pakistan), 129 in 1963 (five Tests and 34 wickets v. West Indies), 127 in 1965 when he was thirty-four years old. These were the vintage years, and the number of wickets Fred took at such modest cost make astonishing reading when set against the advancing years and the great pace he still generated.

Two fellow Yorkshiremen were probably able to exercise greater influence over him than any others he encountered in the whole of a long and spectacular career. One was Sir William Worsley (who, as Captain W. A. Worsley, had skippered the county in 1928 and 1929) became President in 1961 and remained in that office until 1973. During the early part of this period Fred, even after reaching an age of relative maturity, still fought a series of running battles with officialdom. Even the mild-mannered and soft-spoken secretary, John Nash, incurred Trueman's displeasure at times. The bellicose and outspoken Brian Sellers, who ruled Yorkshire cricket like a mediaeval warlord, could make nothing of him and there were some mighty explosions when the two collided. As complaints about Fred's misconduct – real or imagined, and there was no shortage of the latter – arrived in Leeds from other counties, attempts were made by Messrs Sellers and Nash to admonish him. Fred would have none of it. He could defend himself in the same colourful terms as Sellers used to admonish him. And he did. Thus, when all else failed, the error of his ways had occasionally to be pointed out by one of the few administrators – and certainly the only Yorkshire one – he respected.

Sir William was a country gentleman of the old school, and Fred has often recalled with the warmest affection those occasions when he was marched in before the Committee for reprimand, his guilt preconceived by some of his peers, to find the President insisting upon a full and fair hearing of *his* side of the story. Once or twice Fred was given a personal hearing by Sir William at his home, Hovingham Hall, where a young lady of the house was the future Duchess of Kent and Patron of Yorkshire County Cricket Club.

There is no doubt that Fred had an affectionate regard for Sir William and, one suspects, this was reciprocated in some measure. Sir William Worsley was one of the few who *understood* Fred in his playing days and who knew how to handle him. The other was Ronnie Burnet, the man entrusted (at the age of thirty-nine, never having played a first-class match) with sorting out the warring factions within the multi-talented side of the fifties and trying to win back the county championship which had remained with Surrey for most of the decade. He had spent most of his cricketing life in the Bradford League (where temperamental players are not unknown) and if he had yet something to learn about the technical details of the three-day game he at least knew *men*. It is perhaps typical of Fred's natural perverseness that when Burnet courted the strongest disapproval of Yorkshire's membership by telling the gifted slow left-armer, Johnny Wardle, to go, Trueman remained discreetly neutral – much as he respected Wardle's bowling. Where some of his colleagues had 'needled' Fred, provoking him into even more ostentatious aggresssion, or at best left him to get on with it, he now found a leader who encouraged him positively, boosted his morale and advised him. And, almost incredibly considering Ronnie's modest cricketing pedigree, Fred responded.

It is a trifle surprising, perhaps, to find FST adopting a neutral stance on a controversial topic, particularly one which touched so many sensitive areas as the Johnny Wardle affair of 1958. Wardle, one of the stronger personalities in Yorkshire's team of the fifties, was not unreasonable in hoping to become Yorkshire's first professional captain of the modern era when Bill Sutcliffe retired, prematurely, from the leadership. Instead the Committee opted daringly for Burnet who was now required to curb the strident individuality of some of the more senior players, encourage the development of the younger ones and somehow create a winning team when it had been impossible for two other captains to do so in the past decade when the playing strength had been greater.

To Ronnie Burnet must go boundless credit for skippering the side to the 1959 championship – the first success since 1949 (when the title was shared with Middlesex) – but this was only achieved after Wardle, the best slow left-arm bowler in the world at the time, had been dismissed. After Wardle, the next-senior player in length of capped service was Vic Wilson, and then came Close and Trueman, followed by Illingworth and Binks. And as the principal strike bowler, Fred's support (off the field as well as on it) was important to both main figures in the dispute, Wardle and Burnet. It placed him in a difficult position. He liked Wardle personally and had a profound respect for his ability as a slow bowler and as a cricket thinker. He also had great respect for Burnet, whom he regarded as a genuine amateur in an era when shamateurism was rife in some counties to an extent which led to the abolition of the distinction four years later. Fred appreciated, too, the magnitude of the task which confronted the former Second Eleven skipper, and he had a certain admiration for the way Ronnie tackled it despite his shortcomings as a player at that level. He offered public support for neither party but the truth is that Fred would have found it impossible to do less than his best for either protagonist. He was at, or very near, his best in 1958–9 and above all he was steeped in that Yorkshire pride (known as arrogance in other circles) which demanded the winning of the championship at regular intervals.

It is no doubt difficult for a generation which has grown up watching Yorkshire through the seventies and eighties to appreciate the intensity of that feeling. So many shabby performances over a long dreary twenty years have gone a long way towards wiping out the memory of past glories – but not for those who shared those glories (or basked in their reflection) of so many earlier years. The older players in 1958–9 were quick to sense the purposeful and honest approach of Burnet, and the young lions – Padgett, Taylor, Stott, Sharpe, Bolus and Wilson – followed him with an enthusiasm they had hitherto found it difficult to summon. Such is the appeal of that mystical quality called leadership.

While Fred deeply regretted the loss of the skill, the grim determination and the personal friendship of Johnny Wardle, he quickly warmed to the different approach of Burnet. Though required for all five Tests against India that summer (177.4 overs, 53 maidens, 401 runs, 24 wickets at 16. 70) he still bowled 716 county championship overs and took 93 wickets at 19.26. As if that were not enough to demand of any genuinely fast bowler in a summer, Yorkshire called upon him to play, too, against MCC at the start of the season and in the university match at Oxford, against MCC again in the Scarborough Festival and finally, deep in mid-September, against the Rest of England at The Oval, where Yorkshire won by 66 runs at 6 p.m. on the third day. The new county champions had played it out to the bitter end and it was a weary F. S. Trueman who walked off the field with his team-mates as the first autumnal nip was felt in the air. It felt good to be back on top.

One point is worth bearing in mind when looking at the whole picture of Trueman wicket-taking. Yorkshire, having no ground of their own, paid for the use of Headingley, Park Avenue, Sheffield, Hull, Harrogate and Middlesbrough, and of these only the Bradford pitch could be said to provide any sort of help for bowlers on anything like a regular basis. When Yorkshire were away, rarely if ever did they find themselves invited to what one might call 'up-county' grounds such as Dudley, Hinckley, Coventry, Frome, Blackpool, Ilkeston or Kettering, where pitches, less regularly prepared for the big occasion, might be expected to 'do a bit' from time to time. Always Yorkshire were asked to play on a county's No. 1 ground. This meant that, home and away, they were always required to play on pitches which would last three days (i.e. good wickets) so that the host club in Yorkshire and the host county when away could rely on maximum gate receipts. Remember: the white-rose county were the biggest attraction in the game. It must be borne in mind that every other county played that little bit harder against them; no one gave anything away, no one indulged in sporting declarations against Yorkshire.

For people who have started their cricket-watching during the last twenty years this may be a little difficult to understand, but there is no argument whatsoever about the attitude of other counties towards Yorkshire in the first seventy years of this century: it was uncompromisingly hostile. Personal friendships with individuals in other counties were almost unknown. Lancashire were a special case, classified as the ancient enemy for historical reasons far removed from the game of cricket, but it is a fact that all other countries regarded Yorkshire as the side they would most like to beat or the least like to lose to. In games against Middlesex, for instance, there had long been a particular intensity. Consequently Fred (and his colleagues) were not only bowling on pitches which were especially disadvantageous to them; they were attacking opposition which was more than usually determined to resist. And if anyone of a later generation doubts any of this I have to suggest that a word with any former player of twenty-five or more years ago will quickly bring confirmation.

On-the-field contretemps were largely avoided during the two years of Burnet's captaincy, though Fred continued to suffer more than his share of slanderous slings and arrows then, and afterwards. The problems these created within the ranks of county cricket he could handle, though he would have been happier without them. What was particularly unfortunate was that most of them were widely publicised and it was difficult to convince his first wife, Enid, that they had no substance.

One particular instance in which Fred was innocent concerned 'bad language and disgusting behaviour' and brought a thunderous complaint from a Bristol hotel to Yorkshire CCC headquarters, naming FST as a major culprit. It has to be said that the details of this story tax belief – unless one is aware of the feudal stupidity with which county affairs were sometimes handled at that time. Fred was duly hauled before the Committee to answer for his crimes and simply could not believe it. He had actually been playing in a Test Match at Lord's – in fact one of his greatest; he took eleven West Indies wickets for 152 runs – but somehow this had escaped the attention of his masters. They sat in solemn splendour at Headingley to hear an explanation of misconduct in Bristol with the Yorkshire side on 19, 20 and 21 June 1963, when, as the rest of the cricket world knew only too well, he had been playing for England at Lord's from 20–25 June. And if Sir William Worsley had not interrupted proceedings to hear Trueman's protestations of mistaken identity he would probably have been tried and convicted for a crime he most certainly did not commit. Yorkshire's Committee had an unfortunate tendency towards enjoying trampling on the playing peasantry. In the absence of Brian Close, Ray Illingworth *and* Fred, Yorkshire were captained on that occasion against Gloucs at Bristol by Jimmy Binks and he, too, was not guilty of 'bad language and disgusting behaviour'. It was the considerable media following which accompanied Yorkshire at that time who had enjoyed a singing night in the hotel; it might or might not have included refrains of a dubious nature.

Another occasion, at Worksop during a match with Notts, is one where I can personally vouch for Fred. The manageress wrote to say that FST would be banned if he ever tried to darken her doorstep again after 'disgraceful behaviour' in the town's leading hotel during the county championship match. While all the other members of the team, plus camp followers, stayed there, Fred and I in fact stayed at the Station Hotel, a much more modest establishment where the landlord and landlady were old friends of his. We never ventured into the team hotel. I don't think his story was believed by the Committee, though I corroborated it informally to a couple of members, but at least on this occasion Fred had the last laugh. A few weeks later, travelling between games, he called in at the hotel and inquired if the manageress recognised him. Mystified, she said 'No,' and FST, with grim and ponderous satisfaction informed her: 'That's a bit strange seeing as 'ow you've barred me from this place.'

So numerous and so regular were these complaints citing Trueman as a malefactor when he was not that it is difficult to blame him for his conviction, with hindsight, that he was innocent on all occasions. He was not, of course. The legends did not grow without a certain substance. He was high-profile, probably the best-known and most easily recognisable sporting personality in the country, and no matter how he tried to confine that image of ferocity and aggression to the field of play, he simply couldn't. Rarely if ever was he seen with a group of his team-mates when the day's toil was o'er. Fred left on excursions of his own and few knew where or for what purpose. But always there were people who spotted him and asked for autographs. This infuriated him, especially if he were engaged in a conversation or enjoying a quiet meal on his own, and he left no one in the slightest doubt of the extent of his resentment. This offended those who were too stupid to realise that their's was the offence of intrusion in the first place, and away they went to extend and expand the story of Truemanesque brusqueness, often embellishing the tale in the process.

At the same time there can be no doubt that occasionally he went over the top. I remember an occasion at Middlesbrough when two admiring schoolboys asked with admirable politeness for his autograph and were rewarded with a blast which shook them to the core. I was upset as well and gently suggested to my friend that he would not always be at the top. The time would come when he might be glad if someone asked him to sign a book, or a programme, or just a scrap of paper. Fred knew damn well he had over-reacted but would not recant. He grunted, and walked on, leaving two sadly disillusioned little boys in his wake. But the time I forecast has, of course, not yet arrived. He is still a figure of great renown, star of stage, screen and radio; and he still will not tolerate an interruption of his off-duty hours. I have often wondered how the two schoolboys thought of him in later years; was he still a heroic figure on the cricket field, ploughing through the Aussies, laying low the West Indies and terrifying the Indians? Or did the pair grow to adulthood thinking of him merely as a surly and churlish figure, too remote and uncaring to accept their childish homage? These things are important.

Fred was now 'in his pomp', bowling at the highest peak for season after season. Outside the boundary rails he continued to find it an imperfect world, and spent much of his off-duty life complaining about a wide variety of matters. If he could have indulged in a good, wholly uninhibited belly laugh once or twice a week it would have worked wonders for his personal morale and public image. But the best he could manage was a black humour, often self-directed; he enjoyed making others laugh but he could rarely do it for himself and it was a great pity. The epigrams still flowed, but sometimes they misfired through being heard in the wrong quarters, as at Colwyn Bay during Fred's benefit season of 1962. It was a warm and pleasant Sunday afternoon and an elderly lady positioned herself in a deckchair immediately outside the windows of the Yorkshire dressing-room. Conversation inside turned, as it often does on such occasions, to physical characteristics and FST – responding to a gentle jibe – looked down with mock wistfulness and agreed: 'Aye, when they built me they put everything in t'wrong place – like a cart-oss between t'shoulders and a tom cat between t'legs.' The lady outside the windows beat a hurried retreat, no doubt to spread the Gospel of Fred's crude vulgarity amongst her friends. It was during that same game that we saw how his professional pride was never totally switched off.

To give the players an occasional break from six days a week on the county circuit and a day of benefit cricket on the Sunday, a few friends with experience of league cricket used to make up the numbers on benefit match days. Thus it was that I came to open the bowling with Fred in Colwyn Bay, the maestro coming downwind, though at a drastically reduced pace. Upwind, and at about a quarter of the Trueman pace, not unnaturally the ball swung a bit and the Welsh opening batsman – daringly decked in a gaily coloured Cardiff University cap – was generous and friendly enough to offer a little compliment at the end of an over: 'You are moving it much more than Trueman, you know.' Unfortunately he made the remark within earshot of FST as the field changed over and Fred stopped, turned and gave him The Glare. His next delivery to the 'coloured cap', an age-old red rag to any Yorkshire bull, bounced once, soared over the batsman, over the wicket-keeper and almost cleared the boundary fence before long leg had even moved.

From mid-on came the plaintive reproach from Ronnie Burnet (another of those giving up the day of rest to help the beneficiary): 'Fred – it's only a friendly, and it's for *your* benefit after all.' The snarled response was immediate: 'Well, tell that pillock to keep his mouth shut.' Even on the most relaxed of occasions Fred is not to be mocked or despised.

Yorkshire's 1959 championship was followed by other successes in 1960 and 1962 after Vic Wilson had taken over the leadership from Burnet, and the position of runners-up to Hampshire in 1961 was regarded as a major disaster. That is no exaggeration; I recall being asked by my sports editor (of the *Daily Mail*) to fill most of the back page of the then broadsheet newspaper with an 'in-depth' inquiry into Yorkshire's 'failure'. Apart from the captain, and Brian Close, Fred was the next-senior man in the side, and as spearhead of the attack he regarded himself in some ways as even more senior than the others. He did not get on as well with Wilson as he had with Burnet.

He regarded the farmer from East Yorkshire as a bit of a dull stick and Vic, in turn, looked upon Fred as a troublesome 'young' upstart, having served alongside him in the ranks during the whole of the Trueman career – with professional respect but without personal affection. He knew that his orders would be obeyed on the field – albeit grudgingly on occasions! – but he could not rely upon the same deference within the dressing-room.

Like Fred himself, Vic did not mix with other players in his off-duty moments, taking himself off in the evening on unpublicised excursions. Fred took great pleasure in leg-pulling about these mysterious outings in a way which was not always entirely harmless. There was a strong feeling within the camp by the summer of 1962 that before Wilson retired at the end of that season he would find a way of taking revenge. It came on Saturday, 21 July, and one of the greatest moments of the Trueman career was followed immediately by the supreme humiliation.

On the three preceding days Fred had experienced the heady delight of skippering the Players (the professionals) in the last of 137 matches in that series to take place at Lord's against the Gentlemen. It is a game worth recalling, at least for those who took part in it:

GENTLEMEN

The Rev. D. S. Sheppard c and b Titmus	112	b Titmus	34
E. J. Craig b Trueman	4	c Titmus b Trueman	0
E. R. Dexter c Trueman b Shackleton	55	run out	1
M. J. K. Smith run out	44	not out	15
R. M. Prideaux b Trueman	14	b Shackleton	109
A. R. Lewis lbw b Shackleton	2	c Andrew b Titmus	10
R. W. Barber run out	0	not out	3
D. B. Pithey run out	30		
T. E. Bailey c Walker b Shackleton	5		
A. C. Smith c Sharpe b Shackleton	33		
O. S. Wheatley not out	10		
Extras (b 4 lb 6)	10		
TOTAL	323	TOTAL (for five wkts dec)	172

Bowling:

Trueman 13–6–59–2
Shackleton 38–9–101–4
Walker 28–4–64–0
Titmus 20–6–46–1
Gifford 14–4–43–0

Bowling:

Trueman 10–6–8–1
Shackleton 19–8–30–1
Walker 9–2–21–0
Titmus 24–5–69–2
Gifford 7–0–36–0

PLAYERS

Stewart, M. J. c A. Smith b Bailey	0	c A. Smith b Wheatley	3
Edrich, J. H. b Bailey	19	not out	77
Parfitt, P. H. c Sheppard b Dexter	9	c Dexter b Barber	63
Graveney, T. W. c Craig b Wheatley	21	c A. Smith b Bailey	41
Sharpe, P. J. c and b Barber	39	not out	12
Walker, P. M. b Bailey	15		
Titmus, F. J. c Dexter b Bailey	70		
Trueman, F. S. c Wheatley b Barber	63		
Andrew, K. V. c A. Smith b Bailey	17		
Gifford, N. c A. Smith b Bailey	2		
Shackleton, D. not out	1		
Extras (b 4)		Extras (b 1 lb 10)	11
TOTAL	260	TOTAL (for three wkts)	207

Bowling:	*Bowling:*
Bailey 30.3–10–58–6	Bailey 13–1–45–1
Wheatley 19–6–37–1	Wheatley 12–1–46–1
Dexter 18–2–49–1	Dexter 7–0–43–0
Barber 21–7–90–2	Barber 7–0–43–1
Pithey 8–2–22–0	Pithey 4–0–27–0

Match drawn

Fred has a great sense of history and has always been deeply interested in the folklore and statistics of the game, so he came away from Lord's well satisfied with having taken part in a notable match as well as with his captain's innings of 63. After a television appearance he set off, not too early in the evening, to drive to Taunton with his fellow Yorkshireman, Philip Sharpe, as a passenger for the following day's opening of the championship fixture with Somerset. On the Saturday morning Fred was late in arriving at the ground, was left out of the side declared by Vic Wilson before the toss and when he did arrive he was instructed by the captain to return home, where he would be the subject of a report to the Committee. It was probably the greatest humiliation of Fred's career, made a sensational news item and left him spluttering with fury. Wilson had been given the opportunity for revenge and had taken it.

Now, over the years Fred has managed to convince himself that he was the victim of circumstances, that he had taken a wrong turning late at night, had finally got to bed exhausted by the journey and his earlier labours at Lord's and had simply 'slept in' in consequence.

That is not *exactly* the case. At 10.20 on that Saturday morning I was preparing to leave the County Hotel for the ground in Taunton when I met a distracted and harassed-looking P. J. Sharpe in the lobby. 'Isn't it time you were on parade?' I asked, and Philip explained that his kit was still in the boot of Fred's car, Fred was still in bed and – yes – it was certainly time he (or rather both of them) were half a mile down the road at the ground. Now, one of the cardinal rules of life on the circuit was that players presented themselves one hour before start of play on the first day of games, half an hour on the second and third days.

'You shoot off now,' I said to Sharpe 'and I'll get your kit to you in a few minutes.' I went to Fred's room – he was indeed still in bed – and found him, in all truth, feeling a trifle 'bolshy'. He insisted that he was 'knackered' and that it was not *absolutely* essential for him to be at the ground by 10.30. As it was now a few minutes *after* 10.30 it was indeed important for Fred to convince himself of this! I warned, 'It's a breach of team discipline. There's bound to be trouble.'

'Bugger it,' replied Fred. 'I've done my share of the work all season. *I* haven't had a bloody rest. I was late getting here and if they expect me to bowl this bloody lot out today they'll just have to wait till I get there.' It never occurred to him for one moment that Yorkshire would take the field without him. I borrowed his car-keys, transferred Sharpe's bag from Fred's boot to my own, left the keys in reception and drove to the ground.

Fred arrived nearly half an hour later, was given a rocket by the captain, argued his case but was told to return home forthwith. He did not return home. He came round to the Press Box, called me out and we retired to a quiet corner of the ground while Fred poured out his heart. He had so far that season bowled 605 overs for Yorkshire (true) and had taken 84 wickets for his county (true). He had bowled another 111 overs for England in the three Tests played so far and a further 23 in the Gents v. Players fixture just finished. He had played against the bloody MCC and against the bloody 'schoolboys' (i.e. Oxford University) and when Yorkshire met the touring Pakistanis at Bradford it was the slow left-armer, Wilson, who was rested while Fred was obliged to toil on. No rest for Trueman.

All this was perfectly correct. In fact Fred had been in almost perpetual motion since 28 April and this, remember, was 21 July. He had been bowling fast for almost three months, six days a week, with only one rest – Cambridge University – and he was averaging nearly forty overs a game. That he decided on that July morning to chance his arm, to some extent, is undeniable; that he knew he was going to be late in reporting for duty was inescapable. But could anyone dispute that he had a case in snatching an extra half-hour in bed? Whatever the rights and wrongs of the argument. Fred was Page One news once again. The story of his humiliation came early enough for the Saturday evening sports editions to have a field day with it, and cricket-writers of three big-circulation Yorkshire newspapers – the *Evening Post*, the *Evening News* (both Leeds) and the *Star* (Sheffield) – travelled everywhere with the team at that time. Then the Sunday papers had a follow-up go at it and Fred was in the headlines all over the country.

During the whole of Saturday, Fred drowned his sorrows as I had never seen him do before (or since that day). We spent something like six hours together as he opened the flood-gates of resentment and bitterness at what seemed to him to be outrageous and unnecessary persecution. If he felt as rough as I did the following morning there was only one place to be and that was in bed. That was where Fred spent Sunday. His room was not far from that of the captain and Vic knew – everyone knew – that Fred had not returned home, as instructed, but Wilson (wisely, I think) decided not to push his luck with a further confrontation. On the other hand, I had now to compose a story which 'stood up' after the evening and Sunday papers had seemingly milked the incident dry. I got up at 5 a.m. on Sunday (suffering greatly!) and wrote a piece based on Fred's lamentations of the previous day. I checked the figures of Fred's Herculean labours and found them correct to the last detail. And I took the story to his room before setting out on a previously arranged excursion to Portishead, to support a match for the Somerset beneficiary that summer. Fred didn't want to know; he just wanted to sleep.

I insisted that I should read the piece to him: 'Fred, I've quoted you extensively and you know the Committee will come down on you like a ton of bricks. You have criticised the captain and they won't wear that. Let me tell you what I've said and then, if you think we ought to tone it down, we'll do that.'

FST would have none of it. From somewhere underneath the tangled bedclothes he grunted probably the sweetest words any newspaperman could hope to hear: 'If you've done it, sunshine, it'll be reight. I'll stand by what I said.' Still I insisted that he ought to hear what had been written. Still he refused. I went off to Portishead with my Somerset friends, telephoned the story to London before play began and spent the rest of the day knowing that I had done my duty as a reporter but wondering whether I had done it as a friend. I was terribly afraid that I hadn't. At six o'clock I was telephoned in the pavilion at Portishead by J. L. Manning, the *Daily Mail* sports editor, expressing unbridled delight with the story. I was even more unhappy (as a friend).

On the Monday morning the *Daily Mail* used almost the whole of the back page to voice Fred's grievances with a border of Trueman caricatures – the bristling, half-shaven chin, the flopping hair. There was a certain subdued hilarity in the Yorkshire ranks at Monday's breakfast, not noticeably shared by J. V. Wilson. Fred returned North to face the wrath of the Committee before returning to Test duty at Trent Bridge. At the end of the second match, while I travelled first to Bristol, then to Bramall Lane for county cricket, news filtered back that Fred had been confronted by a furious Brian Sellers brandishing a copy of the *Daily Mail* of Monday, 23 July, and had been given the most almighty rocket. We next met on the morning of Wednesday, 1 August, at Middlesbrough, before Yorkshire's match with Kent began. I positioned myself in the room where players, media and umpires had a cup of tea to start the day so that Fred could get everything off his chest. He breezed in cheerfully, got his tea and addressed me thus: 'Na then, sunshine. They tell me you're about as popular wi' Vic as I am.' And he departed for the dressing-room to be reunited after ten days with the team and with the captain. From that day to this he has never uttered a single syllable of reproach. I hope no one ever suggests in my presence that Freddie Trueman is not a loyal friend.

4

Trueman and Statham

Until Clive Lloyd changed the whole concept of Test attacks with his continuous barrage from *four* fast bowlers the history of the game was marked by *pairs* of bowlers, some fast, some slow, but who attacked essentially in tandem. We still think of them in 'twin' terms, rather like a psychologist's word-association test: Gregory and ? A: McDonald; Lindwall and ? A: Miller; Laker and ? A: Lock; Ramadhin and ? A: Valentine. The first name immediately conjures up the second in the cricket-lover's mind. And through the 1950s and '60s the pairing which sprang fastest to the lips of fans everywhere was Trueman and Statham.

They were not paired together as frequently as one might imagine in view of the fact that they are now, with hindsight, invariably associated with each other. At one time or another in his Test career Fred opened the bowling with Alec Bedser, Trevor Bailey, Peter Loader, Frank Tyson, Alan Moss, Harold Rhodes, Les Jackson, Len Coldwell, David Larter, Derek Shackleton, Jack Flavell, John Price and Fred Rumsey. Brian, over roughly the same period, was partnered with the new ball by Bedser, Fred Ridgway (Kent), Bailey, Tyson, Loader, Flavell and David Brown (Warwickshire). The two of them were not allowed a sustained spell of operating in harness as often as some memories might suggest, with one or two notable exceptions like the home series against West Indies in 1957 and South Africa in 1960 and on tour in Australia in 1962–3.

The traditional rivalry between Yorkshire and Lancashire has always added a piquancy to their partnership, at least in the minds of northern cricket people. Twice a year they were opposed in the most important county match for both clubs and no one played those games harder than the two opening bowlers. Otherwise they were linked in the most potent opening partnership England have known in modern cricket. They were ideally suited in that respect because of the entirely different problems they posed. Trueman was fractionally faster (that is Statham's own judgment, not merely that of an observer from the other side of the Pennines) and relied on his natural gifts as the bowler of the outswinger as well as his hostile unpredictability, and his length was a matter of inches shorter than that of Statham so that batsmen were a shade happier watching him from the back foot.

For Brian, on the other hand, movement in the air was something which remained an unsolved mystery to the end of his playing days. When the ball *did* swing for him it was not part of any grand design but a natural process – usually due to atmospheric conditions – over which he had no personal control, and therefore he was rarely happy when it happened. 'George' relied on his pace allied to pin-point accuracy and movement off the seam, and this was something he most assuredly did know something about. His maxim, oft-quoted, was quite simply, 'If they miss, I hit,' but with typical modesty he has dismissed his seam-movement as just enough to find the edge of the bat rather than the middle, and so many of his wickets came from slip catches. His slightly fuller length demanded front-foot defence from batsmen, thus creating over-by-over adjustments in defensive technique when facing the two bowlers in harness.

Temperamentally, they were just as different as they were as attacking bowlers. Trueman was volatile, demonstrative, as free with advice to batsmen as he was with recriminations after an unintentional boundary, a dropped catch or a fortuitous edge; colourful in the extreme with his anguished entreaties for divine aid to desert the batsman, just for an instant; he shunned the commonplace or traditional comment in his mid-wicket invective so that in an age when a lucky batsman was said to have 'more edges than a three-penny bit' Fred coined the more graphic bon mot: 'more edges than a brokken piss-pot.'

Statham, patient and phlegmatic, rarely addressed himself either to opponent or deity. He concentrated his attention on the *next* delivery in the style we were to see later from Richard Hadlee, suggesting an impassive acceptance of unkind Fate. 'George' used the bouncer sparingly and batsmen knew instinctively that they were very rarely in serious physical danger from his bowling; Fred, without overdoing the bouncer, could always be relied upon to let the man at the other end know that it was there in the repertoire, especially if he hit a four, whether by accident or design. Propaganda played a not inconsiderable role in his attacking strategy. It would start in the dressing-room, before the day's proceedings were under way.

Every opposition side could expect a social call by FST on the first morning for (a) an exchange of pleasantries; (b) a selection of jokes from his extensive, and ever-increasing, collection; and, finally (c) a warning of the shape of things to come. This took two forms. The first was a stab of the finger in the direction of a number of players around the dressing-room and an accompanying roll-call: 'That's one, two, three. Oh aye, and *thee*. Well that's four for a start.' The second was even more personal – an imaginary cross marked in baptismal fashion on the forehead of a potential victim with the elaborately casual advice: 'That's where tha can expect it, sunshine.' On the field the psychological battle was marked by the glare, the frown, the pause when half-way back to his mark to cast a look of pure menace over his shoulder at the batsman. It was all very theatrical; sometimes it worked, sometimes it didn't. But whether it did or not, it was all part of Fred's window-dressing, an essential part of the Trueman road show. There were many bowlers around, good bowlers, whom it was possible to dismiss from the mind as *individuals* so that the batsman could concentrate simply on the quality of the next delivery. This was not the case with Fred Trueman; no batsman was ever in the slightest doubt about who had the ball in his hand at the other end. And the spectators found themselves caught up in the whole elaborate charade. One could always sense that tingle of excitement throughout the ground when Fred was in action. Not too many performers have been able to conjure up that reaction and very few indeed during his career or before it.

Although Trueman and Statham presented such a formidable combination on the cricket field, and though they shared a room on tour and home Test occasions many times, they were not particularly close friends in their playing days, though they never quarrelled or even argued. They had not a great deal in common outside plying their trade. Statham was happy in the company of a couple of mates, enjoying a quiet beer, and yearned for nothing more exotic on his travels than an evening at the cinema. We were neighbours, as well as friends, when we both lived in the Denton area of Greater Manchester and I often thought Brian would have enjoyed *watching* Wimbledon just as much as *playing* in a Test Match. He was keen on football, too, and might well have become a Manchester United player if his father had not vetoed the idea in the days when the maximum wage for a League professional was £24 a week.

Fred, a bustling centre-forward, was also keen on football. During his National Service, when he had already made his mark for Yorkshire and was about to be called up by England, his talents were recognised by Bill Anderson, that shrewdest of non-glamour club managers; this resulted in an invitation to play for Lincoln City Reserves, who found themselves, in direct consequence, playing before crowds twice as big as those watching the club's first team! But there the common interests ended. FST was shy of close personal relationships, preferring to address himself to an impersonal group of listeners. The audience might, and usually did, consist of complete strangers and he was happy to hold court for hours an end – providing no one else wanted to occupy centre stage! So the teams he played with, for Yorkshire or England, usually found that Fred would drift quietly away at the end of the day to pursue his own interests, and few of his team-mates ever knew where he went.

At the same time there was an unspoken and unsentimental attachment between the two, perhaps born of mutual respect which remained throughout their retirement years and surfaced, almost dramatically, twenty years later. While Fred and I saw a great deal of each other and, of course, worked closely together during the summer, I then saw Brian perhaps once a year. He worked as a rep for Guinness and, very occasionally, would call at Broadcasting House in Manchester and inquire, diffidently in the extreme, if I had time for a lunch-hour drink. This used to exasperate me. Every time it happened I blasted 'George': 'Don't bloody well creep quietly in here asking if *I* have time to see *you*. Walk in, ten feet tall, and *tell* everybody you have come to have a drink with me. I shall be very proud that you have.' But that was not the Statham way.

Then, in the summer of 1988, we met at Headingley where Brian was judging the Man of the Match in a Natwest Trophy game, and I was appalled to learn that he had had a spell of illness, had lost his job and been on the brink of a complete nervous collapse. Needless to say, the information had to be dragged out of 'George', who neither asked nor expected help or sympathy. A week or two later, my wife and I were with Fred and his (second) wife Veronica and I mentioned the meeting with his old sparring partner.

'How about putting on a Trueman and Statham evening somewhere, Fred?' I asked, 'We could fill a hall anywhere in Yorkshire or Lancashire and raise a bob or two for the old boy. I know he hates speaking in public but you and I could do the talking and then have a question-and-answer session with the audience.' Fred thought about this, quietly, but didn't answer 'Yes' or 'No', which I thought was a bit odd. It was not until three months later, when I was in New Zealand, that I became aware of the extent of Fred's interest. From a newspaper I read that he was busy organising a massive Statham tribute dinner in London and, on my return, I received the terse instruction: 'You'll be there, of course, sunshine. Jonners and Jenkers and Trevor are coming, and a few more.'

A few more! Fred had called up just about every man who ever played with or against Brian Statham and 'sold' eighty or ninety tables at £1,000 a time, with the Minister of Sport to chair the occasion, Leslie Crowther and Rory Bremner to run an auction of an astonishing collection of articles, a cabaret and a series of raffles as well. Not content with that, he staged a similar function in Manchester during the Fourth Test of 1989. The organisational work alone was massive but if Fred sets out to put on a show, for whatever the cause, he does it on a grand scale. Both occasions were the most tremendous tribute to the affection and respect in which 'George' is held, still, throughout cricket; both were a testimony to the fact that FST, sentimentalist or not, is willing to work his socks off to help out an old mate. The Old Firm was still in good working order. My original idea was to make a few hundred pounds; Fred – bless him – thought in terms of tens of thousands.

Statham has ever been a loyal friend and supporter of Trueman, even when their paths have strayed far apart. No wrong word has ever passed between the two of them and I very much doubt if anyone has ever heard Brian speak ill of Fred (or of anyone, for that matter). Indeed, the Lancashire man has championed Fred's cause whenever others have sought to denigrate his partner. Forty years on, he will tell you: 'Fred was *very* much maligned, you know, so often when he least deserved it.' This is not a matter of being blind to Fred's faults, not stubbornly refusing to accept the strictures of 'outsiders' directed at a team-mate. Brian, no less than any close friend of Fred's, is quite aware of his shortcomings, and in the course of refuting a number of ill-founded allegations he slipped in a 'for instance' to illustrate how FST can be infuriatingly boorish – in a context in which Fred would insist with his dying breath that he was absolutely right.

The occasion was the 1959–60 tour to the West Indies, and the two fast bowlers were in a party of seven out for a quiet drink one evening in Jamaica. The round of seven lagers included Alan Moss, the Middlesex paceman, and Roy Swetman, the Surrey wicket-keeper, and the rest of the party were Northerners. Moss and Swetman were not Fred's idea of the perfect touring colleagues. They mocked his heavy South Yorkshire accent and generally 'took the mickey' out of him at every opportunity; the North–South divide was very much in evidence.

'It won't surprise you,' recalls Statham, 'that everyone had bought a round except Fred and when we reminded him that he could no longer avoid shouting in the drinks he grudgingly ordered *five* lagers. "But the round is seven, Fred," we protested. "I'm buying five," Fred insisted firmly. "But why?" we asked. "I'm not buying for them two bastards," he replied, with his eyes fixed on Moss and Swetman. "Never. I'm not buying for them." And he wouldn't. Tommy Greenhough paid for the two extra drinks, "for the sake of peace and quiet".'

Now it is entirely possible to picture that scene. It mattered not to Fred that Moss and Swetman had already bought their round of seven, and that all the canons of drinking etiquette demanded that he pay for the same number as everyone else. What concerned Fred was quite simply that he regarded the two Southerners as unpleasant people bent on taking a rise out of him. He was therefore not disposed to buy a drink for them. QED. And anyone who knows Fred well will understand the situation immediately. You either like a bloke or you don't and if you don't, you don't buy him a drink. Simple! It is not a philosophy calculated to endear Fred to anyone in the round, Northerner or Southerner, but that would not matter a tinker's cuss to him.

Fred had his troubles with tour managers from time to time, notably with Freddie Brown on the 1958–9 trip to Australia and New Zealand. To the eyes of Southern readers, and those of Establishment figures, it might appear more accurate to say that the manager had problems with Yorkshiremen, since he first of all lost the services of Johnny Wardle, whose invitation to tour was withdrawn by MCC (after he had been dismissed by his county) as he had written critical newspaper articles. Then he had a series of difficulties on tour with two Yorkies who disliked him intensely – Jim Laker and Fred Trueman. In one particular dispute, FST once again found Brian Statham backing him wholeheartedly. This was when the party, leaving Melbourne to fly to Sydney, was divided into two groups, one leaving early (7 a.m.) and the other conveniently later. Fred, checking with the roster, found himself on the earlier flight, which did not please him inordinately since early rising has never been his strong suit.

However, he nobly made the effort and so was livid to find himself addressed by the manager as he was about to board the coach for the airport: 'You are not on this flight, Trueman.' Now, if there is one thing that upsets Fred more than most others it is being addressed simply by his surname. He cannot have been a very good National Service airman. Many of his most bitter complaints against Brian Sellers, Yorkshire's cricket chairman, are based on Sellers' penchant for addressing the troops in commanding-officer fashion. And at seven o'clock on an Australian morning he was not in the sweetest of tempers. So a snarling wrangle took place, with dialogue which might have been taken from a Christmas pantomime if the atmosphere had not been so highly charged.

'You are *not* on this flight.'

'Oh yes I am.'

'Oh no you're not.'

'Oh yes I am.'

The problem was finally resolved in a way which saw Fred finally allowed to take the earlier coach – but in a more furious temper than ever. As the snapping pair reached about their sixth 'oh-yes-I-am' Trevor Bailey, one of the five amateurs on tour, appeared on the steps of the hotel, languidly robed in dressing-gown, cigarette in one hand, cup of tea in the other.

'Sorry, old boy,' he blithely informed the manager. 'I can't possibly make the first flight.'

'Doesn't matter a bit, old boy,' replied F. R. Brown. 'Take the later one. Trueman, you may go on this one.'

'I wasn't a bit surprised,' says Statham, 'that it was a seething, muttering, cursing FST who boarded the coach.' It may come as a surprise to many people, probably most of all to F. R. Brown, to learn that Fred is a stalwart supporter of the Conservative Party. And in many ways he has long regretted the passing of the amateur cricketer – or at any rate those who enjoyed his respect. Freddie Brown was not amongst this number.

Statham again presents himself as a staunch ally in the matter of Fred's dispute with Len Hutton, captain in the West Indies in 1953–4, which resulted from a straightforward case of mistaken identity. The players were invited to a rather formal ball at the Yacht Club in Barbados – the sort of occasion most of them disliked intensely, but as an official tour event attendance was mandatory – and Tom Graveney was dancing with an extremely pukka memsah'b who, unfortunately, happened to be a close friend of the Governor (we are still in Colonial days at this point). The smooth Graveney charm beguiled the lady into believing that Tom was an official guest at the ball rather than a touring cricketer and so she launched, unfortunately, into a tirade against the bad manners of the players both on and off the field.

'Have you met many of the players?' inquired Tom, mildly.

'Certainly not.'

'Oh. Well, have you been watching them play?'

'No. I don't like cricket.'

'I see. Well, don't you think it's a little unfair of you to criticise men you don't know?'

End of conversation. End of dance. The lady flounced off to report to her friend the Governor that she had been insulted by an England cricketer 'with black hair'. Now, Fred has always insisted that he was nowhere to be seen at that moment and it is indeed difficult to picture him dancing under a tropical moon at any stage of his life, let alone at the age of twenty-three. But our corroborative evidence from Statham is that the following morning Fred was marched in, left-right, left-right, to be formally reprimanded for rudeness to a lady, without any further inquiries being thought necessary. He had black hair, though there any possible re-semblance to Tom Graveney – in stature, appearance, accent, or Terpsichorean accomplishment – ended.

On the 1962–3 tour to Australia, Fred might well be said, with hindsight at any rate, to have been on a collision-course with the management from the moment the party was selected. The manager was the Duke of Norfolk, Earl Marshal and premier duke of England, and Fred, while despising the *nouveau riche* and devotedly admiring the hereditary peerage, could not really be said to have a lot in common with His Grace. Respecting his lineage was one thing; having to look to him for managerial guidance on a cricket tour was entirely another. The captain was 'Lord Edward' Dexter and much as contemporary players admired his great natural gifts as a cricketer, few had a great admiration for his captaincy.

Even the mild-mannered and relatively uncritical Statham has to confess: 'Ted Dexter was one captain I never fully understood. I don't think anyone else in the dressing-room did, either. He did things at times which were difficult to understand. He made moves, and bowling changes, which were completely out of keeping with the run of the game and which sometimes resulted in the opposition wriggling off the hook.'

And in the side was David Sheppard, now an ordained minister who had been 'signed up' in advance of the tour to officiate at services in Australia on Sundays. Here was a target for Fred's barbed and sometimes ponderous wit which it was impossible for him to resist. Each Monday morning throughout the tour, Fred greeted the future Bishop of Liverpool with an exaggeratedly genial inquiry: 'What sort of gate did you get yesterday, Rev? Was it bigger than Boothie's?' (This was a reference to the Australian batsman Brian Booth, who was a lay preacher). *On* the field, Fred's ecclesiastical references were viewed less tolerantly by captain and manager. Many of them are standards in the after-dinner speaking repertoire to this day, but they bear repetition here because this is the Trueman Story. Thus, when at Melbourne, with ten minutes to go to close of play, Statham found the splice of Richie Benaud's bat and Sheppard spilled the catch, Fred's mournful lament echoed across the ground: 'The only bloody time he can keep his hands together is on Sunday.'

It is true that Fred had a personal cause for bitterness at times on this particular tour because Dexter stationed Sheppard at leg-slip, a position Fred regarded as very much his own. In Adelaide, the Reverend put down two catches there, not chances requiring spectacular dives to right or left, Statham recalls, but straight-forward edges, and finally he was moved to long leg. Fred bowled a bouncer, the batsman hooked and the ball flew high towards the boundary where Sheppard triumphantly held the catch. As he threw the ball high in the air and galloped delightedly after it, it was Statham who called wearily across to him from deep third man, 'You'd better chuck it in, Rev. It was a no ball and they're now running three.' Fred, it has to be recorded, was on this occasion speechless.

The friendship of Trueman and Statham was probably only once in any danger of being breached. This was on a rain-affected pitch at Headingley in a Roses match. Statham bowled to Trueman, the ball took a piece out of the turf, jumped and gave a catch to short leg. Fred cast a long, reproachful look at his mate and growled, 'Bouncers, eh, George? Don't forget thar's got to bat yet.' Did he, in fact retaliate?

'No. He wouldn't waste his energy on me.'

Taking on the West Indies – and Others

One of the major disappointments of Fred's playing career was that he was never selected to tour South Africa, a country he has visited many times (and enjoyed immensely) since retirement both on holiday and as an after-dinner speaker. He was particularly upset when his last chance disappeared in 1964–5. He might have been approaching the end of his career, aged thirty-three, but no one dare suggest that to him when in the previous summer he had become the first man in history to take 300 Test wickets and had headed the bowling averages against Australia with 17 wickets in four Tests at 23.47 while five other quicks had been tried during the series without making a major impact. His 67 wickets for Yorkshire in championship matches had cost 20.05 each and he still believed he could do as good a job as anyone else in The Cape. He was aghast when the Selectors' choice was Ian Thomson, an honest county bowler who had, however, taken 116 wickets for Sussex during the summer at 16.30. Fred looked upon Test bowling as something quite different from the daily round and common task of operating against county batsmen. It was a matter of *class*, allied to experience, and in his view Thomson possessed neither in any great abundance. His horror was complete when, because of a series of injuries, England called up for the last Test in South Africa the Somerset bowler, Ken Palmer, who was coaching in Johannesburg. Twenty-five years later it still causes Fred to choke in near-apoplexy at the memory of England's Test attack being opened by Ian Thomson and Ken Palmer, ungracious as that may seem. It is that sort of ungraciousness which makes him no friends but does line up one or two enemies. It takes a particularly generous spirit to see the situation from Fred's point of view: that he had been deprived of his last chance to tour a beautiful and hospitable country, to give the South African cricket public their only chance to see the great FS in action before he was forced by *anno domini* to call it a day.

As we have seen, his first tour abroad to the West Indies had not been an entirely enjoyable affair, and we have touched briefly upon his problems in Australia. Now perhaps we may look at them in a little more detail.

It was difficult to see how it could ever be a really comfortable tour. The appointment of His Grace of Norfolk seemed to most eyes to be a trifle unusual, and with 'Lord Edward' Dexter as captain it was quickly being suggested that the scorecards should be printed by *Debrett*. Dexter's wife was a fashion model who had a series of professional engagements in Australia at the time the tour was taking place, and with the Rev. David Sheppard's preaching attracting enhanced congregations in the churches the focus of media attention was hardly on the cricket. The Duke's appearances at press conferences, moreover, usually resulted in more questions about his racing connections than about the composition of the England team for the next match.

The holder of the strongest possible view that the real purpose of the tour was being overlooked was, inevitably, F. S. Trueman and, unsurprisingly, he did not hide his opinions too deeply. Thus, an Aussie newspaperman, catching him in an unguarded moment, was delighted to learn that the PBI of the England party were 'not sure whether they were playing under Jockey Club rules, working for Dexter Enterprises or taking part in a missionary hunt'. It did not entirely please the tour management.

Fred's sardonic humour changed to livid rage when he found himself banned from earning a bob or two by endorsing local products or being paid for after-dinner speeches. Apart from his firm belief that his role as the world's top cricketing personality *entitled* him to cash in on his fame, Fred regarded it as manifestly unfair that Mrs Dexter's modelling engagements were carried out during a tour when she was the wife of the touring captain. I don't think he went so far as to suggest that David Sheppard was getting a cut of the collections in church, but he made a few calculations and reckoned he was as much as £1,000 out of pocket because of the management's refusal to sanction his own off-the-field activities. That was a great deal of money in 1962–3. Distinctions between amateurs and professionals might well have been officially abolished, but as far as Fred was concerned the old-boy network had most certainly not been dismantled and he was the poorer for it.

His resentment smouldered, came out into the open from time to time and his indiscretions were quietly noted in the managerial ledger.

It had all started on a much happier note, with thoughtful arrangements of an outward trip by air to Aden and then a leisurely cruise in the *Canberra* to Fremantle – not long enough to get bored at sea but quite long enough for the voyage to be enjoyable.

Unfortunately for Fred's dreams of leisurely sessions in a deckchair, his fellow passengers included Gordon Pirie, one of Britain's most noted distance-runners of his day and a man with some advanced (at that time) theories about training methods. And Dexter thought it was a good idea for Pirie to take charge of the cricketers' fitness programme during the voyage. Twenty years or so later I met Gordon Pirie in Auckland when he came to the commentary box at Eden Park to introduce himself as a fellow Yorkshireman. I said, 'There's one question I've always wanted to ask you . . .' and before I could utter another word Gordon smilingly interrupted, '. . . about my encounter with Fred Trueman on the boat to Australia? Yes, it's perfectly true.'

Gordon had tried to persuade Fred to change his diet from as much steak as he could find on board the *Canberra* to Spartan vegetarian fare, and to perform regular circuits of the deck instead of reclining in a deckchair. It would, he claimed, strengthen Fred's leg-muscles. FS regarded him with severe distaste, then, with the greatest deliberation, replied, 'During the season which finished in September I bowled 1,141 overs and I took 153 wickets at 17.75 apiece. What makes you think my bloody legs need strengthening?' And then, the parting shot. Glancing pointedly up and down the famous Pirie spindleshanks, he added, 'Thar's not much of an example, anyway.' He sought (and received) the sympathetic ear of the assistant manager, Alec Bedser, who knew a thing or two about bowling through an English summer. Manager and captain, however, were less impressed by his logic.

With that little matter sorted out, Fred enjoyed the remainder of the cruise, organising a skiffle group in which he played the bass (a tea chest decked in MCC colours!), as well as acting as compère and resident comedian. He was at the centre of things and he loved it. Such diversions notwithstanding, and despite his brushes with Authority, Fred had an outstanding tour, especially for a man of thirty-two who had been bowling fast for fourteen first-class years. He bowled more overs than anyone except the off-spinner Fred Titmus, took more wickets than anyone else and played a major role in England's Second Test win in Melbourne with three for 83 followed by five for 62. He returned home to England to find that £50 had been deducted from his £150 tour bonus; the same had happened to his fellow Yorkie, Ray Illingworth. By chance I was with them when the news came through. There was a measure of agreement that notable feats on the field of play seemed to be less important on tour than verbal indiscretions off it.

It is not unreasonable to wonder whether Fred ever *really* enjoyed a tour, and it is probable that he could answer with an unequivocal 'Yes – to the West Indies in 1959–60.' The fact that this party was managed by R. W. V. (Walter) Robins had a good deal to do with his enjoyment. A solid Establishment figure – public school and Oxbridge, captain of Middlesex, chairman of Selectors – he seems an unlikely figure to have won Fred's respect and liking, but Robins understood leadership and he could handle men, aided by a sharp wit and sense of humour. Fred responded positively, and with the confidence now of being a senior player. He established a marvellous rapport with the noisy and exuberant spectators in his twin role of supreme practitioner who could also play the clown. When the inevitable riot – worse than usual – occurred in Trinidad and the England team had to leave the field, the flanks were guarded by Trueman and his mate Statham in the fashion of military escorts. Each brandished a stump but the argument was unnecessary; no one thought of attacking the players, least of all 'Mr Freddie'. Twenty years later a Port-of-Spain taxi-driver asked me if I had ever met FST. When I replied that I had he stopped the car, turned round and gave me a huge beam: 'He done ride in my car in 1963. What a maaaan.' And when we ultimately reached my hotel he refused to accept any fare. That probably constitutes the greatest financial favour one Yorkshireman has ever done for another.

England won the series by virtue of victory in the only 'result' Test – a win by 256 runs in Trinidad – where Trueman and Statham took eight first-innings wickets between them and the other two batsmen were run out. Although four Tests were drawn the rubber produced much cricket of heroic quality – the batting of Cowdrey (as an opener) and Barrington on the one hand, that of

Sobers on the other. And there was great fast bowling on both sides, with Trueman and Statham against Wes Hall and Chester Watson. It was, however, all very different from modern cricket warfare. The quick men were used in bursts, essentially as break-through bowlers, while the longer spells were undertaken by the spinners. England included Allen and Illingworth in every Test; the West Indies fielded at various times Sonny Ramadhin, Roy Scarlett and Charan Singh, plus, of course, Sobers who, it seemed, could bowl *anything*. It all gave a greater variety and entertainment value to the cricket.

Brian Statham had to fly home before the end of the tour because of the illness of one of his sons and Fred was formally and officially designated senior professional (to his undisguised delight) with a number of specific duties to undertake, and one he introduced as a purely personal measure: 'T'first thing these buggers'll 'ave to do now is cut out t'bloody swearing,' he informed the accompanying press.

He bowled 342 overs in the three months of that tour, taking 37 wickets at 23.86, this after bowling 808 for Yorkshire during the preceding summer and 177 for England. In the Tests in West Indies he took 21 wickets at 26.14, bowling more overs than anyone else in the party. For the first time in his life he had been given a position of responsibility and had loved it; he got on reasonably well with manager, captains (Cowdrey took over from May when he became ill) and his fellow-tourists; he found he had a huge fan club amongst the West Indian spectators, who formed the biggest crowds ever seen in the Caribbean. Fred returned home a happy cricketer, 19 lbs lighter in weight than when he set out.

From 1959 to 1963 he bowled more than 1,000 overs in each England season with 1960 – starting shortly after his toil in the West Indies – as the most strenuous summer of hard labour. He bowled 873 overs for Yorkshire, another 180 for England and was not spared by his county from the trip to Cambridge to bowl against the university. We spent a lot of time together that summer, and while Fred was at times physically very tired indeed, never once did I see a trace of mental fatigue or loss of appetite for bowling. It really was an astonishing performance. Although he rarely spent much time in the evening in the company of his team-mates he was, nevertheless, just as keen to talk cricket as the others were undoubtedly doing elsewhere. Fred was now a considerable thinker about the game, and about bowling in particular, and those who had known him as the brash, raw, rough-and-ready lad who had come out of the coalfield in 1949 could not help but marvel at the transformation.

At eighteen, Fred had been ingenuous enough to visit a London cinema during that Minor Counties match at Lord's (the seat-prices appalled him!) to see a film called *The Snake Pit*, a thoughtful film on the subject of mental illness in which Olivia de Havilland gave a notable performance. He returned to the team hotel cursing fluently that the film did not show 'a bloody snake from beginning to end'. The next two decades were to make him a more rounded personality in a number of ways without ever smoothing out *all* the rough edges. But in cricketing terms he certainly matured rapidly and it was this that Len Hutton had so shrewdly foreseen. Fred was undoubtedly a far better fast bowler when he was past the first flush of youth than when he enjoyed all his youthful strength and fire.

He learned quickly what the best batsmen of his day were all about, and if he could not beat all of them all of the time he could most certainly deal with most of them most of the time. Throughout his career there was that sense of expectancy whenever he took the ball, new or old; throughout the crowd was the feeling that *something* was likely to happen in the course of the next few overs, and mostly something did. One game sticks in my mind – against Hampshire at Bradford – as a graphic illustration of the point. It was a low-scoring game, as most were at Park Avenue in the fifties and sixties; Hampshire had a first-innings lead of 14 and bowled out Yorkshire for 176 in the second. Derek Shackleton had taken 12 Yorkshire wickets for 145 and this rankled with Fred despite his own impressive first-innings figures of 23.2–9–34–5. 'Shack' was one of the most respected bowlers in the country, especially when there was a little bit of extra grass on the pitch or a touch of moisture in it. At medium-fast pace and invariably on a length he moved the ball in the air and off the seam just sufficiently to make the difference between meeting the middle of the blade or finding the edge of it. Fred, while necessarily respecting the figures which 'Shack' so regularly achieved, could never quite come to terms in his own mind with this type of bowling which was 'neither one thing nor another'. As Hampshire steadily accumulated runs towards victory he chafed visibly at his inability to take a second-innings wicket. The total crept to 127 for four, 155 for five, and Hampshire needed just eight runs to win when Ray Illingworth removed Peter Sainsbury, who had been partnering the opening batsman, Jimmy Gray.

Vic Wilson immediately brought back FST, who responded by getting Gray caught behind for 78. Now, it should be remembered that in the previous summer, 1961, Hampshire had won the county championship for the first time in their history, a success which had left a sense of outrage in Yorkshire where the title was regarded as private property and where there was a strong feeling that Hampshire had succeeded because of other sides' declarations (of a generosity never accorded the team from the Broad Acres). There was very much more to this situation now than simply winning or losing a county match. It was a bit like a play within a play, Hamlet-style. Illingworth would have died rather than give a run away unnecessarily at any time, so he sewed up one end as Fred hurled his thunderbolts from the other. Shackleton came out to bat at 156 for eight, and I remember quite vividly tensing forward on to the edge of my seat. This was not just a matter of championship prospects for 1962; it was not even a matter of who won or lost this particular match. It was entirely about the man who had taken twelve Yorkshire wickets for 145 and the lingering thought that someone, somewhere, might just be misguided enough to be wondering whether Derek Shackleton, on the evidence before us, was a better bowler than F. S. Trueman. It only needed the barest flickering of such a thought to enter Fred's mind. In he came, determination oozing from every pore. No quest for the Holy Grail was undertaken with greater religious fervour than Fred applied to his first delivery to Shackleton – who was very conscious of it, too. He had scarcely started his backlift when the stumps were shattered and left scattered drunkenly all over the place. Fred, to his own immense satisfaction and to Yorkshire's huge and collective relief, had proved his point. 'Shack' was a man who could push and shuffle forward with the best of them when the necessity arose. It had arisen here, but he had been given no chance to move even an inch forward. Illingworth's figures of 22–12–33–5 were largely forgotten in the high drama of Trueman's dismissal of Shackleton. His sense of theatre was always a lively one, but for once it had no special relevance on this occasion. This was personal, very personal.

There was another such time, later in the sixties, when Fred rose to a particular occasion in similar dramatic style. The match was against Warwicks at Middlesbrough and his target was Mike (M.J.K.) Smith, that most likeable and popular of players. I did not know at the time, and I have never been able to discover in later years, what it was that wound Fred up to a high-point of bowling fury, but that first hour gave the crowd one of the most impressive spells of fast bowling that most of them had ever seen. At the end of it his figures were 5–5–0–1. The one wicket was that of Mike Smith, at whom Fred launched an attack of almost demonic proportions, but its effect was such that Don Wilson, the slow left-arm bowler, picked up the best return of his career at the other end as the Warwickshire batsmen sought, with understandable haste, and complete unanimity, to get out of the firing line.

The Trueman career is liberally sprinkled with moments like this, as at Worksop in 1962 when he had nought for 49 overnight and went out on the second morning to take eight for 35. The state of the pitch had not changed to any discernible degree, and the Notts batting was no less resolute on the second day than the first, but Fred roared in and demolished the opposition, breaking a stump in the process. No one, not even amongst the shrewd cricket brains in the side or the most astute of his captains, could ever say what produced these moments of inspiration but they were all grateful for them. So were those privileged to observe, because they were watching true greatness.

Another of his great performances came, like the Warwickshire match, at Middlesbrough against Frank Worrell's touring West Indians. In later years it has sadly become commonplace for counties deliberately to rest their outstanding players against the tourists while they, in turn, use such games to keep their non-Test men 'in nick' and otherwise to get practice out in the middle rather than the nets. Not so in 1963, as the scorecard shows, and at the same time it gives us the opportunity to appreciate Fred as a 'thinking' bowler as well as a fast one. He had a magnificent season in Tests, taking thirty-four wickets at 17.47, but all that was still to come when Yorkshire played West Indies at Acklam Park on 15, 16 and 17 May. There was no question of the England Selectors asking Yorkshire to 'hide' Fred from those tourists who had not previously faced him, any more than there was the slightest chance of Yorkshire resting their greatest bowler. He went out and joyously smote 55 runs in the first innings (20 not out in the second) and then saw the young man he regarded as something of a protégé, the colleague who drove with him around the county circuit at that time, John Hampshire, felled by a bouncer from Charlie Griffith.

Now, Fred was one of the many players who regarded Griffith's quickest deliveries – invariably the bouncer or the yorker – as being bowled unfairly. There was, they reasoned in many long and earnest discussions, no way that a bowler could achieve such an electrifying change of pace from the same ambling approach. Fred is convinced that MCC instructed umpires in that series not to call Charlie for throwing for fear of provoking a black-versus-white furore, and he is not alone in that belief. (Three years earlier the white South African, Geoff Griffin, had been 'called' out of the game by English umpires for throwing). So when his 'mate', Hampshire, was seriously injured at Middlesbrough, and his opening partner, Doug Padgett, was similarly laid low by a blow on the head in the second innings, there was a general belief that Fred would retaliate on a cosmic scale when West Indies came to bat.

It didn't happen. But Fred took ten wickets in the match for 81 runs just the same and enabled Yorkshire to win, with a second-innings declaration, by 111 runs. True, the odd bouncer flew about touring batsmen's ears, but Fred used it as a tactical weapon to disturb concentration and to force the West Indian on to the back foot. He bowled with all his experience and skill and with high intelligence through both innings, dismissing (for example) an accomplished batsman like Rohan Kanhai twice with superb outswingers which had Kanhai playing inside the line and finding the top of his off-stump clipped on both occasions. It was controlled fast bowling of the highest order, and it not only played a major part in Yorkshire's win but served to reinforce the respect which the more experienced West Indian batsmen had conceived for FST during the 1959–60 tour. And this was no touring second string. Look at the names:

YORKSHIRE

First Innings		Second Innings	
Padgett c Allan b King	5	retired hurt	2
Hampshire b King	19	c Solomon b Worrell	25
Sharpe lbw b Griffith	20	lbw b King	10
Close b Griffith	21	lbw b Worrell	23
Taylor lbw b Griffith	10	c Allan b Worrell	13
Stott c Kanhai b Valentine	65	b Griffith	8
Illingworth c Allan b King	1	c King b Worrell	28
Trueman, c Allan b Griffith	55	not out	20
Wilson b Sobers	4	—	
Binks b Griffith	14	not out	13
Ryan not out	5	—	
Extras	5	Extras	3
TOTAL	226	TOTAL (six wkts dec)	145

Bowling:
Griffith 22.2–7–37–5
King 22–4–67–3
Worrell 9–1–19–0
Valentine 17–3–48–1
Sobers 8–1–50–1

Bowling:
Griffith 19–9–33–1
King 20–3–47–1
Worrell 20–3–62–4

WEST INDIES

First Innings		Second Innings	
Worrell c Close b Ryan	22	b Trueman	18
Carew c Taylor b Ryan	8	c Illingworth b Ryan	3
Kanhai b Trueman	19	b Trueman	9
Nurse c Binks b Trueman	7	b Illingworth	26
Sobers c Trueman b Taylor	17	b Taylor	29
Butcher c Binks b Taylor	13	not out	46
Solomon c Sharpe b Taylor	4	c Hampshire b Trueman	12
Allan not out	16	c Trueman b Ryan	0
Griffith hit wkt b Trueman	2	c Binks b Trueman	4

King c Taylor	o	b Trueman	4
b Trueman			
Valentine c Close	o	absent hurt	
b Trueman			
Extras	I	Extras	o
TOTAL	109	TOTAL	151

Yorkshire won before lunch on the third day. It is worth noting that they also won the championship that season, although Trueman and their all-rounder captain Brian Close played in all five Tests, while Philip Sharpe appeared in three.

It was in that same year of 1963 that Fred achieved his most notable batting triumph – one which would have enabled him to collect a bob or two from the unwary if he had been a betting man (he is not) but one which later gave him the chance for a crushing put-down which gave him immense satisfaction. In the late 1980s, during a Test at Trent Bridge, he was roundly denouncing a poor batting performance by England when he was interrupted by one of those people he so cordially detests – a stranger who interrupted, unintroduced and unwelcome, seeking to be clever at Fred's expense. 'And how many centuries did *you* score for England, Mr Trueman?' he inquired, thinking (oh so foolishly) to halt Fred in mid-flow. Without even pausing for breath, without turning to address his inquisitor, FST retorted, 'One – an' it were not out.' And he carried on with his narrative.

On 4 September 1963, at the Scarborough Festival, Fred made exactly 100 for an England eleven against Young England and it was, indeed, not out. It followed his maiden first-class hundred, 104, four months earlier at Northampton, and two years later, again at Scarborough but this time in a county championship match against Middlesex, he made 101 batting at no. 9. He has always been immensely proud of those three centuries, and rightly so when one thinks of the truly abysmal quality of his batting when he first came into the county side. With experience, his technique improved gradually over the years, though he still relied to some extent upon the forward lunge for defence and the summary dispatch of the well pitched-up delivery to accumulate the bulk of his runs.

The area between long-on and wide mid-wicket was his favourite target, as it has been through the ages for those why rely more on power than placement, but he has been known, in periods of loving reminiscence, to dwell fondly on the recollection of the occasional sweetly timed cover drive. He had a good eye, developed a better sense of timing in due course, but most of all he had the confidence born of his conviction that *other* bowlers were lesser mortals. The arrival of F. S. Trueman at the crease in any county match was the signal for a buzz of excitement to run around the ground, second only to the expectancy crowds experienced when he took the ball. Before covered wickets, and an adjustment to the lbw law convinced even the most modest of tail-enders that he could 'hang around' for a while by employing the forward shuffle, most counties had a smiter in the lower regions of the order.

Fred did not include himself in this category. He believed firmly that he could 'bat properly' when the occasion presented itself and that his three first-class hundreds proved the point. Because his main concern was bowling, however, he has always been quick to explain that it served no useful purpose to push and dab at his stage of the proceedings. His job was to make as many runs as he could in the shortest possible time so that he could turn his attention to the real business of the day. Consequently, six-hits were expected in the course of any Trueman innings, and as he was frequently partnered at the death of a Yorkshire innings by Don Wilson, another big blaster, the crowds of the fifties and sixties had something to look forward to at every stage of the batting order. It was great entertainment.

Similarly, Fred's fielding improved out of all recognition – from the raw youngster who put down a catch at mid-on in his earliest days, he became one of the best short-legs in the game. He held 439 catches, mostly in that position, in the course of his career, 64 of them in Tests, which is very nearly one a match. He was inordinately proud of his achievements as a close catcher, and his proficiency in this area had a practical value, too. Between his own overs there was no long trek down to long leg or deep third man such as his friend Statham had to undertake, no energy-sapping chases around the boundary, but merely a short stroll. He enjoyed, too, being a member of the inner Cabinet of usually senior players grouped around the batsman, and made his contribution to their tactical deliberations between deliveries.

If his position was ever usurped his rage was terrible to behold and he recalls his final game (during his National Service) for Combined Services with a mixture of chagrin, at being deposed as short leg, and smug satisfaction at having the last word. The match was against the Australian tourists of 1953 and Fred found himself banished to long leg while 'his' position went to an army officer more senior in rank and years than Aircraftman Trueman. Fred managed a smile of savage satisfaction when the major put down a catch off Keith Miller, but the smile faded as Miller went on to make a double hundred while Fred toiled to remove him. Another catch went down at slip and the more sharp-eyed of his team-mates – those other mutinous dogs of National Servicemen! – noticed that Fred, way out on the boundary, was toying with something which looked suspiciously like a bucket. Nothing which could give rise to a specific allegation, you understand. It just *seemed* that between deliveries the junior airman at long leg appeared occasionally to have a bucket in his hands. It disappeared as quickly as it had materialised. But *the captain*, Lieut. Commander Michael Lionel Yeoward Ainsworth (Shrewsbury, Royal Navy and Worcestershire) had noticed. He waited until the end of the game and then addressed himself to A/C Trueman: 'You will never play for Combined Services again.'

Fred drew himself up smartly to what he fondly imagined was a position of attention: 'Correct, sir. Quite correct.'

'What's that?' demanded the commander. 'What do you mean?'

'I mean you are absolutely right sir. I was demobbed two days ago but I stayed on to play in this game because it was for Service charities.'

One more victim had discovered that no one – but no one – has the final word in an exchange with F. S. Trueman. And one more cricket captain took away the lasting impression that Fred was an insubordinate and undisciplined so-and-so.

6

The Record 300

As we have seen, Fred had had a magnificent season in 1963 and he now had his sights firmly centred on a record which ten years earlier would have been regarded as impossible – most certainly by a genuinely quick bowler: 300 Test wickets. Since Bedser had played his last Test in 1955, his world-record 236 had been the target for all bowlers and it remained intact until January 1963, when Brian Statham reached 237 on the winter tour to Australia. Fred, of course, was in the same party and observed his partner's success with more than passing interest; he was looking further ahead – much further. Statham was one of the players who flew home after the Fifth Test in Sydney, leaving the remainder to go on to New Zealand for three Tests in Auckland, Wellington and Christchurch.

That leg of the trip started inauspiciously with a row between Fred and Colin Cowdrey over a split in the party which now seemed inappropriate: Dexter, Cowdrey, David Sheppard and A. C. Smith occupied a different dressing-room from the 'professionals'. But what was this? Since the previous year there had been no amateurs or professionals; all players were simply 'cricketers'. At the game where the trouble blew up two dressing-rooms were used to give a reasonable degree of comfort to the team as a whole, and it may well have been that those who had been amateurs during the previous season at home had not yet grown accustomed to the all-boys-together situation. But Fred was no quiescent senior professional, and he saw it as gratuitously provocative for the former amateurs to herd together instead of mixing with the other ranks. What the gentlemen did in their off-duty moments was one thing, and he was not interested in that, but a match was an entirely different matter and Fred sailed out with all guns blazing. It is perhaps as well that his fire was directed at the mild-mannered Cowdrey rather than the more explosive Dexter, otherwise the dust-up could have been more serious. Fortunately, an injury gave Fred a cooling-off period while the first Test was played at Eden Park, but he was back in action at the Basin Reserve where his five wickets took him level with Statham. Seven for 75 in the Third Test, followed by two for 16 in the second innings, took him to 250 and now the name of F. S. Trueman led the world's wicket-takers.

Back home in the summer his superb bowling against the West Indies took him to 284 wickets, and he declined to tour India the following winter, where he might reasonably have expected in five Tests, even on placid pitches, to pick up the remaining 16. Ever a man with a sense of occasion, he preferred to wait for the big one – the visit of Bobby Simpson's Australians. As things turned out it was probably a wise decision since the Englishmen in India were mowed down in great numbers by stomach disorders, yet he must be seen as taking a calculated risk by missing the tour. He was thirty-three on 6 February 1964, and now progressing well beyond the normal life-span of a genuinely fast strike bowler.

He had shown three years earlier at Headingley – against the previous Aussie tourists – that, given the right conditions, he could switch to bowling fast-medium cutters, and had done so with great success. But conditions would not regularly be right for that type of bowling, and in any case he knew perfectly well that the Selectors would not pick him for his versatility. It was as a man capable of knocking over two or three or more of the early batsmen and returning later to dismiss the less talented that his reputation stood or fell. Nor could he expect any sympathetic indulgence on the part of the Selectors because he was close to a mightily impressive world record. He had ruffled enough feathers in his time to make it certain that no one would look sentimentally at the possibility of Trueman, F. S., marking up another 'first'.

But he was confident – confident in his ability to take 16 Aussie wickets during the series, confident that his 1962–3 bowling on tour had given him the *right* to selection (even if not to his bonus!) and confident that his early season form had provided the necessary window-dressing: four for 29 against Essex, five for 53 against Leicestershire. In point of fact, his figures overall had not been anything like as impressive as in most of his earlier years, and it may well have been that those five Leics wickets (taken on the day before the Selectors met) had just tipped the balance in his favour. It also helped that Statham was at that time out of touch and the Selectors were forced into a certain amount of experimenting with the Worcestershire pair, Len Coldwell and Jack Flavell, with John Price of Middlesex and Fred Rumsey of Somerset. So Trueman was pretty well assured of selection in the early stages of the tour.

He took three for 58 in the first innings at Trent Bridge, bowling one of the openers (Ian Redpath) for 6 and getting an lbw decision against the no. 4 (Peter Burge). The third wicket was that of the last batsman, Grahame Corling. Rain did not help his cause in the second innings but there was time for Fred to suffer the indignity of being hooked for four successive boundaries by Norman O'Neill – and in his second over with the new ball, too! At Lord's, the scene of a magnificent performance the previous season, he took five for 48 and one for 52, but before his home crowd at Headingley his figures were three for 98 and one for 28. With a total of 297 wickets to his credit he was then dropped for the Old Trafford match! Although there was no one around who looked better, and certainly no one with either Fred's record or reputation, there was now a distinct feeling in the game that he was, at last, a little past his best. He could still, by calling upon astonishing reserves of strength and – even more importantly – pride, make the early batsman jump about a bit, but it seemed that he could not now 'come back' with the old ferocity and reap his due reward by mopping up the tail. There was a widespread feeling that it was very nearly the end of the line for a great bowler and great personality.

The Selectors, in fact, did Fred a considerable favour by leaving him out of the side for the Fourth Test. The Old Trafford wicket was a beauty, and Simpson and Lawry put together 201 for the first wicket, Simpson going on to reach 311 after what was, astonishingly, his first Test hundred. Australia declared at 656 for eight, at which point Price had toiled for 45 overs (three for 183), Rumsey for 35.5 (two for 99) and the medium-fast Cartwright for 77 (two for 118). Fred was well out of it. He was restored to the side for the last Test at The Oval at Rumsey's expense and scored 14 in England's modest first-innings total of 182. Australia replied with 45 for one, 57 for two, 96 for three, 202 for four – and Fred still hadn't taken a wicket. There was, at this time, very little love lost between Trueman and his captain, Dexter, with whom a feud had developed at, and after Headingley.

Fred had reasoned there that he could get Peter Burge's wicket by encouraging him to hook, and pressing hard for a deep backward square leg on what was a fairly easy-paced pitch. Dexter refused the first and subsequent demands and so Fred, seeking to prove a point, dropped an unacceptable number of deliveries short. Burge duly hooked, and hooked in the air. The point was certainly proved to the bowler's satisfaction, but with no fieldsman in the required position it developed into an exercise in expensive futility. Burge reached 160 before he was caught in precisely the position that Trueman had indicated and which was now, at last, occupied.

To appreciate the different points of view in this highly controversial situation it is necessary to go back to the point where Australia, replying to England's first-innings score of 268, were struggling at 187 for seven – Burge, on 38, the only recognised batsman remaining – against Titmus's off-spin. At this point Dexter took the new ball, which was a perfectly rational move to some eyes, though it made less sense to others. In the days when spin bowling played a major part in Test bowling tactics there frequently came a point where a captain faced the difficult decision of whether to continue with the slow men or to take the new ball. This was one of them. In deciding on a return to pace Dexter had not reckoned with Trueman feeding Burge's penchant for the hook shot; in deciding on that sort of approach Fred had not bargained for the captain's refusal to give him the field he wanted. He was playing his sixty-fourth Test, and in his eyes this sort of experience had to count to a high degree and he knew Burge well. From Dexter's point of view, he needed to manoeuvre the tail-enders to take the strike and then expected to see his main fast bowler blast out numbers 9, 10 and 11.

In proving his point – that Burge would hook in the air – Fred saw the batsman quickly steer Australia clear of the crisis, and the first seven overs with that second new ball cost England 42 runs. From 187-7 the tourists reached 389 all out and won the match. It was the only 'result' Test of the series and Australia retained the Ashes. Trueman was widely condemned for having let the opposition off the hook – condemned in a way he had never experienced before. It has to be said that while Fred's *theory* might have found some support, his *execution* merited very little. This was some way below the best use he had ever made of the new ball.

Given the number of times he had been dropped in his career when the silent majority of cricket followers felt he had been treated unjustly, he would have been hard pressed to muster a quorum of his supporters on this occasion. It came as no surprise when he was left out of the side for Old Trafford, though (as we have seen) the Selectors had inadvertently done him a favour.

There was now real concern about his chances of reaching 300 Test wickets. Flavell, too, missed the Old Trafford Test – though because of injury – and with Price adjudged to have stuck gamely to his guns in bowling on that killer of a pitch he was selected for the Final Test. And Fred, to the surprise of many, was recalled. Perhaps it was that the Selectors, well aware of Fred's sense of occasion and knowing the depth of his ambition to take 300 Test wickets, felt it would be very much in the interests of the side to let him loose once again. And so here he was on the third morning at The Oval without a single victim yet in the bag – twenty overs for 80 runs and no wickets. With minutes to go before the lunch-break, Dexter was pondering over what to do next. It seemed to Fred that he was going to offer the ball to Parfitt, and it would have occasioned no great surprise to the crowd if he had done so. The Middlesex batsman, an occasional off-spinner at Test level, might have seemed as likely as anyone to achieve a breakthrough, but that was more than Fred could stomach. He virtually snatched the ball from the captain and, in effect, put himself on at the pavilion end. His first ball bowled Ian Redpath, his second saw Graham McKenzie caught at slip – and at that cliff-hanging point the umpires, Charlie Elliott and Jack Crapp, led the players from the field for lunch, praying, no doubt, that neither of them was called upon to give a hairline decision off the first ball after the break.

It is a pretty safe bet that no one at The Oval on Saturday, 15 August 1964 lingered over the last crumb of lunch or the final dregs in a glass. Neil Hawke, the next man in – subsequently to live for a time in the North of England and become a very close friend of Fred – ate no lunch. 'To be on a hat-trick is not a pleasant experience at the best of times,' he confessed later, 'and this, if Fred could do it, would be a very, very special hat-trick.'

Now, the Aussies' match immediately before the Test had been against Yorkshire at Bradford and during the game Fred, who astonishingly was 'resting', mentioned to Hawke, in an elaborately conversational manner, that he needed only three wickets at the Oval. The Test team at that time had not been announced, but FST reckoned he had some inside information.

'Well,' grinned Neil, 'if you are just needing one when I come in I'll look after you.' The reply startled him: 'There'll be a bottle of champagne for you if that happens, sunshine.' Fred was not renowned for buying the drinks.

The conversation now came back to Hawke as he walked out to the middle after lunch to take up the non-striker's position. Cartwright bowled an over and then Dexter set the stage with a tight-packed close field, while Trueman gave an Olivier-like performance of all the preliminaries. His first ball, the hat-trick ball, the 300th wicket ball, passed wide of the off-stump. According to the anguished bowler it was no more than the finest coat of paint wide; to those less personally and emotionally concerned it was two or three inches. Fred bowled on until the new ball became due and neither Dexter nor ten thousand demons could have prised the ball out of his hand by this time. Indeed, it would have required a very brave man to try. No such effort was necessary. An outswinger found the edge of Hawke's bat, Cowdrey made the catch and Trueman made history.

Neil Hawke was the first to congratulate him with the comment: 'Well, there was no way I was going to get into the history books on my own, Fred. Now I'm there for all time. Oh – and don't forget the champagne.' True to his word, Fred duly delivered a supply to the Australian dressing-room at close of play with a personal bottle for Neil. 'We all understood how delighted he was,' says Hawke, 'but we were still a bit overwhelmed by a generosity for which Fred was not particularly noted. It was only later that I learned the bubbly had been supplied by Harry Secombe! We were actually relieved to find Fred hadn't changed character *that* much.'

The last wicket of the Australian innings, that of Grahame Corling, also fell to Fred, by means of a catch by Parfitt, another of his closest friends of his post-playing days, but rain made it impossible to add to a total of 301 wickets in sixty-five Tests.

Years later – when Dennis Lillee overtook his record around Christmas, 1981 – I heard Fred complain that when *he* reached 300 'nobody sent him a telegram'. That serves to show that his memory, brilliant on some matters, can be exceedingly fallible on others.

Yorkshire had been playing Sussex at Hove while Fred was achieving cricket immortality at The Oval and had celebrated on a limited scale, reserving their energies for the festivities which were to follow when Fred returned to the ranks for the championship match with Kent, at Dover. Almost unnoticed in the general euphoria (though not by the man most concerned), Geoffrey Boycott had scored his maiden Test century in England's second innings at The Oval and, since he had not yet achieved the unpopularity which was to dog his career, it was to be a double celebration. John Hampshire takes up the story: 'There had been quite a lot of champagne left over from the celebrations at The Oval, and a couple of Yorkshiremen were never going to let it be wasted, so a fair supply of bubbly found its way to Dover in Fred's car. *With it came the biggest pile of congratulatory letters and telegrams anyone has ever been. They just about filled the back of Fred's Jaguar, and I spent most of the day opening and sorting them for him.*'

It would, perhaps, have been pleasant for Fred to do a lap of honour, so to speak, by mowing down Kent, but it was very much a spinners' wicket at Dover and it was Ray Illingworth who stole the headlines with 135 runs in Yorkshire's total of 256, which was enough to win by an innings (Illingworth seven for 49 and seven for 52), while Trueman bowled just five overs in the first innings, only two in the second. There was no championship that year, either, Worcestershire's runaway success relegating Yorkshire to fifth place in the table. Fred's championship haul of 67 wickets cost 20 runs apiece. Time was beginning to take its toll, and although his bag of 301 Test wickets looked likely to stand for all time, at least for a genuinely fast bowler – unless (a) someone else came along with a remarkable ability and physique, and there was no one of that nature on the horizon or (b) a fast bowler was accorded the privilege of being chosen for fifty or sixty Tests in rapid succession, which did not look likely to happen to anybody – this was probably the time to take stock.

There were no real doubts in Fred's mind at this time. Nearly fifteen years of heady success through a combination of ability and sheer weight of bowling personality had convinced him that there was no county side, at any rate, which could withstand him if he were on song and the gods were not conspiring against him. Occasionally he permitted himself to look three and four years into the future and to ponder, for a moment, the remote possibility that his bowling *might* lose some of its potency, but he did not dwell for long on such heresy. His faith in his God-given talents was implicit. He could, he reasoned, switch to cutters and seamers, if – and it was always a very big 'if' – weariness dared to inflict itself upon him. His natural ability to bowl the late outswinger remained his trusty sword, and he was convinced that it would serve him to the end of his days.

The Selectors, not unnaturally, did not see things in exactly the same light and there were only two more Tests for Frederick Sewards Trueman to play – against New Zealand, on their three-match tour at the beginning of the 1965 summer. At Edgbaston, on a wicket which favoured batsmen, he took one for 49 from 18 overs and three for 79 in a marathon 32.4 overs. In the first innings, slow, low wicket or not, he caused the retirement of Bert Sutcliffe by hitting him on the ear – an injury which probably caused Fred more personal distress than any other blow he inflicted. He had a considerable affection for the left-hander who probably made just one tour too many; his ability to deal with fast bowling was not what it had been in his earlier days, even after dropping down the order from opener to No. 5.

Fred finally bowed out of Test cricket at Lord's on 22 June 1965 with two for 40 and no wicket for 69. He had been the most colourful personality and the most prolific wicket-taker on the international scene for thirteen years. He did not reflect upon past glories; he railed bitterly against those who had denied him the opportunity of making it 400 wickets. He still does.

7
The Last Lap

If his Test career was over, Fred's life in first-class cricket was most assuredly not. There were still great glories to come – one of them perhaps his finest achievement and certainly the one which ranks most prominently amongst his fondest memories – as well as moments which are still relished by the collectors of Trueman-lore. In the next three years, 1966, 1967 and 1968, Yorkshire won three successive championships, and if Fred's name no longer figured in the top ten of the national averages he nevertheless played his part by knocking over one, two or more of the early batsmen while taking pleasure in seeing the names of colleagues like Tony Nicholson, Ray Illingworth and Don Wilson amongst the leading wicket-takers. Yorkshire were a formidable combination of elder statesmen like Close, Trueman, Illingworth, Padgett and Binks. The young lions who had developed from the late 1950s were now mature and accomplished players – Taylor, Sharpe, Wilson and the new players of the sixties, Hampshire, Boycott and Richard Hutton, were developing dramatically.

Fred had had during his career more than forty opening partners. One of them, Bob Platt, the Beau Brummel of county cricket in his day, is now part of the inner circle of close friends, but the longest-lasting and most successful of the men with whom Fred shared the new ball was Tony Nicholson. He bowled huge outswingers from the most improbable-looking delivery stride, and after one season (when county batsmen thought they had sorted him out) he added an off-cutter to his repertoire which made him a very useful customer indeed. His displayed many of Fred's personal characteristics – exasperation when a ball failed to find the edge, his belief that every ball merited a victim, a conviction that Fate and umpires joined forces in conspiring against him – but without Fred's finely honed touch of antagonism. There was a complete absence of malice in A. G. Nicholson. Cricketers respected Fred; they liked

1a 'I could out-jump the lot of 'em' – playing for Lincoln City, 1951–2.

1b England v. Australia, 1953. *Back row (l. to r.):* Bailey,
May, Graveney, Laker, Lock, Wardle, Trueman.
Front row (l. to r.): Edrich, Bedser, Hutton, Compton, Evans.

2a The perfect cartwheel action . . .

2b . . . and the naked hostility.

3a *top opposite* FST leads out his team in the last Gents *v.* Players match. Lords, 1962.

3b *bottom opposite* Fred leads England back to the dressing-room after taking his 300th Test Wicket. The Oval, 1964.

4a Life after
cricket –
stand-up comedian
at the Club Fiesta
Stockton-on-Tees,
1969.

4b Charity
appearance –
as Dick Turpin,
for the Variety Cl
of Great Britain,
1973.

5a The birth of the Courage Old England XI, 1981. Denis Compton bowled Trueman. Fieldsmen John Edrich, Dick Richardson, Godfrey Evans, Fred Titmus.

5b In the garden of Fred's home in the Yorkshire Dales, sculptress Betty Miller puts the finishing touches to the bust of FST.

6a Broadcaster Fred with the BBC's *Test Match Special* commentary team, 1984.
Back row (l. to r.): Lewis, Blofeld, Illingworth, Martin-Jenkins, Baxter, Frindall.
Front row (l. to r.): Mosey, Bailey, Johnston, Trueman, Cozier.
6b Fred the affectionate father with daughter Karen . . .
6c . . . and grandfather with Karen's daughter Sarah.

7a The old firm: Statham and Trueman.

7b Fred with old friends and adversaries
Keith Miller and Bert Sutcliffe.

8a FST, OBE, with Veronica after the investiture, 1989.

8b Fred with his daugh[...] Rebecca, Neil Harvey, Veronica and Ray Lindw[...] at his home in 1989.

'Nick'. Consequently, they made a good pair. Fred cherished a gruff affection for Nicholson, whom he described as 'the best bowler never to play for England'.

With this pair leading the attack and under Brian Close's leadership – at times intuitive, at others inspired, and always with the knowledgeable back-up of Illingworth and Binks – Yorkshire were probably as harmonious an outfit in those years as at any time in their history.

Laughter and song played a major part in their more relaxed moments, even though grim determination attended all their work on the field. Every county still tried harder to beat Yorkshire than any other opposition; declarations which gave them a sporting chance of victory were unknown – and would have been regarded with utter astonishment if they had been made. Yorkshire in the 1960s were content that this attitude towards them was their birthright, their pride and their burden. They would have had it no other way. They were great and glorious days and every member of the side revelled in their successes. The membership of the county club – well, it was what they expected, wasn't it?

Fred's retirement at the end of 1968 was followed by Illingworth's angry and disillusioned (with Committee decisions) departure to Leicestershire and the dismissal of Close in 1970. Yorkshire had pressed the self-destruct button and the years which followed were to bring a disintegration of morale and the loss of the very soul of the club. Not one of those players of the 1960s would have believed it possible. No one has been more deeply affected by it than Freddie Trueman.

Throughout his playing days he enjoyed a strange sort of love–hate, respect–contempt relationship with Brian Close. Even the 'hate' part had an element of half-amused, half-affectionate regard. Each knew only too well the qualities of the other, and in general, over the course of a season, the fusion of leadership and individual talent was seen to work well enough to bring the required success to the side. There would be occasional eruptions but they were quickly suppressed by the overwhelmingly important requirements of the common cause. Those of us who were camp-followers in the considerable media following which Yorkshire enjoyed did not publicise these insurrections and saw to it that our colleagues in the London offices of the national daily papers were kept in ignorance of them. Fred nursed the belief, with no great pretence at secrecy, that he was a better, and more suitable candidate for the captaincy, than Close. Brian, for his part, regarded Fred's furies with smiling tolerance without surrendering one shred of respect for Fred's ability.

Close, in fact, rather enjoyed winding Fred up – sometimes for a specific purpose, sometimes just for the hell of it. In the 1964 Scarborough Festival (and what a significant year it had been for Fred) he went to the Festival needing three more first-class wickets for his 100 in that season, and dismissed Keith Fletcher early in the MCC innings after Tony Nicholson had taken the wicket of Brian Bolus. With the Festival crowds in mind, and not wanting to have to enforce a follow-on, Close rested Fred with two more wickets still required, much to the disgust of the bowler. For the next three hours he grumbled and spluttered on the long-leg boundary, regaling the crowd with highly colourful descriptions of his captain's less endearing characteristics. He did not lower his voice. At one stage half the Yorkshire team were laughing their socks off between trying to dismiss the MCC side. Finally, with two wickets remaining, Close called Fred up from the boundary: 'Come and finish it off. You can get your two wickets.' By this time Fred, however, had worked up a towering rage and he bawled his reply from the far distance: 'Bollocks. Stick your adjectival ball. I'm not bowling.' Well, it *was* a Festival match. Close humoured him, gave the ball to Illingworth and the MCC innings was duly polished off. It took Fred a fair amount of energy to get those two wickets he so badly wanted when MCC batted for the second time.

Sometimes Close's handling of Fred took a different course. At Taunton in 1963, for instance, the game was drifting towards an inevitable draw on the third day with neither side able to get into a position to produce a positive result. Fred decided to enjoy himself by smashing the disinterested bowling around the field, and rattled up 42 in no time at all. The Somerset skipper, Harold Stephenson, however, had a sense of humour, too. Calling up his fastest bowler, Fred Rumsey, he suggested letting Fred have a playful bouncer, and Rumsey obliged. The drowsy crowd sat up; even in the press box we stopped writing our short accounts of a pointless draw. Had we been premature to think there was no 'story' in the game? Were we now to have high drama in the closing half-hour? From the look of things out in the middle, the answer was 'Yes'. We put down our pens and watched with re-awakened interest as Fred threatened his namesake with direst retribution. Rumsey, secure in the knowledge that he was Somerset's no. 11 and only a short time remained, answered outraged fury with an amiable grin.

The last wicket duly fell, leaving time for just two overs to be bowled with Somerset nearly 200 in arrears. In the dressing-room, Stephenson's black comedy now moved into the second act. 'Right,' he said to Rumsey. 'You've had your little joke. Now you can go and open the batting.'

'And it had been *his* idea to bowl the bouncer,' recalls Rumsey.

Amidst the laughter from his team-mates, the loudest was that of Brian Langford, the off-spinner.

'And you can go with him,' ordained the Somerset captain. Delight was unconfined in the Somerset ranks, and the whole team crowded on to the balcony to watch the final few moments. They saw Fred marking out an even longer run than usual, muttering dark threats as the unusual opening pair emerged from the pavilion. The crowd who were drifting away now turned back; in the press box we tore up our reports and sat with pens poised over a blank sheet of paper. The Yorkshire team looked at Rumsey and Langford and the grins grew broader. Only two men were not smiling – at least not openly, D. B. Close ignored Fred completely, affected not to notice that he was rarin' to let go the biggest, fastest bouncer in the history of the game. Leaving Fred to rage at the start of that enormous approach, not even bothering to indicate his place in the field, Close tossed the ball to John Hampshire for the first over, Duggie Padgett for the second. Rumsey was bowled by Padgett's fifth delivery – one of the only six wickets he took in the course of a twenty-year career – and everyone returned to the dressing-rooms, where the last to arrive was F. S. Trueman, offering gratuitous, if uncomplimentary, views on the subject of captaincy. He did, however, have the last word with Rumsey: 'There's always next season, sunshine.'

Fred's personal, on-the-field, humour was a touch more mordant. Peter Parfitt, a noted after-dinner speaker these days with a script which owes half its entertainment value to the career of Denis Compton, the other half to that of FST, remembers his earliest encounter with Fred, when he played as a young man for

Middlesex against Yorkshire at Lord's. He unwisely tried to hook a short-pitched ball and departed the scene (with assistance) spitting out blood and teeth. He returned after a couple of wickets had fallen, somewhat to the surprise of the bowler who had taken them. 'Are you all right, sunshine?' inquired Fred, more in astonishment than solicitude.

Parfitt (who has never been known to use a couple of words when twenty-five will do) replied, 'It's good of you to ask, Fred. Thank you. I'm fine.' But before he could move on to the wicket to take guard again he saw Fred stroke his chin and muse to anyone who might happen to be listening, 'I don't know – they don't usually come back so soon when I've 'it 'em.' He seemed genuinely perplexed.

One of the hoariest of cricketing stories is of the young university batsman, patronising a grizzled Yorkshire veteran who had just dismissed him: 'Well bowled. That was a very good one.' The response is reputed to have been, 'Aye, but it were wasted on thee.' Fred had, of course, to give us an updated and improved version of this when, in 1954, he gazed in fascination at the sight of a Middlesex batsman (one of the mid-summer recruits from public-school and Oxbridge) advancing to the middle wearing a gaily coloured hooped cap, matching cravat, and brand new, pristine pads and gloves. Having duly demolished his stumps from the pavilion end in no time at all, FST waited until the young man was passing him to inquire, conversationally, ' 'Ardly worth gettin' dressed up for, were it?'

In 1961, when Don Wilson broke a hand at Worcester, his place was taken for the remainder of that season by a slow left-arm bowler from Huddersfield called Keith Gillhouley. A talented player, who was also a useful batsman, Gillhouley was disappointed when at the start of the 1962 season he was not called upon again. He had taken 77 wickets in 1961 at 22.10 and scored 323 runs and he felt, quite rightly, that he had never at any time let the side down. But Wilson was the capped player and there was no questioning the Yorkshire policy of playing the senior man. Gillhouley spent a season mulling over his belief that he was good enough to play first-eleven cricket for a county, then accepted a contract with Notts.

He was a man with a wry sense of humour and he nursed a secret ambition – to hook a six off all the leading fast bowlers of the day.

During his four seasons with Notts and three-quarters of a season with Yorkshire he had gone a fair way towards fulfilling these hopes and it has to be borne in mind that there were a lot of pretty useful quick men around at the time. But Fred? Well, that was a bit different. Having spent the best part of his cricketing life respecting the great man's ability, and most of one season sharing a dressing-room with him, Keith was all too well aware of the blood-curdling threats uttered by Fred against those ambitious, or foolhardy, enough to attempt cavalier treatment. But the thought flickered dangerously but deliciously through his mind from time to time.

On 15 July 1964, Notts found themselves batting first against Yorkshire at Scarborough on a very flat wicket indeed. Those dangerous thoughts now invaded Gillhouley's mind as never before. There was no help for Fred in *this* pitch; he was thirty-three years old and nearing the end of his Test career. Was this now the time to chance his arm? He chanced it – and scratched a bottom-edge single to mid-wicket. He tried it again: precisely the same result. And then, just a *little* closer to success, he mistimed a bottom edge to fine leg – for four. That did it. By this time Fred had realised what it was all about. Distant memories were recalled of the young Gillhouley, when a Yorkshire player three years earlier, voicing his ambition to hook all the great fast bowlers for six. It hadn't meant anything at the time – the idle ramblings of an ambitious youngster. If Fred had reacted at all at that time it would have been to wish Keith luck, because they were both on the same side and Fred believed that most 'other' fast bowlers were mere journeymen.

But this was something else altogether. The cheeky kid was now a Notts player, he was on the other side, and he was thinking – actually daring to think – about hooking the great FST for six. As the mis-hit scuttled away to the fine-leg boundary, Fred followed through to a point only a couple of yards from the batsman. He stood and he glared. Gillhouley refused to look up. He pottered about around the crease, flicking away imaginary pieces of loose turf. 'Is he still there?' he asked Jimmy Binks, the wicket-keeper, who was trying hard to keep his face straight. 'He is,' replied Jimmy. 'Well, I'm not looking up till he's gone,' maintained the batsman. He pottered about some more. 'Is he still there?' 'Aye.'

It took Fred several minutes to realise that this was one potential victim who was not going to succumb to Medusa-style tactics.

Gillhouley might well turn to stone if he turned to face the glowering rage, but he simply wasn't going to look up. Fred finally turned away, tramped back for fourteen or fifteen yards of the pitch and then another twenty-five into the middle distance. He roared in and the bouncer flew across the bridge of Gillhouley's nose. The batsman turned to look at Binks who returned an amiable smile. 'Well, what did you expect?' The next ball whistled past Gillhouley's ear. He tried to count. How many more balls were there in the over? One. It screamed over his head and Binks had to leap to take it. On a flat, flat pitch. From a 33-year-old bowler. And this time, knowing the over was complete, Fred followed through to address Keith from a distance of approximately two feet. There was no way to escape the wrath now. But the ordeal was, for the moment, over. 'Ah thowt thar could hook?' snarled FST. Tremulously, Gillhouley replied, 'Not you, Fred. Not you. You're far too quick for me.'

Fred pondered this for a moment before marching off to short leg. Honour, he decided, was satisfied. Tribute had been paid. He bowled no more bouncers to *that* batsman.

These are just some of the legends that Fred has bequeathed to the game, and which today are heard with undiminished delight around the after-dinner circuit. There is no one around today who can provide new ones, and if there were, there is no one available to record them, for modern writers are unfortunate in not enjoying the same intimacy with players that existed twenty and thirty years ago. Present-day writers are usually admitted to the inner playing circles only if they can provide a service to the practitioners – as a ghost-writer or agent. It is for the most part strictly business in the 1980s–90s; the game and its folklore is the poorer for it.

While the fires of competition burned as brightly as ever for Fred in the last few years of his county career, the fact had to be faced that he could no longer conjure up the same physical fear in opposition batsman. Close 'nursed' him at times (though Fred would have fiercely denied it) when, on good pitches, players of modest pretension but long experience of earlier humiliations sought to 'get after' Fred. Not all of them succeeded, but some did and I have to say I squirmed with actual distress when it happened.

I had admired and respected the man too much and for too long to find the idol teetering on its pedestal. If he could have come to terms with advancing years and the toll taken by those 16,000-odd overs, if he had been content to become a fast-medium bowler of great experience and no little guile, he might well have carried on for two, three or perhaps even more years. But then that would not have been Fred. He was, as John Arlott said (and no one has ever put it more succinctly) 'purely a fast bowler in method, mind and heart'. And even if he was winding down in those last three seasons, perhaps because he was no longer called upon to raise his game in England's cause, there were still moments of glory, and of glee, to be savoured. Against the 1967 Indian tourists at Sheffield he found a bit of life in the pitch and was suddenly transported back fifteen years. Two or three deliveries reared sufficiently to trap knuckles against bat-handle, to the acute discomfort of Rusi Surti, an elegant left-hander who had spent some time in English league cricket. This had given him a fair grasp of the idiom, and after the second painful blow he rounded on Fred with as fine a flow of invective as anyone in the vicinity had ever heard. Fred gazed at him in disbelief, then stamped off to the umpire in a condition of high moral indignation to complain about bad language. The umpire, and to my intense regret I have forgotten who it was, listened with grave attention and a completely straight face, then solemnly forwarded an official complaint to Lord's. It was received there with total disbelief – but the story went round the dressing-rooms of England, where there was great rejoicing.

But the end of an era was now beginning to look increasingly inevitable, even if some of us found it difficult to contemplate county cricket without F. S. Trueman. To an entire generation of Yorkshiremen it was unthinkable that the county side should take the field without him; how could we look at our evening or morning papers without expecting to see his name there amongst the wicket-takers? And how could some of those papers view a season without an explosion of some kind, on the field or off it, in which Fred was involved?

There was another acrimonious dispute with Brian Sellers in the dressing-room at Bramall Lane in 1966, when the chairman accused Fred of dawdling in the field, and a monumental row with Close at Middlesbrough in 1968 when he made Fred twelfth man so that the promising Chris Old could have a run in the first team. It was the first time that it had ever happened; Close felt strongly that he was justified and Fred felt equally strongly that he had been unnecessarily humiliated. His thoughts now began to turn to retirement.

It was right that he should go out on a high – nothing could have been more right after twenty seasons of brilliant fast bowling in a career which, admittedly stormy, often because of his own lack of self-control and judgment, had seen him develop from an ingenuous boy from the coalfields into the best-known personality in cricket around the world. Close's absence on Test duty and because of injury had given Fred a number of opportunities to lead Yorkshire, and he had loved each and every one of them.

His greatest moment was still to come, however; with Close a casualty, he led Yorkshire against Bill Lawry's 1968 Australians at Sheffield, won the toss and decided to bat. At 271 for four on the first day he knew he had not enough runs in the bag for any quixotic move; the following morning he batted on, staking everything on his, and his other bowlers' ability to dismiss the tourists twice. He opened the attack like the man he had been fifteen or sixteen years earlier – bowling flat out to a field which, with its ultra-attacking placement would inevitably concede runs. But in giving the Aussies a half-hour's batting before lunch he had manoeuvred a tactical and psychological advantage. He dismissed Redpath himself and took a magnificent flying catch to send back Doug Walters. A storm delayed the re-start (36 for two) but when play resumed Fred caught Paul Sheahan, ran out Ian Chappell, caught Lawry and gathered in the last two wickets of Gleeson and Connolly. Amidst all these personal triumphs the moment he savoured as much as any was when the groundsman approached, at the fall of the ninth wicket, to ask which roller was required. In the grand manner of Toscanini admonishing an intrusive fiddler Fred dismissed him in the direction of the Australian captain. He asked the tourists to follow on, 212 behind. With twenty minutes of the day remaining Fred once again marked out the long, long run, discarded for many years. In his mind it was 1952 and Lawry's men were as vulnerable as Hazare's had been.

It was Richard Hutton who took the wicket Yorkshire so badly needed now – that of the obdurate Lawry – and on the final morning Fred was asked to forecast how the day would unfold. He replied with grim emphasis that Yorkshire would win by half-past three.

Hutton again took an early wicket, and Walters and Sheahan put on 50 for the third wicket until Fred returned to remove Sheahan's middle stump. Next he had Walters caught in the gulley off the outswinger. The match was won, with Illingworth mopping up but Fred still contriving to take the wicket of McKenzie, at precisely half-past three. He had directed his bowling superbly, played his own part by dismissing some of Australia's most accomplished batsmen, flung himself about the close-field to take outstanding catches and effected a run-out by a swift return from extra cover. He had led his county to victory over the Australians.

If he had simply walked away from that game and announced his retirement he could have left first-class cricket at the high-point of that long and brilliant career. But he was contracted for the season; he played *out* the season and, not knowing his intentions, the Yorkshire public felt no sense of anti-climax in the remaining games because Yorkshire won the county championship for what has proved to be the last time. His old England sparring-partner, Brian Statham, then announced that he would retire after that season and Fred watched with interest during the Roses match at Old Trafford when Statham was given a hugely emotional farewell by the crowd. For reasons I have never been able to understand, Fred then decided to follow suit, but to do it unobtrusively.

If he had announced publicly that the 1968 season was to be his last there would have been an emotional farewell on every ground where he played. The emotions might, perhaps, have varied from one county to another and they might not always have indicated the immense, affectionate attachment that Lancashire's public felt for 'George' Statham. But there can be no doubt at all that the cricketing membership of all the other sixteen counties would have paid a tribute to the greatest fast-bowling talent the country had produced and a man who had never been out of the headlines, back page or front. And in Yorkshire there would most certainly have been a gala farewell during the Scarborough Festival. It would have been possible to fill the ground three or four times over.

Yorkshiremen may not be as sentimental as their Lancastrian neighbours, but they cherish their heroes in their own way. They felt in some way cheated when Fred delayed the announcement until cricket had finished for the summer of 1968. They actually resented being deprived of the opportunity to pay their respects to *their* Freddie Trueman. It may well be the very perverseness of the man that induced him to retire in this way. There is an innate touch of masochism in Fred which probably gave him pleasure from the pain of retiring with a whimper rather than a bang. His followers were left with six months or more to contemplate the awfulness of life at Headingley, Park Avenue, Bramall Lane and points south without him. By the following April they had sadly and grudgingly accepted the fact, even if they had not come to terms with all its implications. *I* resented the way in which Fred had left us, and so did the hundreds of cricket-lovers I knew. It was not just that we would no longer thrill to the sight of his bowling. Somehow we had been robbed of our opportunity to show him how we felt about his departure. Astonishingly, perversely, Fred had offended those who admired him most. As I walked morosely round Park Avenue the following season, watching those who succeeded him, a venerable member looked up and asked, wistfully, 'Eee, Mr Mosey, weers t'next Freddie Trueman comin' from?' With unreasonable anger I snapped back, 'There's only been one in over a hundred years. What right have we got to expect another for a bit?'

Yet Fred had done it all consciously, with deliberation, if not with logic. He composed a polite letter of resignation, telephoned the man he respected above all others in authority at the County Club, Sir William Worsley, and asked if he might see the President. At first Sir William refused to accept his decision, insisting that Fred could continue for several years and hinting that he might be made captain. That jolted Fred. He would have valued that honour above all others. But he had already informed the Sunday newspaper for which he wrote a column of his intention. It was now Saturday night and the *People*'s early editions would already be rolling off the presses. It was too late for him to change his mind. The one thing which would have persuaded him to postpone retirement was the Yorkshire captaincy, a position which at that time meant more to a player than skippering England. But, just as much as the prestige, Fred actually loved captaincy for its own sake, the tactical involvement, the moving of the pieces in the great chess game of long-range strategy.

However, if he could not go on as Yorkshire's skipper for a couple of years or more, now *was* the time to bow out. He had fought the good fight, and fought it spectacularly and superbly. It is worth dwelling for a moment on some aspects of the statistics of that remarkable career, detailed in the following pages by Robert Brooke, and one which immediately catches the eye is the chart of Fred's victims in Test cricket. All three men who were dismissed by him on nine occasions were front-line specialist batsmen. So were the five he dismissed on seven occasions; two of the four he claimed six times were batting specialists and one an all-rounder. Throughout that particular table his striking-rate against top-of-the-order batsmen emphasises just how valuable he was to the England sides in which he played. Consider, too, his overall striking rate and the low cost of his Test wickets – and this from a man who might well have been rejected by Yorkshire because of the runs he conceded in his earliest days. And then, consider if you will, the sheer physical effort he put into those twenty seasons – 2 million yards of sprinting in to bowl, and Fred's approach was no window-dressing. He *ran* in, accelerating to the point where he cartwheeled into the delivery stride without any braking, any stuttering, any changing step. From his first stride to the moment the ball was released from his hand the whole action was one continuing, co-ordinated process of bowling a cricket ball – laden with menace yet beautiful to watch, unless, of course, one happened to be at the other end with a bat in the hand. But *2 million yards*! And 2 million more yards trudged back to the mark. No marathon runner can have covered anything like the distance involved in the course of an entire athletic career.

If Fred had lingered, if he had been able to stop that newspaper announcement and if he had, in fact, been appointed captain, how many years could he have enjoyed before the Committee said to him, 'That's enough'? One would like to believe that the Committee might then have suggested gently to him that he should retire, but there is no guarantee of that. The shameful, cruel and utterly disgraceful dismissal of Brian Close in 1970 is the best pointer to the fate which might have been Fred's. No – it was right for him to retire when he did. If we were left to regret the lack of opportunity to honour him properly in 1968 we were at least spared the terrible possibility of his departure in the same unspeakable way that Close was compelled to leave. Yorkshire cricket has never been the same without the two of them, and the rejected Illingworth. We are faced with a future which may never bring the restoration of the glory that was theirs.

Statistics

THE RECORD OF F. S. TRUEMAN IN FIRST-CLASS CRICKET

FREDERICK SEWARDS TRUEMAN
Born Scotch Springs, Stainton, near Maltby, Yorkshire
6 February 1931

Debut Yorkshire 1949
Debut England 1952
67 Test matches for England 1952–65

100th Test wicket in 25th Test, *v.* New Zealand, Christchurch 1958–9
200th Test wicket in 47th Test *v.* Pakistan, Edgbaston 1962
242nd Test wicket, to overtake then Test record held by J. B. Statham in 56th Test *v.* New Zealand, Christchurch 1962–3
First player to take 300 Text wickets, in 65th Test, *v.* Australia, The Oval 1964

Best first-class bowling performances

8 wickets in an innings
8–70 Yorks *v.* Minor Counties, Lord's 1949
8–58 Yorks *v.* Notts, Sheffield 1951
8–53 Yorks *v.* Notts, Trent Bridge 1951
8–31 England *v.* India, Old Trafford 1952
8–28 Yorks *v.* Kent, Dover 1954
8–84 Yorks *v.* Notts, Worksop 1962
8–45 Yorks *v.* Gloucs, Bradford 1963
8–36 Yorks *v.* Sussex, Hove 1965
8–37 Yorks *v.* Essex, Bradford 1966
8–45 MCC *v.* Otago, Dunedin 1958–9

13 wickets in a match

14–123 Yorks *v.* Surrey, The Oval 1960
14–125 Yorks *v.* Northants, Sheffield 1960
13–77 Yorks *v.* Sussex, Hove 1965
13–79 MCC *v.* Otago, Dunedin 1958–9

Hat-tricks

Yorks *v.* Notts, Trent Bridge 1951
Yorks *v.* Notts, Scarborough 1955
Yorks *v.* MCC, Lord's 1958
Yorks *v.* Notts, Bradford 1963

Season-by-season career record

	Mtch	Inn	N.O.	Runs	H.S.	Av'ge	100	50	Ct	Overs	Mdns	Runs	Wkts	Av'ge	5in	10mch	B/B
1949	8	6	2	12	10	3.00	—	—	2	243.3		719	31	23.19	1	—	8/70
1950	14	15	9	23	4*	3.83	—	—	5	290.1	43	876	31	28.25	—	—	3/28
1951	30	24	7	115	25	6.76	—	—	21	737.4	166	1852	90	20.57	6	1	8/53
1952	15	4	3	40	23*	—	—	—	5	282.2	57	841	61	13.78	5	—	8/31
1953	8	16	2	131	34	9.35	—	—	15	447.1	77	1411	44	32.06	1	1	6/47
1953–4	33	9	3	81	20	13.50	—	—	7	319.4	81	909	27	33.66	—	—	5/45
1954	31	35	5	270	50*	9.00	—	—	32	817.2	187	2085	134	15.55	10	—	8/28
1955	31	38	8	391	74	13.03	—	1	26	995.5	214	2454	153	16.03	8	3	7/23
1956	31	30	3	358	58	13.25	—	—	21	588.4	133	1383	59	23.44	2	—	5/34
1956–7	2	4	2	96	46*	48.00	—	—	1	61	9	204	8	25.50	—	—	3/38
1957	32	41	14	405	63	15.00	—	1	36	842.2	184	2303	135	17.05	9	2	7/37
1958	30	35	7	453	61	16.17	—	3	22	637.5	176	1414	106	13.33	6	—	6/23
1958–9	17	21	2	312	53	16.42	—	1	16	26.1	30	1067	57	18.71	4	1	8/45
1959	30	40	9	602	54	19.41	—	1	24	1072.4	269	2730	140	19.50	6	—	7/57
1959/60	10	13	2	153	37	13.90	—	—	11	342.3	86	883	37	23.86	—	—	5/22
1960	32	40	5	577	69	16.48	—	3	22	1068.4	274	2447	175	13.98	12	4	7/41
1960–1	4	5	1	139	59	34.75	—	—	2	114.4	16	326	22	14.81	1	—	5/59
1961	34	48	6	809	80*	19.26	—	4	13	1190.1	302	3000	155	19.35	11	1	7/45
1962	33	42	4	840	63	22.10	—	1	24	1141.5	273	2717	153	17.75	5	1	8/84
1962–3	12	14	0	194	38	13.85	—	—	9	229.3	19	1020	55	18.54	4	1	7/75

Year	M	I	NO	Runs	HS	Avg	100	50	Ct	Overs	Mdns	Runs	Wkts	Avg	5wi	10wm	Best
									35	121.2							
1963	27	41	6	783	104	22.37	2	2	15	844.3	206	1955	129	15.15	10	5	8/45
1963–4	2	2	0	28	28	14.00	—	—	2	49	12	124	9	13.77	—	—	4/27
1964	31	39	4	595	77	17.00	—	4	19	834.1	171	2194	100	21.94	3	—	5/48
1964–5	3	2	0	24	23	12.00	1	—	1	79.3	18	253	11	23.00	1	—	5/78
1965	30	39	2	636	101	17.18	1	2	17	754.4	180	1811	127	14.25	10	1	8/36
1966	33	43	4	448	43	11.48	—	—	22	859.5	203	2040	111	18.37	2	1	8/37
1967	31	33	5	342	34	12.21	—	—	31	595	135	1610	75	21.46	2	—	5/39
1967–8	1	2	0	42	33	21.00	—	—	1	18	2	58	1	—	—	—	1/10
1968	29	30	5	296	45	11.84	—	—	16	510	116	1375	66	20.83	3	—	6/20
1969	1	1	0	37	26	18.50	—	—	1	21	1	93	2	46.50	—	—	1/41
										494.4	49						
	603	713	120	9232	104	15.56	3	26	438	15981.2	3706	42154	2304	18.29	126	25	8/28

NB Trueman's overseas first-class cricket was played as follows:

1953–4	MCC in West Indies
1956–7	C. G. Howard's team in India
1958–9	MCC in Australia
1959–60	MCC in West Indies
1960–1	Cavaliers in Rhodesia & South Africa
1962–3	MCC in Australia & New Zealand
1963–4	Cavaliers in Jamaica
1964–5	Cavaliers in West Indies
1967–8	Charity match in India

Test career – match by match

1952 v. India

	Runs	Catches	Overs	Mdns	Runs	Wickets
Headingley, Leeds	0*	—	26	6	89	3
Lord's, London	17	—	9	1	27	4
		—	25	3	72	4
Old Trafford, Manchester	—	—	27	4	110	4
		—	8.4	2	31	8
The Oval, London	—	1	8	5	9	1
		—	16	4	48	5

	Mtch	Inns	N.O.	Runs	H.S.	Av'ge	Ct	Overs	Mdns	Runs	Wkts	Av'ge	5in	10mch	B/B
TOTAL	4	2	1	17	17	—	1	119.4	25	386	29	13.31	2	—	8/31

1953 v. Australia

	Runs	Catches	Overs	Mdns	Runs	Wickets
The Oval, London	10	2	24.3	3	86	4
			2	1	4	0

	Mtch	Inns	N.O.	Runs	H.S.	Av'ge	Ct	Overs	Mdns	Runs	Wkts	Av'ge	5in	10mch	B/B
TOTAL	1	1	0	10	10	—	2	26.3	4	90	4	22.50	—	—	4/86

1953–4 v. West Indies

	Runs	Catches	Overs	Mdns	Runs	Wickets
Kingston	18	—	34.4	8	107	2
Port-of-Spain	1	—	6	0	32	0
		—	33	3	131	1
Kingston	19	—	15	5	23	1
		—	15.4	4	39	2
	0*	—	29	7	88	3

	Mtch	Inns	N.O.	Runs	H.S.	Av'ge	Ct	Overs	Mdns	Runs	Wkts	Av'ge	5in	10mch	B/B
TOTAL	3	4	1	38	19	12.66	—	133.2	27	420	9	46.66	—	—	3/88

1955 v. South Africa

Match	Mtch	Inns	N.O.	Runs	H.S.	Av'ge	Ct	Overs	Mdns	Runs	Wkts	Av'ge	5in 10mch	B/B
Lord's, London	1	2		2*			—	16	2	73	2			2/73
				6*				19	2	39	0			
TOTAL	1	2	2	8	6*	—	—	35	4	112	2	56.00	—	2/73

1956 v. Australia

Match	Mtch	Inns	N.O.	Runs	H.S.	Av'ge	Ct	Overs	Mdns	Runs	Wkts	Av'ge	5in 10mch	B/B
Lord's, London				7			1	28	6	54	2			5/90
				2				28	2	90	5			
Headingley, Leeds				0			2	8	2	19	1			
							1	11	3	21	1			
TOTAL	2	3	0	9	7	3.00	4	75	13	184	9	20.44	1	5/90

1957 v. West Indies

Match	Mtch	Inns	N.O.	Runs	H.S.	Av'ge	Ct	Overs	Mdns	Runs	Wkts	Av'ge	5in 10mch	B/B
Edgbaston, Birmingham				29*			1	30	4	99	2			5/63
								5	3	7	2			
Lord's, London				36*			2	12.3	2	30	2			
								23	8	73	2			
Trent Bridge, Nottingham				—				30	5	63	5			
								35	5	80	4			
Headingley, Leeds				2*			1	17	4	33	2			
							1	11	0	42	0			
The Oval, London				22			2	5	1	9	1			
								5	2	19	2			
TOTAL	5	4	3	89	36*	—	7	173.3	34	455	22	20.68	1	5/63

1958 v. New Zealand

	Runs	Catches	Overs	Mdns	Runs	Wickets
Edgbaston, Birmingham	0	1	21	8	31	5
Lord's, London	8	2	17	5	33	1
			4	1	6	1
Headingley, Leeds	—	1	11	6	24	2
			11	5	18	1
Old Trafford, Manchester	5	1	14	6	22	0
			29.5	4	67	3
The Oval, London	39*	—	2	1	11	0
			16	3	41	2
			6	5	3	0

	Mtch	Inns	N.O.	Runs	H.S.	Av'ge	Ct	Overs	Mdns	Runs	Wkts	Av'ge	5in	10mch	B/B
TOTAL	5	4	1	52	39*	17.33	6	131.5	44	256	15	17.06	1	—	5/31

1958–9 v. Australia

	Runs	Catches	Overs	Mdns	Runs	Wickets
Sydney	18	—	18	3	37	1
Adelaide	0	—	4	1	9	0
	0	—	30.1	6	90	4
Melbourne	21	—	3	1	3	—
	36	3	25	0	92	4
			6.7	0	45	0

	Mtch	Inns	N.O.	Runs	H.S.	Av'ge	Ct	Overs	Mdns	Runs	Wkts	Av'ge	5in	10mch	B/B
TOTAL	3	6	0	75	36	12.50	3	87	11	276	9	30.66	—	—	4/90

1958-9 v. New Zealand

	Mtch	Inns	N.O.	Runs	H.S.	Av'ge	Catches	Overs	Mdns	Runs	Wkts	Av'ge	5in	10mch	B/B	Ct
Christchurch				21			1	10.5	5	39	1					
							2	8	2	20	1					
Auckland				21*			1	26	12	46	3					
TOTAL	2	2	1	42	21*	—		44.5	19	105	5	21.00	—	—	3/46	4

1959 v. India

	Mtch	Inns	N.O.	Runs	H.S.	Av'ge	Catches	Overs	Mdns	Runs	Wkts	Av'ge	5in	10mch	B/B	Ct
Trent Bridge, Nottingham				28			1	24	9	45	4					
								22.3	10	44	2					
Lord's, London				7			—	16	4	40	1					
								21	3	55	2					
Headingley, Leeds				17			1	15	6	30	3					
								10	1	29	1					
Old Trafford, Manchester				0			—	15	4	29	2					
					8		1	23.1	6	75	2					
The Oval, London				1			1	17	6	24	4					
								14	4	30	3					
TOTAL	5	6	0	61	28	10.16		177.4	53	401	24	16.70	—	—	4/24	5

1959-60 v. West Indies

	Mtch	Inns	N.O.	Runs	H.S.	Av'ge	Catches	Overs	Mdns	Runs	Wkts	Av'ge	5in	10mch	B/B	Ct
Bridgetown				3			1	47	15	93	4					
Port-of-Spain				7			1	21	11	35	5					
					37											
Kingston				17			1	19	9	44	1					
								33	10	82	2					
Georgetown				4			—	18	4	54	4					
				6			1	40	6	116	3					
Port-of-Spain				10*			—	37.3	6	103	2					
				2*			2	5	1	22	0					
TOTAL	5	8	2	86	37	14.33		220.3	62	549	21	26.14	1	—	5/35	6

1960 v. South Africa

	Mtch	Inns	N.O.	Runs	H.S.	Catches	Overs	Mdns	Runs	Wkts	Av'ge	5in	10mch	B/B
Edgbaston, Birmingham				11			24.5	4	58	4				
				25			22	4	58	3				
Lord's, London				0			13	2	49	0				
Trent Bridge, Nottingham				15		1	17	5	44	2				
							14.3	6	27	5				
Old Trafford, Manchester				10		2	22	3	77	4				
				14*			20	2	58	3				
The Oval, London				0		1	6	1	10	0				
				24			31.1	4	93	2				
							10	2	34	2				
TOTAL	5	8	1	99	25	4	180.3	31	508	25	20.32	1	—	5/27

1961 v. Australia

	Mtch	Inns	N.O.	Runs	H.S.	Catches	Overs	Mdns	Runs	Wkts	Av'ge	5in	10mch	B/B
Edgbaston, Birmingham				20		1	36.5	1	136	2				
Lord's, London				25			34	3	118	4				
							10	0	40	2				
Headingley, Leeds				4			22	5	58	5				
							15.5	5	30	6				
Old Trafford, Manchester				3		1	14	1	55	1				
				8			32	0	92	0				
TOTAL	4	6	0	60	25	2	164.4	21	529	20	26.45	2	1	6/30

1962 v. Pakistan

	Mtch	Inns	N.O.	Runs	H.S.	Catches	Overs	Mdns	Runs	Wkts
Edgbaston, Birmingham				—		1	13	3	59	2
							24	5	70	2
Lord's, London				29		1	17.4	6	31	6
							33.3	6	85	3

	Mtch	Inns	N.O.	Runs	H.S.	Av'ge	Ct	Overs	Mdns	Runs	Wkts	Av'ge	5in 10mch	B/B
Headingley, Leeds				20				23 & 10.4	2 & 4	55 & 33	6 & 3			
Trent Bridge, Nottingham				29			2	24 & 19	4 & 1	71 & 35	3 & 5			
TOTAL	4	2	0	49	29	24.50	6	164.5	37	439	22	19.95	1	6/31

1962–3 v. Australia

	Mtch	Inns	N.O.	Runs	H.S.	Av'ge	Catches	Overs	Mdns	Runs	Wkts	Av'ge	5in 10mch	B/B
Brisbane				19			2	18	0	76 & 59	3 & 0			
Melbourne				6			1	15	1	83 & 62	3 & 5			
Sydney				32 & 9			2	23 & 20	1 & 2	68 & 20	0 & 2			
Adelaide				38			1	6 & 19	1 & 1	54 & 60	1 & 4			
Sydney				30 & 8			1	23.3 & 11	3 & 0	33 & 6	1 & 1			
TOTAL	5	7	0	142	38	20.28	7	158.3	9	521	20	26.05	1	5/62

1962–3 v. New Zealand

	Mtch	Inns	N.O.	Runs	H.S.	Av'ge	Catches	Overs	Mdns	Runs	Wkts	Av'ge	5in 10mch	B/B
Wellington				3			—	20 & 18	5 & 7	46 & 27	4 & 1			
Christchurch				11			—	30.2 & 19.4	9 & 8	75 & 16	7 & 2			
TOTAL	2	2	0	14	11	7.00	—	88	29	164	14	11.71	1	7/75

	Mtch	Inns	N.O.	Runs	H.S.	Av'ge	Ct	Overs	Mdns	Runs	Wkts	Av'ge	5in	10mch	B/B
1963 v. West Indies															
Old Trafford, Manchester				5, 29*			—	40	7	95	2				
Lord's, London				10, 0			—	44, 26	16, 9	100, 52	6, 5				
Edgbaston, Birmingham				4, 1			1	26	5	75, 0	5, 0				
Headingley, Leeds				4, 5			1	14.3, 46	2, 10	44, 117	7, 4				
The Oval, London				19, 5			1	13, 26.1	1, 1	46, 65	2, 3				
TOTAL	5	10	1	82	29*	9.11	3	236.4	53	594	34	17.47	4	2	7/44
1964 v. Australia															
Trent Bridge, Nottingham				0			1	20.3	3	58	3				
Lord's, London				4, 8			—	5, 25	0, 8	28, 48	0, 5				
Headingley, Leeds				4, 12*			—	18, 24.3	6, 2	52, 98	1, 3				
The Oval, London				14			2	7, 33.3	2, 4	28, 87	1, 4				
TOTAL	4	6	1	42	14	8.40	3	133.3	25	399	17	23.47	1	—	5/48
1965 v. New Zealand															
Edgbaston, Birmingham				3			1	18, 32.4	3, 8	49, 79	1, 3				
Lord's, London				3			—	19.5, 26	8, 4	40, 69	2, 0				
TOTAL	2	2	0	6	3	3.00	1	96.3	23	237	6	39.50	—	—	3/79

Test figures against each country

	Mtch	Inns	N.O.	Runs	H.S.	Av'ge	Ct	Overs	Mdns	Runs	Wkts	Av'ge	5in	1omch	B/B
Australia	19	29	1	338	38	12.07	21	399.4	63	1999	79	25.30	5	1	6/30
								245.3	20						
India	9	8	1	78	28	10.14	6	297.2	78	787	53	14.84	2	—	8/31
New Zealand	11	10	2	114	39*	14.25	11	361.1	113	762	40	19.05	2	—	7/75
Pakistan	4	2	0	49	29	24.50	6	164.5	37	439	22	19.93	1	—	6/31
South Africa	6	10	3	107	25	15.28	4	215.3	35	620	27	22.96	1	—	5/27
West Indies	18	26	7	295	37	15.52	16	764	176	2018	86	23.46	6	2	7/44
TOTALS	67	85	14	981	39*	13.81	64	2202.3	502	6625	307	21.57	17	3	8/31
								245.3	20						

Test record – ground by ground in England

	Mtch	Inns	N.O.	Runs	H.S.	Av'ge	Ct	Overs	Mdns	Runs	Wkts	Av'ge	5in	1omch	B/B
Edgbaston	7	8	1	93	29*	13.28	6	284.5	55	798	39	20.46	3	1	7/44
Headingley	9	10	3	68	20	9.71	11	294	66	795	44	18.06	2	1	6/30
Lord's	12	16	3	160	36*	12.30	7	514.3	113	1394	63	22.12	5	1	6/31
Old Trafford	6	9	2	82	29*	11.71	5	198.4	39	532	21	25.33	1	—	8/31
The Oval	8	9	1	134	39*	16.75	10	207.2	42	543	30	18.10	1	—	5/48
Trent Bridge	5	4	0	47	28	11.75	5	216.3	52	528	32	16.50	2	—	5/27
TOTALS	67	85	14	981	39*	13.81	64	2202.3	502	6625	307	21.57	17	3	8/31
								245.3	20						

Test record, overseas

	Mtch	Inns	N.O.	Runs	H.S.	Av'ge	Ct	Overs	Mdns	Runs	Wkts	Av'ge	5in	1omch	B/B
Australia	8	13	0	217	38	16.69	10	245.3	20	797	29	27.48	1	—	5/62
New Zealand	4	4	1	56	21*	18.66	4	132.5	46	269	19	14.15	1	—	7/75
West Indies	8	12	3	124	37	13.77	6	353.5	89	969	30	32.30	1	—	5/35
TOTALS	67	85	14	981	39*	13.81	64	2202.3	502	6625	307	21.57	17	3	8/31
								245.3	20						

Dismissals in test cricket

Total 307: 161 caught, 103 bowled, 40 lbw, 3 hit wicket.

Batsmen dismissed by Trueman in test cricket

9 times: R. Kanhai (W. Indies), N. C. O'Neill (Aust), F. M. M. Worrell (W. Indies)

7 times: R. N. Harvey (Aust), W. M. Lawry (Aust), Pankaj Roy (Ind), R. B. Simpson (Aust), G. S. Sobers (WI)

6 times: R. Benaud (Aust), W. W. Hall, C. C. Hunte (both WI), P. R. Umrigar (Ind)

5 times: K. D. Mackay, G. D. McKenzie (Aust), V. L. Manjrekar (Ind), S. Ramadhin (WI)

4 times: P. J. P. Burge (Aust), P. R. Carlstein (S. Africa), J. W. D'Arcy (N. Zealand), C. C. McDonald (Aust), R. A. McLean (S. Africa), E. D. A. McMorris (W. Indies), D. L. Murray (W. Indies), E. D. Weekes (W. Indies)

Batsmen dismissed by Trueman on three occasions or fewer are now listed by country.

3 times: G. S. Ramchand, R. G. Nadkarni, S. P. Gupte (India); R. R. Lindwall, A. T. W. Grout, A. K. Davidson, G. C. Corling (Aust); B. H. Pairaudeau, O. G. Smith, F. C. M. Alexander, C. C. Griffith (WI); D. J. McGlew, S. O'Linn, J. E. Pothecary (SA); L. S. M. Miller, W. R. Playle (NZ); Hanif Mohammed, Mohammed Farooq (Pak)

twice: V. S. Hazare, M. K. Mantri, M. H. Mankad, H. R. Adhikari, D. G. Phadkar, P. K. Sen, R. B. Desai, J. M. Ghorpade, N. S. Tanhane, R. Surendra Nath (India); K. R. Miller, I. R. Redpath, N. J. N. Hawke (Aust); A. L. Valentine, J. K. Holt, J. D. C. Goddard, M. C. Carew, B. F. Butcher, L. R. Gibbs, J. S. Solomon (WI); T. L. Goddard, G. M. Griffin, N. A. T. Adcock, J. P. Fellows– Smith (SA); T. Meale, J. C. Alabaster, J. R. Reid, R. W. Blair, G. T. Dowling, B. W. Sinclair, A. E. Dick, F. J. Cameron, R. O. Collinge (NZ); Imtiaz Ahmed, Nasim-ul-Ghani, Javed Burki, Mushtaq Mohammed, Wallis Mathias, Ijaz Butt (Pak)

once: C. D. Gopinath, S. G. Shinde, R. V. Divecha, P. G. Joshi, D. K. Gaekwad, A. A. Baig (India); G. B. Hole, J. H. de Courcy, I. W. Johnson, J. W. Burke, I. Meckiff, B. C. Booth, R. M. Cowper (Aust); J. B. Stollmeyer, N. S. Asgarali, DstE. Atkinson, S. M. Nurse, C. L. Walcott, Charan Singh (WI); J. H. B. Waite, H. J. Tayfield (S. A.); J. A. Hayes, B. Sutcliffe, E. C. Petrie, R. M. Harris, S. N. McGregor, J. T. Sparling, A. M. Moir, P. T. Barton, M. J. F. Shrimpton, R. C. Motz, R. W. Morgan, B. R. Taylor (NZ); Saeed Ahmed, Mahmood Hussain, Shahid Mahmoud, Alim-ud-Din (Pak)

Record for Yorkshire against each team

	Mtch	Inn	N.O.	Runs	H.S.	Av'ge	100	50	Ct	Overs	Mdns	Runs	Wkts	Av'ge	5in	10mch	B/B
Derbys	24	27	4	338	58	14.69	—	1	17	755.2	178	1850	108	17.12	7	2	6/59
Essex	20	21	4	288	54	16.94	—	1	9	591.4	120	1492	96	15.54	7	2	8/37
Glamorgan	17	20	0	180	37	9.00	—	—	13	371.1	100	858	54	15.88	4		7/15
Gloucs	23	29	3	488	77	18.76	—	4	22	527.1	122	1331	91	14.62	5	2	8/45
Hants	23	32	6	581	58*	22.34	—	4	20	622.5	176	1361	91	14.95	6	1	6/28
Kent	20	21	0	264	69	12.57	—	1	10	491.1	92	1265	82	15.42	3	1	8/28
Lancs	35	38	11	400	54*	14.81	—	—	18	973.3	226	2307	128	18.02	8		6/109
Leics	22	25	2	417	74	18.13	—	2	18	593.2	131	1536	88	17.45	6	1	7/45
Middlesex	28	35	2	555	101	16.81	1	1	20	754.5	159	2037	89	22.88	2		6/49
Northants	18	23	3	396	104	19.80	1	—	22	548.3	132	1372	65	21.10	4		7/60
Notts	29	26	7	266	34*	14.00	—	—	22	786.4	190	1826	131	13.93	10	3	8/53
Somerset	25	27	3	372	63	15.50	—	—	22	676.4	164	1572	108	14.55	3		6/42
Surrey	32	44	3	434	50	10.58	—	—	28	915	221	2272	107	21.23	5	1	7/41
Sussex	21	26	3	362	43	17.23	—	—	12	612.4	146	1557	79	19.70	4	1	8/36
Warwicks	24	29	6	266	57	11.56	—	—	11	654.1	183	1542	109	14.14	7	2	7/42
Worcs	21	26	7	330	56	17.36	—	—	15	597.3	122	1193	62	19.24	2		7/46
Cambridge	14	13	3	181	49	18.10	—	—	10	319.1	92	757	55	13.76	3		7/37
Oxford	9	6	1	56	23	11.20	—	—	4	263.5	91	482	50	9.64	3		6/23
Australians	9	7	1	64	33	10.66	—	—	3	134.2	25	367	13	28.23	—		3/32
Canadians	1	1	1	16	16	—	—	—	1	14	2	43	4	10.75	—		2/12
Indians	1	1	0	2	2*	—	—	—	—	31	4	92	3	30.66	—		3/47
N. Zealanders	3	2	0	60	60	30.00	—	1	3	23	6	58	2	29.00	—		2/26
Pakistanis	2	2	0	35	35	17.50	—	—	1	47	15	96	3	32.00	—		3/80
S. Africans	2	2	0	4	4	2.00	—	—	4	47.1	11	96	7	13.71	—		5/19
W. Indians	5	8	4	85	55	21.25	—	1	4	111.3	23	313	14	22.35	2	1	5/38
MCC	29	38	5	362	43	10.96	—	1	14	677.3	143	1795	81	22.16	2		6/41
Minor Cos	2	2	—	1	1	0.50	—	—	1	38.3	4	128	9	14.22	1		8/70
Scotland	2	3	1	—	—	—	—	—	—	40.1	6	115	7	16.42	1		5/52
The Rest	2	3	0	50	45	16.66	—	—	1	74.4	18	177	9	19.66	1		6/54
TOTAL	459	533	81	6853	104	15.16	2	21	325	12204.0	2902	29890	1745	17.12	97	20	8/28

Record for Yorkshire ground by ground (home games)

	Mtch	Inn	N.O.	Run	H.S	Av'ge	100	50	Ct	Over	Mdns	Runs	Wkts	Av'ge	5in 10mch	B/B
Bradford	57	68	10	889	60	15.32	—	3	52	1362.4	321	3349	212	15.79	12	4	8/37
Harrogate	12	11	8	248	57	27.55	—	2	8	295.1	94	619	44	14.06	3	—	6/59
Headingley	39	47	8	611	63	15.66	—	2	35	1030.1	245	2573	137	18.78	6	1	6/50
Huddersfield	5	6	2	25	12	6.25	—	—	4	161.3	32	432	32	13.50	2	—	7/30
Hull	20	23	1	182	39	8.27	—	—	10	550.2	129	1280	80	16.00	2	1	6/45
Middlesbrough	12	16	1	325	55	21.66	—	2	10	303.3	74	696	54	12.88	4	—	7/57
Scarborough	39	46	11	549	101	15.68	1	—	34	945.4	200	2432	140	17.37	9	2	7/23
Sheffield	53	53	8	806	77	17.91	—	4	45	1560.3	355	3954	225	17.57	17	4	8/68
TOTAL (HOME)	237	270	43	3635	101	16.01	1	13	198	6209.3	1450	15335	924	16.59	55	12	8/37
TOTAL (AWAY)	222	263	38	3218	104	14.29	1	8	127	5994.3	1452	14555	821	17.72	42	8	8/28

Record for Yorkshire ground by ground (away games)

	Mch	Inn	N.O.	Runs	H.S.	Av'ge	100	50	Ct	Overs	Mdns	Runs	Wkts	Av'ge	5in 10mch	B/B
Bath	2	3	0	11	6	3.66	—	—	2	61	16	121	7	17.28	—	—	3/8
Bournemouth	6	11	2	222	53	24.66	—	2	6	136.4	37	331	16	20.68	1	—	5/23
Brentwood	1	1	0	—	—	—	—	—	1	30	4	144	6	24.00	—	—	5/91
Bristol	9	10	2	143	61	17.87	—	2	5	180.4	37	479	28	17.10	1	—	4/8
Bristol (Imp)	1	1	0	5	5	1.00	—	—	—	26.2	11	30	4	7.50	—	—	4/30
Burton	1	2	0	33	33	16.50	—	—	1	45.1	3	171	6	28.50	—	—	3/38
Canterbury	2	2	0	—	—	—	—	—	1	29.1	7	85	7	17.00	—	—	2/25
Cambridge	12	11	2	167	49	18.55	—	—	7	282.2	87	629	45	13.97	2	1	7/37
Cardiff	3	4	0	63	37	15.75	—	—	3	49	7	143	5	28.60	—	—	2/38
Cheltenham	1	2	2	0	0	0.00	—	—	2	9	1	35	0	—	—	—	—

	M	I	NO	Runs	HS	Avge	100	50	Ct	O	M	R	W	Avge	5wi	10w	Best
Chesterfield	7	7	1	79	48	13.16	—	—	3	206.4	51	439	22	19.95	—	—	3/16
Colchester	2	4	2	100	54	50.00	—	1	1	90.2	18	230	14	16.42	1	—	5/65
Coventry	1	2	1	2	2	—	—	—	1	36	8	87	8	10.87	1	—	7/67
Derby	4	4	0	29	20	7.25	—	—	—	30	8	72	0	—	—	—	—
Dover	1	2	0	28	24	14.00	—	—	2	67.3	4	168	12	14.00	1	—	8/28
Eastbourne	2	2	0	34	26	17.00	—	—	—	20	3	79	3	26.33	—	—	3/55
Edgbaston	10	11	4	68	28	9.71	—	—	3	252.5	63	693	40	17.32	3	—	6/18
Gillingham	2	3	0	78	69	26.00	—	1	—	56.2	12	141	7	20.14	—	—	2/21
Gravesend	2	3	0	34	26	12.55	—	—	1	62.2	10	151	8	18.87	—	—	3/48
Hove	10	12	3	113	34	12.55	—	—	2	347.2	86	850	46	18.47	4	—	8/36
Kidderminster	1	—	—	—	—	—	—	—	—	15.3	4	46	2	23.00	—	—	2/11
Leicester	12	15	2	223	74	17.15	—	1	10	304.2	61	770	36	21.38	2	—	5/41
Leyton	2	2	0	21	12	10.50	—	—	—	56.4	14	123	10	12.30	—	—	4/37
Lord's	31	39	2	482	54	13.02	—	1	13	813.5	169	2246	108	20.79	3	—	8/70
Lydney	1	1	0	39	39	39.00	—	—	—	13	6	18	2	9.00	—	—	1/8
Neath	1	1	0	3	3	3.00	—	—	1	25.1	11	30	8	3.75	1	—	7/15
Northampton	8	10	0	255	104	31.87	1	1	8	249.2	57	637	23	27.69	2	—	5/34
Old Trafford	17	21	6	199	40*	13.26	—	—	9	488.4	115	1155	58	19.19	2	—	5/26
The Oval	18	26	1	225	45	9.00	—	—	17	527	130	1186	65	18.24	5	—	7/47
Oxford	9	6	1	56	23	11.20	—	—	4	263.5	91	482	50	9.64	3	—	6/23
Portsmouth	4	3	1	37	13	12.33	—	—	—	128.3	38	247	27	9.14	3	—	6/28
Romford	1	—	—	10	10	—	—	—	3	10	1	32	0	—	—	—	—
Southend	3	3	0	36	29	12.00	—	—	3	103.1	22	255	21	12.14	3	—	6/42
Swansea	4	6	0	14	10	2.33	—	—	4	79	28	149	11	13.54	1	—	6/41
Taunton	8	8	1	114	42	16.28	—	—	9	208	55	453	28	16.17	—	—	4/27
Trent Bridge	11	9	2	69	31	9.85	—	—	—	301.5	75	704	45	15.64	3	—	8/53
Westcliff	1	1	0	32	30	16.00	—	—	1	33	8	84	3	28.00	—	—	3/57
Worcester	9	13	3	144	43	14.40	—	—	2	254	59	606	25	24.24	—	—	4/50
Worksop	3	4	1	81	34*	27.00	—	—	1	101	25	254	17	14.94	1	—	8/84

Record for other first-class teams in England

	Mtch	Inn	N.O.	Runs	H.S.	Av'ge	100	50	Ct	Overs	Mdns	Runs	Wkts	Av'ge	5in	10mch	B/B
England XI	7	10	4	133	100*	22.16	1	—	7	143.1	16	580	17	34.11	1	—	5/57
Int. Cavaliers	1	2	0	37	26	18.50	—	—	1	93	1	93	1	46.50	—	—	1/41
MCC	2	2	1	5	5	—	—	—	1	49.2	7	167	4	41.75	—	—	4/62
T. N. Pearce's XI	11	15	5	356	80*	35.60	—	2	1	236.1	34	834	33	25.27	1	—	4/32
Players v. Gts	11	13	6	161	63	23.00	—	1	8	257.5	57	731	34	21.50	1	—	5/47
Services	2	2	1	12	6*	—	—	—	1	14	2	95	0	—	—	—	—
The Rest v. Eng	2	3	1	1	1	0.50	—	—	1	40	11	107	1	—	—	—	1/18
The Rest v. Surrey	3	5	1	21	9	5.25	—	—	1	84	19	223	12	18.58	—	—	4/71
TOTAL	38	52	19	726	100*	22.00	1	3	20	845.3	147	2830	103	27.47	2	—	5/47

Ground records for other first-class matches in England

	Mtch	Inn	N.O.	Runs	H.S.	Av'ge	100	50	Ct	Overs	Mdns	Runs	Wkts	Av'ge	5in	10mch	B/B
Bradford	1	2	1	1	1	1.00	—	—	1	9	3	18	1	—	—	—	1/18
Edgbaston	1	1	0	0	0	—	—	—	—	31	8	89	0	—	—	—	—
Hastings	1	2	1	8	6	—	—	—	2	23.1	4	86	5	17.20	1	—	5/57
Kingston	2	4	1	15	6*	5.00	—	—	2	40	3	215	20	10.75	—	—	1/46
Lord's	7	7	4	95	63	31.66	—	1	4	159	41	468	20	23.40	1	—	5/47
The Oval	2	3	0	8	6	2.66	—	—	1	53	14	122	8	15.25	—	—	4/71
Old Trafford	2	3	1	5	5	—	—	—	1	49.2	7	167	4	41.75	—	—	4/62
Scarborough	22	31	11	594	100*	29.70	1	2	9	481	67	1565	63	26.42	—	—	4/48
TOTAL	38	52	19	726	100*	22.00	1	3	20	845.3	147	2830	103	27.47	2	—	5/47

Grounds used for Yorkshire & other first-class matches – combined records

	Mtch	Inn	N.O.	Runs	H.S.	Av'ge	100	50	Ct	Overs	Mdns	Runs	Wkts	Av'ge	5in 10mch		B/B
Bradford	58	70	11	890	60	15.08	—	3	53	1371.4	324	3367	213	15.80	12	4	8/87
Edgbaston	18	20	5	161	29	10.73	—	—	10	568.4	126	1580	79	20.00	6	2	7/44
Headingley	48	57	11	679	63	14.76	—	2	46	1324.1	311	3368	181	18.60	8	1	6/30
Lord's	50	62	9	736	63	13.90	—	2	24	1487.2	323	4108	191	21.50	9	1	8/70
Old Trafford	25	32	9	286	40*	12.43	—	—	15	736.4	161	1854	83	22.33	3	—	8/31
The Oval	28	38	2	367	45	10.19	—	—	28	787.2	186	1851	103	17.97	6	1	7/47
Trent Bridge	16	13	2	116	31	10.54	—	—	14	518.2	127	1232	77	16.00	5	—	8/53
Scarborough	61	77	22	1143	101	20.78	2	2	43	1426.4	267	4097	203	20.18	9	2	7/23

Record in first-class matches on West Indian grounds

	Mtch	Inn	N.O.	Runs	H.S.	Av'ge	50	Ct	Overs	Mdns	Runs	Wkts	Av'ge	5in 10mch	B/B
Bridgetown	4	5	1	33	9*	8.25	—	2	132	30	401	7	57.28	—	4/93
Georgetown	3	3	0	36	20	12.00	—	5	83	19	209	6	34.83	—	3/116
Grenada	1	1	0	16	16	—	—	2	16	1	49	6	8.16	1	5/22
Kingston, Melbourne Pk	2	1	0	12	12	—	—	1	60	18	162	8	20.25	—	4/54
Kingston, Sabina Pk	7	9	1	92	28	11.50	—	3	268.4	70	762	37	20.59	2	5/78
Montego Bay	1	1	—	—	—	—	—	—	25	8	63	1	—	—	1/30
Port-of-Spain	5	7	3	97	37	24.25	—	8	206	51	523	19	27.52	1	5/35
TOTALS	23	26	5	286	37	13.61	—	21	790.4	197	2169	84	25.82	4	5/22

Record in first-class matches on Australian grounds

	Mtch	Inn	N.O.	Runs	H.S.	Av'ge	50	Ct	Overs	Mdns	Runs	Wkts	Av'ge	5in 10mch	B/B
Adelaide	4	5	0	112	39	22.40	—	4	123.1	16	348	19	18.31	1	5/46
Brisbane	1	1	0	19	19	19.00	—	2	33	0	135	3	45.00	—	3/76
Hobart	1	—	—	—	—	—	—	—	9	0	36	3	12.00	—	3/36
Launceston	2	1	1	29	29*	—	—	3	26	8	57	6	9.50	—	4/13
Melbourne	4	4	0	72	36	18.00	—	4	125.3	4	490	20	24.50	2	5/42
Perth	3	5	0	86	53	17.20	1	1	66	7	211	6	35.16	—	3/42
Sydney	6	10	0	127	32	12.70	—	5	112	14	319	10	31.90	—	2/20
TOTALS	21	26	1	445	53	17.80	1	19	494.4	49	1596	67	23.82	3	5/42

Record in first-class matches on New Zealand grounds

	Mtch	Inn	N.O.	Runs	H.S.	Av'ge	50	Ct	Overs	Mdns	Runs	Wkts	Av'ge	5in 10mch	B/B
Auckland	1	1	1	21	21*	—	—	1	26	12	46	3	15.33	—	3/46
Christchurch	2	2	0	32	21	16.00	—	3	68.5	22	150	11	13.63	1	7/75
Dunedin	2	2	0	1	1	0.50	—	1	61.5	13	162	24	6.75	4	8/45
Hamilton	1	1	0	3	3	3.00	—	1	15	5	26	1	26.00	—	1/26
Wellington	2	3	0	4	3	1.33	—	—	50	14	107	6	17.83	—	4/46
TOTALS	8	9	1	61	21*	7.62	—	6	221.4	66	491	45	10.91	5	8/45

Record in first-class matches on South African grounds

	Mtch	Inn	N.O.	Runs	H.S.	Av'ge	50	Ct	Overs	Mdns	Runs	Wkts	Av'ge	5in 10mch	B/B
Johannesburg	2	2	0	76	59	38.00	1	2	54.4	7	164	15	10.93	1	5/59
Durban	1	2	0	44	39	22.00	—	—	23	3	74	3	24.66	—	3/49
TOTALS	3	4	0	120	59	35.00	1	2	77.4	10	238	18	13.22	1	5/59

Record in first-class match in Rhodesia

	Mtch	Inn	N.O.	Runs	H.S.	Av'ge	50	Ct	Overs	Mdns	Runs	Wkts	Av'ge	5in 10mch	B/B
Police Ground, Salisbury	1	1	1	19	19*	—	—	—	37	6	88	4	22.00	—	3/30

Record in first-class matches on Indian grounds

	Mtch	Inn	N.O.	Runs	H.S.	Av'ge	50	Ct	Overs	Mdns	Runs	Wkts	Av'ge	5in 10mch	B/B
Bombay	2	4	0	81	33	20.25	—	1	48	8	153	4	38.25	—	2/66
Calcutta	1	2	2	57	46*	—	—	—	31	3	109	5	21.80	—	3/38
TOTALS	3	6	2	138	46*	34.50	—	1	79	11	262	9	29.11	—	3/38

The Man

The Man

8
Husband and Father

Everything about Fred, from his earliest days, was seriously competitive, and he never changed. Even in the twilight years, when he led his Courage Old England Eleven around the country playing charity matches – he was past the half-century mark in years – there was fierce pride to find 'the old outswinger' working, and he was quick to draw the attention of his colleagues to it. The fact that they did not always treat such occasions with the respect Fred felt they merited was more a matter of affection than exasperation. Everyone in the game knew Fred for precisely what he was, and it would have seemed a kind of heresy if he had changed. In the Yorkshire camp he was looked upon in many different ways by many different players, but the one common factor in all attitudes was respect for his ability to take wickets when they were most required.

For two larger-than-life public figures who quarrelled publicly, if by proxy in 1985 (in the *Sunday People* and the *Sun* respectively), Fred and Ian Botham had a lot in common. The cult of personality in modern newspaper journalism might have become more pronounced by the 1980s, but the fact is that both men were haunted and pursued wherever they went by reporters keen to detail everything they did whether it concerned cricket or not. Both enjoyed (in fact *courted*) publicity when they were in action, but were considerably less enthusiastic about the reporting of their off-duty moments. They were not alone in this, of course, but newspaper coverage is not selective when dealing with world-famous personalities.

Fred in the 1950s suffered more from word-of-mouth rumour than from actual newspaper sources, but the effect was equally devastating. Such was his world-wide reputation that any conversational reference to any aspect of his life-style was pretty certain to get a good reaction from those who heard (or over-heard) it. That is the way legends grow. During Peter Sainsbury's benefit year in

Hampshire, John Arlott asked several of the Yorkshire team – engaged in a weekend championship match in Bournemouth – to take part in the Sunday benefit game, including Fred. His presence alone was guaranteed to increase considerably the 'gate' and John, who had asked Fred to play as a personal favour, was a little concerned when he didn't arrive for the pre-match lunch. His apprehension was increased when one of the Yorkies tossed out a throw-away line, 'Fred might be a bit late. When I came in at half-past three this morning he was just going out for the second time.' Now that was undoubtedly untrue. It was the sort of remark made, not with malice, but it was what the audience expected to hear and it brought a laugh all round. But *someone* was quite certain to go away from that occasion believing it to be true and he or she would, without the slightest doubt, pass it on to a third party in due course – perhaps as an indication of admiration: Fred was the chap who was starting on a second round of Saturday night partying at 3.30 a.m. He could still mow down the batsmen. Ergo: he is a bit of a superman, very much a jack-the-lad, and we take our hat off to him.

Even those who were close to Fred, who knew him well, subscribed at times to this inverted admirers' club. They were not intending any disrespect to his cricketing ability. Rather were they paying tribute to a man who could live life to the full and still be county cricket's most feared bowler. To be scrupulously, but perhaps brutally honest, Fred didn't *mind* being regarded as supernaturally fit and strong and virile so long as the stories remained in private circulation around the country's dressing-rooms. They strengthened the image, extended the legend, built up the character. But at the same time the real truth is that he was *not* a heavy drinker – no matter what one might have heard from a chap whose third cousin knew a bloke whose sister's husband had been in a pub where Fred had been seen. And he most certainly would not have been going out for the second time at half-past three on Sunday morning. Sunday on the cricket circuit in the 1950s and well into the sixties was a rest day for fast bowlers, the day when they put their feet up or lay langorously for hours in hot, soothing baths.

Most players, it is true, engaged in a bit of celebration on Saturday night and many of them enjoyed a round of golf on Sundays. Fred, who became extremely keen on golf after his retirement, rarely played at all when he was hurling down 1,000 overs a season. No one was surprised; his captains were glad. And the time that Fred could spend in bed was precious to him. He rarely, if ever, appeared at breakfast in the team's hotel, preferring to have a meal delivered to his room while he indulged himself in an extra hour's rest. He worked hard during a cricket season – agonisingly hard, excruciatingly hard, exhaustingly hard, debilitatingly hard. And he didn't whinge about it. A bit of a grumble, perhaps, from time to time when something was amiss, but it was rarely a serious grouse. Fred loved fast bowling; he revelled in it, gloried in his position as the best-known practitioner in the business. If he had been a serious drinker or smoker, if he had been a consistent late-nighter, he could not have carried on plying his trade with such incisiveness for twenty seasons. It never came to a conflict between what he wanted to do and what he would have preferred to do. He took his work far too seriously for that. If there had ever been a choice between a good party and taking six wickets the following morning the bowling analysis would have won hands down, every time. Fred Trueman was a fast bowler with every waking thought, every ounce of energy he possessed. It was his Life.

No one who lived, worked and played with him in those days would claim that he qualified for enrolment in the Little White Ribboners or unquestioned admittance to the monastery of La Trappe, either. What they will and do say is that The Job came first, and Fred would have shot himself rather than follow a sustained lifestyle which took anything away from his bowling. Nevertheless, the rumours and the legends grew, followed him and, inevitably, reached his home.

The Scarborough Festival (est. 1871) is regarded with affection by almost everyone who has played or watched cricket during that final fortnight of the summer season. It has been the setting for friendships and romances, the place where 1,000-runs-in-a-season, or 100 wickets (sometimes both), have been gratefully completed, where touching farewells have taken place, where lovers of the game who never otherwise see each other in the course of a year expect once more to join in joyous reunion. Apart from the ground at North Marine Road (or its short-lived predecessor at Castle Yard), the focal centre of Festival life was for many years the Balmoral Hotel, sadly a shopping complex these days. There the landlord, Ken Gill, saw more fun and heard more laughter, watched more burgeoning romances and witnessed more tempestuous break-ups, dispensed more wine and listened to more song in one fortnight than many hotel-managers do in a lifetime. He was a friend of Fred's from his earliest days and watched over the budding romance of Yorkshire's cricket hero and the attractive daughter of Scarborough's Mayor, Alderman Rodney Chapman, which began in 1951 – at a mayoral reception. During the Festival of 1954 the couple became engaged. They married in 1955 and made their home close to the town, which was understandable since Fred was always likely to be away for long periods in both summer and winter and Enid did not want to find herself away from family and friends she had known all her life during these absences. Headingley and Park Avenue were something like a two-hour drive away from Scarborough in the 1950s, Sheffield even more so, and what was a 'home' game to most of the team based in the West Riding was in effect an away game for Fred. It was not the easiest of starts for a young married couple.

Apart from being a beauty, Enid was a strong and dynamic character. She had enjoyed a good social life in the town before marriage, and after enduring days and weeks without her husband she felt she was entitled to expect a bit of a whirl when he returned home. Fred, on the other hand, was looking for something on the lines of a haven of rest from his labours. Thus, there was a conflict of interests rather than a tranquil domestic scene, especially after their first child, Karen, was born. Enid felt more than ever tied down by domesticity, and if she could not enjoy a change of scene when her husband returned to the fold she resented it. Most young wives would understand that.

Fred bought a bigger house, nearer the middle of Scarborough and then, to cut down the travelling from Yorkshire's 'home' games he moved the family to Heworth, a suburb of York. He did not help his own cause at times. Jack Mewies, his solicitor, adviser and close friend, has a vivid memory of joining Fred for a social drink in a York club when FST (in his lady wife's eyes at least) might well have been spending the time in the bosom of his family. Anticipating that his welcome might not be as cordial as some he had known, Fred plucked a bunch of flowers from a vase as the pair were leaving the club, opened his front door and held out his peace-offering. Jack, standing a step behind him, never got beyond the threshold:

'Suddenly, flower-heads were being showered over me as Enid let Fred have it with his bouquet. She was not happy. I thought it would be better if I got into my car and drove fifty miles back home to Skipton.'

It was not all like that, of course. Enid was a bright, intelligent and lively lady. Without the fireworks and histrionics they made an attractive couple and it had been, originally, a match which made delighted headlines – a union of Yorkshire cricket and Scarborough Society. But public rows, all *too* public, with powerful personalities and colourful vocabularies ranged in fierce and acrimonious combat, became too frequent. When Fred found time to be at home there was no respite from the ringing of the telephone or callers at the door. (Again, it is necessary to stress that he was the most spectacular figure in English – perhaps even world – cricket). When they went out together there was always someone trying to take Fred on one side for a private word. Enid, and her family, were considerable figures in the social round of East Yorkshire; she was naturally miffed at having to take a back seat so frequently.

And always there were the stories, the reports, the rumours, that while she waited at home Fred was living it up and having a high old time around other parts of the country. Individually, Enid might have been able to cope with the many problems; collectively they became too much of a burden. Fred's homecomings became steadily more strident occasions and he started to miss opportunities to return to Heworth. To be fair to him, it has to be said that he *understood* his wife's frustrations and anger; he didn't blame her for them. Gradually and ominously it became clear that there was not enough tolerance on either side for the marriage to last. Fred moved out for a time, staying with Jack Mewies or other friends in a different part of Yorkshire from that where he had made his home. On a visit to see their daughter Karen he learned that Enid was pregnant and he moved back into the matrimonial home.

The birth of the twins, Rodney and Rebecca, in 1965 held the family together for another five years, not least of all because FS has a genuine and deeply-sentimental love of children. His charity work (which is considerable) has long centred largely on young people and, whatever accusations may be levelled against him, he has always been a remarkably generous and caring father and step-father. But sadly, none of the problems had been removed. The arrival of another two children had, if anything, exacerbated them as far as Enid was concerned and the late fifties to early sixties, when the children were beginning to grow, was the time at which Fred's career reached its high-point. More than ever it was necessary for him to spend long periods away from home; more than ever was he lionised in the press and on TV and radio; more than ever Enid felt shut out of so much of his life.

It is probably true to say that Fred was not ready for the responsibilities of and commitment to a wife and young family until he was past thirty years of age. He would not have been alone in that. Enid and the children were important to him, very important indeed, but in an entirely different way from that in which cricket and fame were important to him. Consequently he was leading a schizophrenic existence and some of us wondered how he did not crack up under the strain of it all. His work-load as a bowler was phenomenal; the focus of public attention upon him was glaring; and when he returned home there were rows, and more rows. Perhaps it can be said that at that time neither he nor Enid fully understood the other's point of view; certainly it can be said that neither of them *accepted* the other's case.

In the midst of all this the BBC made a television programme about Fred's life and it included a dazzlingly frank interview with Enid which was a talking-point around the country the following day. Her bitterness at the destruction of all semblance of privacy in her family life was lacerating; her anguish at the way her own strong and vibrant personality was being submerged in the ocean of Fred's fame was poignant in the extreme. And yet it was not some wildly emotional outburst. The grim, matter-of-fact tone in which so much of the interview was conducted enhanced the bitterness and the anguish. Away on the county championship circuit I watched the programme with Fred – and he was profoundly shaken. The other members of the Yorkshire team watched it elsewhere. But they watched it. Everybody in cricket, it seemed, had watched it.

The Second World War provided a great watershed in attitudes. Those whose childhood covered the 1930s grew up with the conviction that because our mothers had always been at home to care for us, so would our wives in due course always be there to care for our children. Certainly in working-class West Riding that was the natural order of things. We (and FST was one of 'us') emerged from wartime Britain as adults, but with our attitudes unchanged. We were unprepared for an emancipation which had seen women drive trucks and fly aeroplanes, direct searchlights, barrage balloons and guns. Fred, as a middle-order batsman, so to speak, in a large and loving family, did not question his belief that the next generation of women would be precisely the same. So with hindsight, he and Enid might well have been on a collision course from the start, because not all women by any means were any longer content to sit at home with the kids. Sadly, the marriage now broke up finally.

For all the brave face he put on it, Fred was left miserable and bewildered. Getting away with his friends (especially in the Dales which he had discovered and come to love) was fine when the other anchorage of home and family remained – in Scarborough, or York. Moving from one pied-à-terre to another between matches was something quite different. He spent a lot of lonely nights in a lot of hotels where he literally cried himself to sleep. That is something a generation or two of batsmen will find difficult to visualise but it is literally true. Tough guy he might have been; awkward and uncompromising he might have appeared – images which, if he had not entirely created, he had cultivated. But right down at the bottom of F. S. Trueman, for those prepared to dig hard enough, is just a great big softy – a hugely sentimental man, vulnerable, malleable.

It was now that he needed his friends. His career in cricket had come to an end and no ready-made substitute immediately presented itself. There was enough natural vanity in the man for him to believe that after so long at the top, after twenty years of being a leading personality in the world of sport, something similar would naturally follow. He decided that the music hall was his forte (or at least as much of the music hall which remained – it was now largely centred on social drinking clubs where weekend cabaret 'turns' were popular). He will hate me for saying so but I regard that brief episode as one of the major disasters of his life.

Fred's repertoire of jokes was by far the most extensive on the cricket circuit; he acquired them from a variety of sources but delighted in conjuring up many of them himself, and it has to be said that he was good – if one likes that sort of thing. The jokes were mostly of the variety known in polite company as 'risqué', liberally sprinkled with racial overtones. It is doubtful, for instance, if Fred would ever be invited to read the lesson (or whatever the equivalent is) in one of the mosques of Bradford. But he had friends in 'the business', notably the Lipthorpe brothers, who owned clubs in Sheffield and Stockton-on-Tees, and they gave him a booking. They devised an act which started with film of Fred in his prime being shown on a thin, paper screen and the climax arrived with him leaping *through* the screen to announce himself. Fred actually thought it was an effective bit of show business; his friends thought it was a prostitution of the artistry he had shown on the cricket field for so long. We were relieved and grateful when it came to an end.

At this time, Jack Mewies proved to be not only a good solicitor but a good friend, too, involving Fred in a number of business enterprises – a sports-goods shop, a garage – as well as handling the divorce from Enid which, mercifully, went through quietly without any laundering of dirty washing or recrimination. This was not through any lack of zeal on the part of the popular press. While there was a bare minimum of what could be reported about an undefended petition there was no restriction on 'quotes' after the granting of a decree, and in this connection there was always the hope of something juicy. Fred and Jack went to London and then, to avoid the reporters, flew to Jersey. A whole planeload of news-papermen followed and, with a neat sidestep, the pair of fugitives returned to London on the plane which had brought the press!

'I had never seen Jersey,' reflects Jack, wryly. 'I was looking forward to it, but all I saw was the airport. When we got back to Heathrow there was an even bigger crowd of newsmen and we wondered how they could have got wind of our return so quickly. As things turned out, the Queen was flying in from a visit to Canada, and even Fred could not compete with that!'

In the meantime, a meeting had occurred which I regard as the best thing that has ever happened to Fred in his life. He met Veronica, who was to become his second wife.

9
Veronica

Veronica Wilson was not only a most attractive auburn-haired lady; she was an extremely shrewd businesswoman when Fred first met her, for which he has had reason to be profoundly grateful over the past twenty years. Veronica and her friend Pat Bromley worked together in a solicitor's office in Bradford in the early 1960s. They had known each other all their lives; their parents and their grandparents had been friends. And both were determinedly ambitious ladies with a need to express themselves in a way which progressed beyond shorthand, typing and filing. They searched for a business they could run together, finally settling on management of a public house (since running a more ambitious hotel-type project was not at that time a practical proposition). They pursued every brewery, many of them at that time, with licensed outlets in Yorkshire but got no encouragement at all. 'What? Two women running a pub? Impossible.'

But Veronica and Pat have never been the type to give up easily. They wrote and wrote, pestering one brewery after another, until finally, and no doubt deciding it was the best way to discourage them, Hammond's offered them The Swan in the winding main street of Addingham, between Skipton and Ilkley. It was badly run down at the time and Veronica believes it was offered in the belief that the two women would never take it on. If that was the case, Hammond's were very wrong indeed. Since only one of them could be the licence-holder they tossed a coin – 'to the brewery's horror'. Pat won, and she and her partner set to work to prove a point.

Between the two of them they knew a very large number of people, who were duly invited to the grand re-opening of The Swan. All accepted and all came: barristers and solicitors, professional men as well as tradesmen, not forgetting the locals to whom the thought of one of the five pubs which adorn Addingham's main street being run by a couple of appealing ladies was something of a novelty. The street – one of the most tortuous thoroughfares in the West Riding at the best of times – was jammed. The following day the police expressed a certain displeasure at the traffic problems thus created, while the joint manageresses, naturally enough, hoped to see the patronage increase, rather than diminish. The brewery, hoist on their own petard, built them a car-park at the back of the pub. It wasn't large, by any means, but at least it reduced the cause for complaint.

Veronica and Pat, like good publicans of a village local, got themselves involved with the life of the community as much as possible, and this took in the support of various causes. One of their enterprises was raising funds for Keighley Rugby League Club, eight miles away, and in pursuit of this they went to see, perhaps paradoxically, a soccer match involving the Showbiz Eleven in which one of the players was Freddie Trueman. A mutual friend, Malcolm Davies, brought FS back to The Swan for a drink afterwards. If this were a work of fiction we might now find ourselves reporting love at first sight or, at any rate, an instant mutual attraction. It was, however, around another couple of years before the two saw each other again. By that time Fred had faced the final break-up of his marriage and Veronica was facing the fact that her own was rocky. It was not so much a matter of spectacular rows, as had happened in Fred's case, but there was a definite conflict of interests. Veronica felt that she was ambitious in a way which her husband did not share. They had two children, Sheena and Patrick, so they did not part without considerable efforts on both sides to make the marriage work. Gradually, however, Veronica faced up to the fact that all was not well.

Fred, in the meantime, had started to drop in at The Swan, often with Jack Mewies, whose home was only five miles away, but sometimes on his own as he put off a return to *his* matrimonial home. With his retirement from cricket, not only had his marriage started to disintegrate but his life generally, without a really firm and constructive guiding influence, was getting into something of a mess. He invested money in a frozen-food business which went in for bulk-supplying to hotels and other catering establishments. He lost his money. The sports shop and the garage business were not in those first years wildly successful, and one way and another the career of F. S. Trueman, fast bowler extraordinary and major sporting personality, seemed to be drifting aimlessly in no particular direction.

By 1970 Veronica decided that her marriage was irretrievably lost and she and Fred set up home together – scarcely a year since he had promised himself that he would never again tie himself up completely with one woman! They moved into a bungalow in an idyllic setting halfway between Airedale and Wharfedale, with an entourage of, as Fred put it, 'five kids, a dog, a parrot and thirty bob in the bank.'

In this context we may perhaps allow our hero a little licence. The three children of his marriage remained, for the time being, with their mother, who was now living in Scarborough again. The 'parrot' was, in fact, a budgerigar. And while we have no information on Fred's personal finances, Veronica's bank balance was rather more than thirty bob – it was £10. Within a few weeks she had a summons from the Department of Inland Revenue (Burnley bureau) which called upon her to explain how she proposed to pay off a debt of £250. She presented herself, trembling with anxiety ('By this time I hadn't even 250 pence!'), and to her considerable relief was courteously and gently interviewed. The Inspector of Taxes expressed a willingness to be paid in instalments and Veronica explained, 'I am now living with someone. He'll help.' She returned home feeling a good deal better than when she had set out.

At five o'clock, that same afternoon, there was a knock at the door of the bungalow and, opening it, Veronica found herself gazing at the very man she had faced across his desk in Burnley three hours earlier. Simultaneously they both gasped, 'I don't believe this.' The Inspector was calling upon another of his 'clients', F. S. Trueman. They sat, over a coffee, pondering on the mysteries of coincidence until FST arrived; an amicable interview took place and both of them were able to pay off their tax arrears. With that nightmare out of the way Veronica started on the major task of putting the various FST enterprises on some sort of firm financial footing.

People who wrote to Fred now, for the first time, began to receive replies. True, they were not written by Fred, but they did provide a Yes or No to suggestions or proposals. 'Fred had no commercial experience,' Veronica recalls. 'He had no business sense. He had only fame and, beyond his stage appearances, he had no idea how to harness it. He had an agent who charged £30 a time for public appearances by Fred but not many bookings were coming in. I wrote to him to say it might be a good idea to end the contract and I took over myself.' Her first move was to increase his fee from £30 to £50 and Fred nearly had a fit. 'I'll never get another booking,' he choked. But Veronica knew her product and she knew her market. She also read the shoals of letters which arrived asking for FST to speak at functions of all kinds – letters which had so often gone unanswered.

Not *all* her organisational skill was properly rewarded, however. She accepted an invitation for both of them to attend a dinner at Elland, near Huddersfield, and asked whether it was to be formal or informal dress. After a short hesitation the answer was given, 'Formal.' Only later did Veronica realise that no Yorkshireman, faced with a choice he did not understand, was going to opt for an 'in' or an 'un'. That would be negative! The engagement called for a dash by Fred from Old Trafford, where he was involved in one of the early Test Match commentaries, so Veronica made her way independently to Elland bearing Fred's dinner jacket and her own long dress (de rigeur at that time for most occasions). It was a hurried bath and change for FST before the two of them swept majestically into the foyer, immaculate in black tie and flowing ball gown respectively. The entire ground floor of the hotel was deserted – 'It was like the *Marie Celeste*,' recalls Veronica. However, from up the stairs emerged the buzz of conversation, a clatter of crockery and a clink of cutlery. They followed the sounds – and found the audience Fred was due to entertain happily wading into a good hearty West Riding meal. If the guest speaker was late, that was his look-out. Ignored by the assembled throng, Fred and Veronica found places at the top table, ate what was left of the meal and then gazed, fascinated, as an electric organ was wheeled out from concealment and the gathering prepared all too obviously for an evening of music, dance and merriment.

'Now then, Freddie,' said the chairman – at last acknowledging the presence of the two over-dressed latecomers, ' 'ow long dusta reckon to speak for?'

'How long d'you want?' inquired the professional, willing to accommodate any requirement.

'Mek it ten minutes, lad. No more, 'cos when all's said and dun we're 'ere to enjoy us sens.'

Some of the engagements went rather better than that one, and the demand for Fred's services as an after-dinner entertainer grew rapidly. The fee went up to £75 and still people wanted Fred. His charge increased to £100 without any slackening of the demand and he began to extend his field, and his repertoire. He was, after all, not simply, as Harold Wilson put it, 'the greatest living Yorkshireman'; his reputation as a cricketer had been truly international and it seemed only reasonable now to reflect that in his new role as a professional entertainer of another kind.

At any given time in his life FST has always had, stored away in his mind, a huge stock of blue and not-so-blue 'jokes'. He developed, over a long period of trial and error, a sense of timing, a polishing-up of his delivery and a professional presence, whether it was on stage or on the top table after a dinner. Veronica saw that there was going to be a demand for his services at least in the foreseeable future, but there was another side to Fred – a most important side – which had yet to be developed. He was (and is) a quite brilliant retailer of purely cricketing anecdotes, and since he had been personally involved in so many of the occasions he described the stories carried so much greater authenticity and conviction than the second-hand tales of the non-practitioners. There has always been a great deal of the exhibitionist in Fred. His chosen profession and the way he carried it out called for that in the first place. He had confidence in abundance in facing an audience, no matter who its constituents were. As Veronica puts it, 'I am not saying he didn't have nerves, but he was never short of confidence.' He did not try to polish up his ripe South Yorkshire accent because that was an integral part of his character. He did not strive for wit in the way that, say, John Warr employs it as a gifted after-dinner speaker. Indeed, some of us with good memories and fair libraries can still turn up a *Playfair Cricket Annual* in which J. J. Warr (Middlesex) is described as 'RHB, RFM, wit and raconteur', which is, I think, still a unique entry in that invaluable little reference book. Fred simply gives his audiences the Essential Trueman – himself.

As a purely personal preference, I do not particularly enjoy his non-stop, effortless stream of rude jokes – an hour of them is as nothing to Fred, without the aid of any prompter or crib-card – though one has to confess that it is impossible not to laugh at the sheer outrageousness of some of them. But Fred talking Cricket –

Ah! Now, that's something else altogether. It can be a humorous narrative, as when he puts together a script made up entirely of stories about Brian Close's adventures in driving a car, which makes absolutely hilarious entertainment, or it can be serious – for let us not forget that Fred was a very serious cricketer indeed. And it is then that Fred, preferably with one other, a man he respects, can be absolute magic. He once spent an hour during one of those rain-stops-play sessions on *Test Match Special* talking pure cricket with Alan McGilvray, ex-captain of New South Wales and a superb commentator, while the rest of us just sat back entranced by the dialogue. We shall look at Fred the broadcaster in more detail later, but in the context of *serious* cricket talk that occasion deserves a mention at this point.

He and Veronica had been together for about two years (waiting for the time when her divorce was finalised and they could marry) when his career as a media entertainer began to take off. He had fairly quickly become a regular contributor to Yorkshire Television programmes like *Sometimes You Win* (which largely concerned itself with football pools), *Yorkshire Speaks* (interviews with well-known characters from the Broad Acres) and commentaries on esoteric local pastimes like knurr and spell; then came his appearances as anchorman on a series called *Indoor League*. In these programmes he was largely involved in studio links, a continuity role in which he introduced contests in anything ranging from darts to arm-wrestling, *re*-introduced them after the interval advertisements and signed off at the end by hoisting his gimmick, a pint of ale, and intoning his catch-phrase, 'Reight? Ah'll sithee.'

A slight digression is called for at this point, first to translate for those not familiar with Yorkshire argot, that 'Reight' is pronounced to rhyme with 'weight' and not 'reet' as in 'neat,' which is a Lancashire pronunciation. It is a distinction which not all London-based drama producers (amongst others) understand, and it is one which makes us rather cross from time to time when we are being unnaturally intolerant! 'Ah'll sithee' (if a translation is necessary there it is 'I'll see you', otherwise simply 'Goodbye') is an expression familiar to Yorkshiremen of all sorts and conditions, but *Indoor League* gave it a new vogue.

It was a farewell which appealed particularly to Philip Sharpe, for ten years a team-mate of Fred's with Yorkshire, who in 1975 moved to play for Derbyshire and he used it with some frequency although it was far from a natural part of his everyday vocabulary. When, in 1976, Sharpe was summoned before the Derbyshire Committee to be told – completely to his surprise – that his services were not to be retained the following year he was dumbfounded enough to be unable to think of anything to say except, 'Reight. Ah'll sithee.' It was a response which I like to think startled the Committee in turn, coming as it did from the polished (Worksop College-educated) P. J. Sharpe.

This period in Fred's career had an effect on which one other comment is called for. The pint which he raised, before the TV cameras, in greeting and farewell was simply a prop. It was most certainly not 0.568 litres of the real stuff which Fred was engaged in drinking in whole or in part. Yet an entire generation of Yorkshire TV viewers gained a distinct, and understandable, impression that FST was very much on his home ground with the glass in his hand and the impression, with many of them, has lingered despite Fred's fury in later years at being so misunderstood. I have often wondered idly, a decade or more later, whether John Thaw, the actor who so engagingly portrayed the TV detective Inspector Morse, was similarly affected. The inspector's role was that of a pint-loving officer who at some stage of every episode was seen in a pleasant, usually riverside pub with a glass or two of the amber nectar. Yet one of the Sunday supplements irreligiously informed us at the time that Mr Thaw actually disliked beer and was simply doing his Thespian best with his character. Alas, Sunday supplements did not exist when Fred was introducing *Indoor League* and thus his real preference (for a glass of white wine or perhaps a whisky) remained unpublicised.

With or without the image, the Trueman appearances on television were becoming more regular and extensive: *Emmerdale Farm*, *Dad's Army*, the Esther Rantzen show *That's Life*, *Blankety Blank* (in which he is always hugely proud when he assists a contestant to a prize). In more serious vein he featured on *Nationwide*, and he began to become involved with TV advertising: hair cosmetics, tobacco, beer (!). Apart from the fees themselves for such appearances, they all helped with the natural spin-offs of personal appearances.

These, plus a public relations tie-up with British Airways, began to take him to all parts of Great Britain as well as all round the world: Australia, New Zealand, South Africa, West Indies, Mexico, the Sudan, the Persian Gulf, Hong Kong, Singapore, Malaysia, Thailand, the Persian Gulf. The schedule became unbelievably punishing and it is important to remember that he was not simply making a living from all these jet-set engagements – he was sandwiching in a very large number of charity engagements as well. One such trip saw him fly to South Australia, do two charity dinners on consecutive nights and fly back the following morning! This sort of programme goes on, winter and summer. In the middle of a Test Match (where his role as a summariser takes a lot of concentration) he will suddenly work a quick switch of duties with Trevor Bailey towards the end of the day and drive off, up or down the motorway, to carry out a speaking engagement 100 miles or more away, rise at the crack of dawn and be back on parade in the commentary box before the start of play. These excursions, it must be confessed, cause the *Test Match Special* producer a certain amount of anxiety, but Fred has not yet failed to return. His stamina is incredible. Just as in his playing career, whatever else anyone said of FST, no one could ever complain that he gave less than 100 per cent, so it is with his later working life.

It would all be totally impossible without (a) the constitution of an ox and (b) the administrative genius of his wife. Fred has great difficulty in saying 'no' to people and his informal acceptance of invitations has been known to lead to double bookings. Most of his life is lived in a tearing hurry, so much of Veronica's can be spent pursuing him to Leeds/Bradford Airport at Yeadon with essential items of equipment (a dinner jacket, for example) which he has overlooked when setting out. One example, in March 1990, graphically shows Fred's lifestyle and Veronica's problems. On the 6th FST drove to Worcestershire to speak at a luncheon for the cricket Benefit of Chris Smith, the Hampshire batsman. He drove back 100 miles in late afternoon to speak at an hotel about fifteen miles from his home at a dinner to raise money for an eighteen-year-old Craven League cricketer who had been struck on the head in the previous season and seriously incapacitated. Peter Parfitt and I joined Fred in an effort to try to make life a little bit more comfortable for the young man.

Now, on the evening of the 7th, Fred was due to speak at a dinner in Bristol and there must have been a great temptation to turn down the Craven League function and drive gently from rural Worcestershire into Bristol. But no – he came back those 100 miles and arranged to fly to Bristol on the morning of the 7th. We finished at the hotel near Gisburn, close to the Yorks–Lancs border, around midnight, because apart from the three speakers there was an auction and a raffle; then Parfitt (who had nobly stayed on Perrier water all evening) drove us back to Fred's, where I was to spend the night. We stayed up chatting until about 1.30 a.m. and at 8.30 the following morning Veronica knocked on the door of my room: 'Fred has driven off to the airport without his overnight bag. I am going to try to catch up with him before the plane takes off.' And off she went – but not before she had telephoned Sheena, her married daughter living three miles away in the next village, to come round to make my breakfast! She is not only a brilliant and indefatigable organiser; she is also the perfect hostess.

Such vicissitudes (which are by no means rare) have given her a fund of stories which rival, and in some instances surpass, Fred's personal repertoire – like the time Fred bought, in Mexico City, an onyx dining table which weighed nine hundredweight and arranged for it to be shipped to his remote outpost in the Yorkshire Dales. Unfortunately he could not arrange for it to be delivered when he was at home. It duly arrived, with Veronica husbandless in the house, and the delivery-squad consisted of one, solitary little man. By the grace of God, Maison Trueman was at that time having a kitchen extension built so, with seven workmen around, labour (over and above their call of duty) was not the main problem. Manoeuvring in the table *was*. It was finally achieved by the use of a long-discarded skateboard which had belonged to her son, Patrick!

On a trip to Germany, Fred forgot his passport. They let him in after a bit of debate; getting out proved a trifle more difficult. Adventures of a more exotic nature came on a visit to Jamaica. But it's Veronica's story:

> We flew with British Airways to Miami and then had to transfer to an Air Jamaica flight. Their lounge was filled with Jamaicans going home after a fruit-picking season in Florida, and the noise they made tearing open the parcels of presents they were taking back was deafening. It was then that we were approached by an airline official to be told that we could not be accommodated on

the flight. I waited for the explosion, but Fred simply dismissed the man: 'I've *got* to be on it. I'm playing there tomorrow.' I don't know what sort of impression this might or might not have made because a man sitting near us heard the exchange and he turned out to be a senior official of Air Jamaica. He simply said, 'Mr Trueman *must* be on the plane. *I* am going to watch the game.' So at least we got as far as the aircraft.

Then came a very large West Indian to sit in the next seat to Fred. And he carried a very large holdall – very large indeed. He struggled with the impossible task of trying to stow the bag under the seat when it was perfectly obvious that it couldn't be done. I was fascinated as Fred watched with a sort of idle curiosity until finally he remarked, 'It's *not* going to fit under there, sunshine.' The Jamaican gentleman was in no way put out. He started to unpack the bag – a huge doll, a coffee table, books – you have never seen such a collection of articles. And as he took them out, one by one, *he placed them on Fred's knee!* This time I didn't wait for the explosion. I grabbed the doll, the coffee table and the rest. It seemed the best way to avoid trouble.

When we reached Jamaica we discovered that our luggage was still in Miami. Fred was wearing the heavy winter suit in which he had left home and so he was a bit hot under the collar in every way.

Fred and Veronica had been on a Tom Graveney-organised trip to Kuwait, where they became friendly with the British Minister, Graham Burton. On a subsequent visit to Abu Dhabi they found that he had moved a few hundred miles down the Gulf and was now Minister to the United Arab Emirates. He invited them to a reception to mark the Queen's birthday – one of the notable events in an ambassadorial calendar. Mr Burton proposed Her Majesty's health, first in Arabic with a substantial reference to his distinguished cricketing guest. He then explained in English that he had just told 'the Gunga Din story'. This, as aficionados will know, is a completely untrue tale which has dogged Fred for nearly forty years – the claim that Fred, at a formal dinner, had once requested the Indian High Commissioner in London, to 'pass the salt, Gunga Din'. If there is one apocryphal story more than any other which is calculated to send Fred into a paroxysm of fury it is that one, and this time Veronica dreaded the explosion which seemed inevitable. She reproached Her Britannic Majesty's Plenipotentiary Extraordinary: 'That was a bit below the belt,' and was hurriedly assured that it was intended as a joke and had been taken as such by the other guests. Fred, to his eternal credit, did not explode. A distinguished member of the Diplomatic Corps could count himself exceedingly fortunate.

If controversy has sometimes (mercifully) eluded him in his travels to all corners of the earth, drama has usually taken its place: an earthquake in Mexico, a visit to India shortly after the assassination of Mrs Gandhi when he and Veronica were escorted on a shopping expedition by a huge Sikh guard. But it was an occasion when they were just sitting quietly in the lounge of their hotel on that trip that Veronica remembers most vividly: 'There was a wedding reception taking place in the hotel and scores of the guests filed quietly into the lounge where we were sitting. They didn't say a word; they just stood in a semi-circle and looked at Fred.' It is a story which reminds one irresistibly of the occasion in 1968 when, before his final season of first-class cricket, FST went to India as part of an international team to play a match for the Flood Relief Fund. Sitting with him in the lounge of the Taj Mahal Hotel was the Australian Norman O'Neill, and O'Neill said, 'Fred, I believe those two Indians at the next table are talking about you.' With an unostentatious simplicity which refuted any allegation of big-headedness Fred replied, 'Ay, they talk about me all over t'world, Norm lad.'

Canada, the Channel Islands, the Caymans, Tasmania, Oman – the travels read like a tour catalogue, and still they go on. Incredibly, he finds time to snatch an occasional day or two of relaxation. The ideal is a sunny summer's day in the garden of his home, enjoying the extensive bird life it attracts (with well over 100 species logged by the Craven Naturalists when a survey was made), and a close second comes a week or two with friends in southern Spain during the worst of the winter weather in England.

Golf is a game which Fred largely ignored as a needless expenditure of energy in his cricketing days. After retirement it became increasingly one of his greatest interests. He plays with the same ferocious competitiveness and determination to win which he showed in his Yorkshire and England days. Scores of partners testify in hushed tones to the single-mindedness of his pursuit of glory, no matter how modest the prize. The growth of the Celebrity Am-Am type of tournament has become a great money-spinner for charity and for cricket beneficiaries alike and Fred, quite naturally, is on everyone's invitation list. He could play just about every day of the week in an English summer if his schedule allowed it, and his home is something like Aladdin's Cave with the treasures he has brought back from golf days. Once, in the wildly improbable location of a ferry boat crossing from Tahiti to Moorea in the South Pacific I got into a conversation with an English fellow-tourist who mentioned that he had a villa near Marbella and played golf there. 'Do you perchance see Fred Trueman playing on your course?' I inquired – and he sat up as if he had suddenly found a drawing-pin underneath him. 'Let me tell you about a tournament I played with Mr Trueman in my four,' he said in the tones of one who has undergone a profound spiritual experience. No one who has shared the experience will require any further elaboration. Suffice it to say that Fred plays to win, and very often does. He has not, however, yet managed to win his own tournament, the Fred Trueman Classic, which takes place in June at Harrogate and raises very large sums for charity, but that is another part of our story.

In business matters, he likes to think on a grand scale. One of his many interests (which may startle a few people) is a directorship of a firm of financial consultants. At Godfrey Evans's seventieth birthday celebrations in London in 1990 he startled his chairman, Claude Brownlow, by announcing, 'There's a chap over there I think we ought to have as another non-executive director of the company. I'll bring him across and introduce you to him.'

He disappeared into the throng of guests and returned a few minutes later with his nominee – John Major, Her Majesty's Chancellor of the Exchequer!

In showbiz terms he received the accolade of *This is Your Life* in 1979 when, with his family round about him and a host of friends and colleagues ushered on stage by Eamon Andrews, he hovered between heart-catching emotion and glimpses of the old bravado.

Keith Miller was flown in from Australia, Neil Hawke delayed his departure overseas (and was glad he had done so when he was introduced as 'the great Australian *all-rounder* – *This is Your Life* research is occasionally less than precise!) and Yorkshire and England cricketers clustered on the set: Graveney, Edrich, Laker, Barrington, Parfitt, Wardle, Brennan, Sharpe, Wilson, Nicholson, Burnet. Bill Anderson provided the link with his footballing days at Lincoln, Leslie Crowther the warmth of a cricket-loving enter-tainer and friend. And Sir Harold Wilson, in a filmed interview, repeated to the programme's massive audience his 'greatest living Yorkshireman' tribute. From a Labour prime minister to a dyed-in-the-wool lifelong Tory voter, as Fred is, it was one of those masterly strokes of Wilsonian PR for which he was noted.

Perhaps more surprising was the last line of a conversation between FST and 'Red Ken' Livingstone which was: 'Any time you want a bed for the night in my house, you are welcome.' That was from Fred to Ken. The occasion was Russell Harty's televised Christmas party at Russell's home in Giggleswick, less than twenty miles from Fred's. At the very outset of the evening Fred announced to his wife that under no circumstances would he talk to that so-and-so Ken Livingstone. Fate decreed (or was it a mischievous host?) that they shared a table at supper and Fred, his earlier avowal forgotten, succumbed to the Livingstone charm, or so we are assured by Veronica. Thus disarmed, he mentioned that one or two oblique suggestions had been put to him in his time about going into politics and he was promptly assured by Mr Livingstone: 'Don't even think about it, Fred. You are too honest and they would destroy you.' A new, if unlikely, bond was formed. Undoubtedly he impressed Fred, and Veronica, too: 'I asked him why he had gone into politics and he said he was a non-sporting, non-athletic type but he had a determination to get to the top.'

So much for dining out. What of dining in, chez Trueman? Fred is a generous host, Veronica a brilliant hostess. The buffet is always superb, the drinks seemingly limitless. The guest list is always a pleasant mix of types, professions, opinions, interests and styles in best cocktail-party fashion, but it is drawn from a circle of friends who are liked – and even more importantly *trusted* – by Fred.

He is content to leave all the detailed planning to his wife, who knows that under no circumstances will he dissemble in the presence of people he dislikes. No requirement of diplomacy would induce F. S. Trueman to invite into his home anyone with whom he was not at ease. At sixty he is no more house-trained today than he was forty years ago. On trips abroad he will happily tour the souks and bazaars, but he has never been in a supermarket in his life, and feels no burning desire to experiment in that direction. So much time is spent haring up and down the country and round the world that when he is at home with no engagements in prospect he will very happily sit for half the day in dressing-gown and slippers.

Anyone fixing up an outing – for a social round of golf, say – and arranging to pick up Fred from his home can reckon with absolute certainty on his not being ready at the appointed time. His affection and concern for his wife sometimes takes a magnificently ambiguous form. For example, Veronica at home 'dying of 'flu', and wondering what time to be prepared to serve an evening meal, gets a phone call: 'Don't worry about *me*, darling. I'll eat out.' And who would seek to explain to Fred that that was not *really* being considerate? No one of my acquaintance.

It was a surprise to many of us that after retiring from the first-class game, Fred continued to dabble in cricket at a less exalted level – several of them in fact. Most surprising of all was to find him turning out in a couple of Sunday League matches, not exactly a bowler's favourite form of the game, and with Derbyshire! Foresaking my personal policy of refusing to have anything to do with that comic-opera nonsense I went to Bradford to watch Fred perform against his own county, against which he was not, at that time, as deeply embittered as he is today, and I spent the afternoon moving around the crowd to see what people thought of this re-appearance. Without exception, the reaction was one of regret, genuine regret, that FST should have chosen to come back for another county and in such a deplorable form of the game he loved.

Ex-players are not good watchers. There are, of course, those who move into managerial or coaching roles when their playing days are over and thus stay close to cricket, but very few are to be found in the ranks of spectators, certainly not those who achieved Fred's eminence. No one expected to see him at matches purely as an uninvolved observer. But at the same time no one expected to see him performing on the smaller stage of the out-of-town theatre when he had topped the bill on Broadway for so long. The competitive spirit was unquenchable, however. Fred *had* to keep on playing the game, and not for fun, either. Quickly discarding the trappings of Derbyshire, and the John Player League, he started to show his artistry to the public schoolboys of the North of England on the playing fields of Sedbergh, Ampleforth, Giggleswick, Rossall, Stonehurst and St Peter's, York among others. In some cases this involved his playing under the banner of MCC (which must have caused a number of inner conflicts), but more frequently he flew the colours of The Saints CC, a club founded and administered by Desmond Bailey, ex-Army officer, Yorkshire Committee member, legendary host and close friend of FST. Having persuaded Fred to turn out for MCC sides, Captain Bailey of the West Yorkshire Regiment (after a notable career in Service cricket and rugby circles) embarked upon the fusing of amateur and professional *types* to play cricket together on a more regular basis and The Saints were born, an absolutely typical Bailey concept, 'at 5.30 a.m. on Easter Sunday, 29 March 1959, dear boy'.

To any of the hundreds of cricket aficionados who know Cap'n Bailey, it goes without saying that the birth of the club resulted from night-long deliberation rather than early-morning inspiration, and that the whole process was attended by prolonged head-wetting. It took place in the home of Major Duncan Pocock, with whom Desmond was staying at the time, in Harrogate, and the first decision centred upon the club colours: light blue and orange (representing the ideal conditions of cloudless sky and sunshine), red (the halo of Leslie Charteris's Saint), yellow (colour of Harrogate's cockerel emblem) and brown (representing bitter beer, which was to be the lifeblood of the club).

It was perhaps symbolic of the philosophy of the new club that before caps, sweaters and blazers had been designed and ordered, one of the earliest members, Bob Platt (former opening bowling partner of Fred's with Yorkshire) had ordered beach shorts in the club colours to be worn on visits to holiday villas in Spain! Desmond wrote to twenty-five acquaintances with both amateur and professional cricket backgrounds, inviting them to membership; most accepted, a few (probably those of more orthodox and abstemious life-styles) declined. Fixtures were arranged with schools and with a select handful of other clubs of a similar esoteric nature, but the highlight of The Saints year was from the first, and has remained, the annual dinner in mid-winter. Desmond Bailey – as president, founder, convenor – undertakes to provide the principal speaker, a task which has become progressively more difficult over the years as word has gone round that wit and repartee, merry quip and jest, are less important than a voice loud enough to shout down the hecklers, prominent amongst whom are R. K. Platt (beach-shorts designer) and J. B. Bolus (ex-Yorkshire, Notts, Derbyshire and England). The dinner is held on a Saturday night in a Dales hostelry. Cap'n

Bailey arrives on Friday afternoon and books in until Monday morning ('There is a lot of organisational work to be done, dear boy').

This, then, was to be a part of the new cricketing career of F. S. Trueman, holder of the world record for Test wickets. It gave some of his schoolboy opponents great pleasure to write home to their parents that they had batted against the great man. One or two were able to report that they had played against him with some distinction, like a big Rhodesian boy called Schmidt, for instance, pupil of St Peter's. He hit the first ball he received from *the* Frederick Sewards Trueman for six – and grinned at him. Not a friendly, or pleasant grin. A malicious, gloating grin. The next ball he top-edged over the wicket-keeper – for six. And grinned.

'Then,' recalls Desmond, 'there really was bother – especially as Fred couldn't get him out.'

On one occasion at Leeds Grammar School (Bill Sutcliffe the captain), the Saints openers had proved a trifle slow against some good school bowling and Fred was promoted to no. 5 in the order to quicken the pace. He reached 88 at lunch and announced, 'I'm going to get a hundred now.' Desmond, with malice aforethought, quietly persuaded the captain to declare and briefed all other members of the side. Ten Saints, with absolutely straight celestial faces, earnestly read newspapers or gazed silently into space as Sutcliffe announced the declaration, while the anguished and expectant FST roared, 'You rotten lot of four-letter-words.' Fred took his batting, as well as his bowling very seriously indeed.

He even took The Saints colours seriously. Fred was a throw-back to Hirst and Rhodes, Robinson and Macaulay in his professional contempt for the gilded youths who performed against them wearing the multi-hued hoops of school, college and university caps. 'Coloured-caps' was the ultimate term of dismissal by the hoary pros for the gentlemen who played cricket without thought of payment. By Fred's day the term had been modernised to 'Jazz 'ats', but the sentiments were precisely the same. By 1969, however, Fred's membership of The Saints had converted him to a 'Jazz 'at' himself and, with typical perverseness, he revelled in it.

When Platt revealed his design of the beach shorts, FST was quick to place an order: 'Ah'll 'av one o' them.' When the blazers were unveiled: 'Ah'll 'av one o' them.' I have yet to see FST thus arrayed in all his finery, but it is an intriguing possibility.

Sometimes with The Saints, sometimes with MCC, or perhaps with the Craven Gentlemen, or the Forty Club, Fred extended his playing career into his forties and fifties. His team-mates on these occasions testify to the amount of time Fred devoted to helping schoolboys, coaching as the game progressed, and the final verdict is that he was 'very good' with the boys, except, of course, on occasions of *lèse majesté* such as that involving the boy Schmidt at St Peter's! Nor were the epigrams forgotten in this relaxed atmosphere of public school and country house cricket. The captain of The Frogs (an Oxbridge origination), Bob Levy, searched for a ball which had been hit for six into a thick hedgerow at Brighouse and bent lower and lower to his task until the bawled comment came from FST: 'Hey, Bob, I see you haven't brushed your teeth today.'

Finally he came into his own with the formation, in 1981, of the Old England Eleven sponsored by Courage Brewery (captain: F. S. Trueman). It was his own idea and he found a quick supporter for it in Reg Hayter, one of the best-known names in cricket-writing, to whom Fred put the suggestion in El Vino's – a favourite Fleet Street watering hole when the national newspaper industry of Britain was still centred in EC4. Reg consulted David Wynne-Morgan, a public-relations specialist, who in turn approached Brian Baldock, of the Courage company. There was enthusiastic backing from Fred's contemporaries and a couple who in fact preceded him into Test cricket. Reg Simpson (Notts 1946–63) and Don Brennan (Yorkshire 1947–53) had been amateurs during their playing careers. Now, at the age of sixty-one, both of them in effect surrendered their amateur status because Courage paid a match fee to the Old England players! In a very short space of time FST had collected thirty-four players willing to turn out, perhaps a little creaky in some of their joints but imbued with the spirit of auld lang syne: Compton, Graveney, D'Oliveira, Titmus, Price, Close, Illingworth, Sharpe, Wilson, Richard Hutton, Swetman, Murray, Parfitt – great names from two or three decades after the war. In some cases new flannels with more generous waist-measurements were required, and MCC sweaters were taken proudly out of their display cabinets (or out of mothballs), along with long-discarded caps.

Requests for a meeting with these golden oldies poured in from all parts of the country. They played for charities of all kinds, for cricketers' benefits, but always for the sheer love of the game and the reminiscences which could be shared during the course of play and, perhaps, for an hour or two afterwards. During one season I provided the public-address-system commentary on the Old England Eleven matches – a difficult job because it is so easy to be banal or trite and very easy indeed to talk too much. But the end-of-season party, 'sponsored' by Courage and organised by Reg Hayter, with Sharpe and Wilson providing the cabaret, made it all something more than worthwhile. They were great days which provided at least one innovation: instead of fathers asking for autographs 'for my young son', we now had small boys being pushed forward to ask for signatures 'for my dad'. Some of the sides fielded could muster over 300 Test appearances in all; some of the greatest names in post-war cricket were paraded, a little greyer, looking in some cases a trifle well-fed but – the batsmen in particular – always evoking memories of the most treasured kind as they conjured up a long-dormant sense of timing and grace and elegance. The effortless placement of Tom Graveney's cover-drive, for instance, evoked nostalgic sighs on every ground, while Fred's occasional re-discovery of the late outswinger resulted in a bellow of triumph as – the crowd momentarily forgotten – he drew the attention of his contemporaries to his achievement. Happy days.

In the final game of the 1981 season Old England met England Ladies in a classic encounter at the Lansdowne Club in Bath, to help the girls raise funds for a World Cup trip to New Zealand. Fred's boys totalled 209 for seven and the game took an immediate turn for the worse when the Ladies opened their innings against the bowling of Harold ('Dusty') Rhodes, of Derbyshire and England. Tom Graveney, out of action with a broken finger but taking over public-address-system broadcasting for the day, takes up the story: 'I have always regarded fast bowlers as thick. No disrespect to my captain, of course, but they have never impressed me as being amongst the brightest members of the human race. And now Dusty proved the point. He ambled in from two or three yards but let the ball go like a thunderbolt. Stumps went flying in all directions and two or three wickets fell in his first over. From all sides came cries of, "Come off it, Dusty," so he bowled a couple of gentle leg-breaks to the ladies' captain, Rachael Heyhoe-Flint, and then let another one go. Another wicket. England Ladies were 5 for three wickets and Rhodes had taken three for 0. He was banished to the outfield, never to return, and quite right too.'

Let us record that the girls finished on a respectable 158–8 and gallantry had achieved a notable victory. 'Praise be,' said Mrs Heyhoe-Flint, 'that Freddie Trueman played the game in the right spirit.' And our hero, blushing modestly, experienced a number of different emotions in a unique moment of his career.

It would not be right to leave an account of Fred's post-first-class career without reference to his brief, but inevitably spectacular, excursion into the Dales Evening League. It is highly unlikely that more than the merest handful of players in the League has ever had a formal introduction to the game of cricket; more than 90 per cent of them are there simply to make up the numbers. Brown trousers and matching suede shoes are not unknown; reminders that the field has been occupied earlier in the day by herds of cattle are everywhere underfoot. As a bowler of that parish, Fred was invited to represent the village of Cracoe against their neighbours at Linton on a pitch where the ball was as likely to take off over the batsman's head from a length as it was to shoot straight along the ground after landing on precisely the same length. Fred, bowling with ultra-circumspect daintiness, removed five batsmen for no runs but also broke the spectacles of the wicket-keeper standing some thirty yards distant near the boundary edge. At the premature end of the game the teams repaired to the Devonshire Arms, where a three-man deputation addressed its collective self to FST: 'You should not be allowed to play in this League. It's not right for us to have to face a man who has bowled for Yorkshire and England.'

Fred defended his presence with admirable restraint. 'I'm forty-eight years old, you know, an' I don't get all that much practice,' he replied, but the villagers of Linton were having none of it. They took their complaint to the League, who solemnly decreed that they might be prepared to review the situation when FST had reached fifty (years of age). By the time his eligibility could be reviewed he was lost to the Dales Evening League, as the Courage Old England Eleven now flourished in the land. The old competitive fires flickered briefly, however, when he was told, years later, that a star player had been unavailable to the opposition on that celebrated occasion and if *he* had been laikin', well, there would have been a different tale to tell. He at once threatened to return to the League.

With British Airways Eccentrics Eleven Fred trotted round the world, playing in Khartoum, Mexico City, Hong Hong, Singapore, Kuala Lumpur and Thailand, and with other sides he performed in Oman, the Cayman Islands and South Africa (where he took part in one of the earliest multi-racial games), and always it was cricket followed by speaking engagements in the evening. Everywhere in the world there was an audience to watch the ageing FST put on his flannels once again; everywhere there was an audience to listen when he had exchanged his whites for a dinner-jacket. He played his last cricket in 1988, but the speaking goes on.

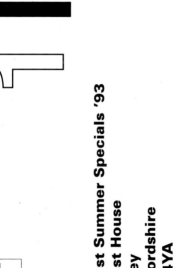

Everest Summer Specials '93
Everest House
Cuffley
Hertfordshire
EN6 4YA

10

Writer . . .

F. S. Trueman, journalist and author, has been a literary figure for
more than thirty years. It was in the late fifties that the *People*
(subsequently the *Sunday People*) published four articles, the
material for which was furnished by Fred and amounted, in effect,
to a brief autobiography. They contained enough that was interesting and entertaining to induce the *People*'s legendary editor, Sam
Campbell, and the gifted sports editor, Frank Nicklin, to offer FST
a contract as a regular contributor to the newspaper. A cricket
column in summer and match reports on Rugby League in winter
then followed, not without a series of journalistic adventures born
of Fred's rather sketchy literary experience and an inability to cope
with such matters as deadlines and edition times!

Initially his words were ghosted by Phil King, as heinous a traitor
as ever was born in Yorkshire (Guy Fawkes notwithstanding), since
he played cricket for Lancashire in 1946 and 1947! This was an
inspired pairing of personalities in once sense, since Phil reported
cricket in summer and Rugby League in winter, but it was not the
most efficient partnership that the world of newspapers has ever
known. Benjamin Philip King was born in Leeds, had extensive
family connections with the Bradford area and, like so many
talented cricketers from the industrial West Riding in pre-war days,
had to move further afield to make his mark in first-class cricket. He
played for Worcestershire from 1935 to 1939, scoring 1,000 runs
in a season twice, and after the war returned to the West Midlands
hoping to be re-engaged. When the offer of his services was turned
down Phil (who loved a sporting wager) offered to play for nothing
until he had reached 1,000 runs if the county would pay him £1 a
run thereafter. He was astonished to be turned down again, high in
his indignation at the refusal of Worcs to take a sporting chance,
and joined Lancashire. When his playing career ended he turned
(as another Lancashire cricketer, George Duckworth had done) to

newspaper-writing, with the twin interests of cricket and Rugby League.

Phil was a character I found fascinating because he made me laugh, not always *with* him, it has to be confessed because quite frequently one had to laugh at him. His firm conviction that the Fates conspired against him in so many ways resulted in long monologues of bitter complaint which were often so illogically reasoned that they became simply, but hilariously, funny. He nurtured a career-long and almost pathological hatred of Eddie Waring, his rival Rugby League columnist and reporter with the *Sunday Pictorial*, more particularly when Eddie became the best-known personality in the game through his colourful, if eccentric, commentaries on BBC Television. The very mention of Eddie's name was sufficient to drive Phil into a paroxysm of choking fury. Once, covering a tour of Australia with the Great Britain team, he stepped off a plane in the far-flung RL outpost of Townsville to be met by a local broadcaster, microphone in hand. 'G'dye. Mr Waring?' he inquired, civilly but inaccurately, prepared to do an on-the-spot interview with the well-known representative of the British Broadcasting Corporation. Phil, already hot and sticky in the sub-equatorial temperature, drew a deep breath and roared into the microphone: 'Waring? Not for a —— million pounds.' I am reliably informed that in that moment the listening public of Northern Queensland took B. P. King to its collective antipodean heart. At last – a Pom who spoke their language.

Phil's invocation of a favourite descriptive term – whether as a noun, verb or adjective – more usually associated with an act of sexual intercourse made him an interesting partner for Fred Trueman in the realm of creative writing. John Maddock – who, over the last quarter of a century, has been variously Fred's sports editor, ghost writer, agent and friend – recalls his first encounter with the partnership with brilliant clarity:

> I had just arrived in Manchester to join the *People* after a time with the *Sunday Express* in London. Phil King was not always happy if called upon to sit down and actually write a piece. He much preferred to dictate, over the telephone, to a copy-taker. When he was occasionally summoned to the office he would still nip out of the sports room, find a quiet office, pick up the telephone, ring through to the *People* switchboard and dictate his

match-report to a copy-taker sitting perhaps twenty feet away. The Northern Sports Editor, Harry Peterson, was a good journalist but a man of unpredictable temper. He was regularly affronted by Phil King's idiosyncratic method of operating; he was frequently driven spare by Fred's failure to recognise that copy had to be delivered in time for the appropriate edition. And most of all he was deeply affected if Blackburn Rovers, his 'home' team, lost a game. On this occasion, Rovers had lost, Phil King had disappeared into another office to dictate his copy and it was getting dangerously close to the Yorkshire edition-time, while they still had no copy from FST on Wakefield Trinity versus Featherstone Rovers. The Northern Sports Editor was not happy. And I was having my first taste of Saturday in the Manchester office of the *People*.

Harry Peterson snarled at John: 'Get Trueman's copy – NOW.'

John took their reporter into a corner and said: 'Right, Fred. Let's start with who won?'

Fred, with the smug satisfaction of one who is about to encapsulate the whole occasion in one succinct phrase, replied: 'They ——ed 'em right.' (Phil's adjective had now been translated into a verbal context). Deeming it politic to inquire in the same idiom, John asked: 'Who ——ed whom?' This elicited the news that Wakefield Trinity had beaten Featherstone Rovers by 26 points to 14. It is a measure of the impression the occasion left on John Maddock that he remembers the scoreline without a second's thought.

'Fred had made three lines of notes on the game,' he recalls. 'They weren't of absolutely vital relevance or significance but with the help of Press Association copy on the game I was able to cobble together a piece with Fred.'

In due course John succeeded Harry Peterson as Northern Sports Editor, while Neville Holtham took over from Frank Nicklin in London. They made the joint decision that ghost-writing would be dispensed with and Fred in future would write his own copy. In the meantime Rugby League had switched its match-day from Saturday to Sunday, so FST's winter reporting had now to centre on association football. Although he had played the game pretty well for Bill Anderson at Lincoln City, and in the Showbiz and Yorkshire CCC Elevens amongst others, he had not the same fondness as a spectator for soccer that he had for the men of Rugby League. He could identify more readily with their strength, fitness, willingness to take knocks and lack of histrionics than he could with the prima-donna posturing of more highly-paid denizens of the Football League. Although I have never managed to get him to a Rugby Union match, Fred has maintained a great affection for League and is an annual, honoured guest at the game's cup final.

He approached the reporting of football matches in the Second, Third and Fourth Divisions conscientiously but, in modern popular newspaper terms, in an unsophisticated style. As a professional sportsman himself he followed an understandable natural inclination to talk about the game, its quality and its mechanics. What the *People* wanted was personality stuff and if it was controversial, so much the better. His two sports editors then gave him a specific brief: if any 'incidents' occurred, they had to be built up; if any visiting managers or scouts were present their names had to be noted and, if possible, the player they were watching had to be pin-pointed. His next game was at Barnsley. Fred duly turned in the name of one manager and eleven scouts who were on parade, embellishing the list with the *middle* name of one of the scouts. Unfortunately, his report contained no reference to the player they had all come to watch!

Now, it would be easy enough for the professional journalist, formally trained and experienced, to scoff (as so many of us have done with great frequency) at such ingenuous excursions into our territory, so let us point out straight away that, after having the error of his ways pointed out to him, Fred, in the very next game, discovered the name of a player who was being specially watched, got the appropriate 'quote' from the scout who was doing the watching and his story made second lead on the back page of the *People*. But all in all it was harder work for Fred than he has ever allowed himself to acknowledge. He has always managed to convince himself, if not others, that he was a natural at whatever he has turned his hand to. The truth is that he was not happy 'digging' for the story behind the story. Reporting a match as he saw it – *and* getting paid for doing so – was a not unpleasant way of spending his winter afternoons. Following the scent of a more dramatic story by hounding officials and players for 'quotes' was not to his liking at all. And, accustomed as he was to the big occasions, the great crowds of his cricket career, he chafed at week after week spent in the unfashionable and less densely populated stadiums of Rochdale and Doncaster, Barnsley and Halifax. He tired of these duties while at the same time his journalistic mentors were accepting that it had been a good idea but one which had not worked to everyone's complete satisfaction. The decision was made to concentrate on Fred's cricket-writing. John Maddock admits that:

> Asking Fred to cover football on the same basis as a full-time professional sports reporter was like asking me to open the bowling for England. With his cricket-writing we had an entirely different problem. His match reports (after his retirement from playing) and his weekly column were far too technical. He could tell readers how an outswinger should be bowled, when a batsman was caught with his feet in the wrong position, where a bowler ideally needed his short-leg positioned. In the pure cricketing sense it was brilliant. But it wasn't the stuff to present to readers of a popular Sunday newspaper. We had to provide him with a ghost again – a man who could understand and interpret Fred's technical and tactical knowledge in terms which our readers could appreciate – and since then it has worked well.
>
> At the same time, I firmly believe that in a 'quality' paper and with the right ghost-writer, Fred's column would have been exceptional.

The 'contacts' which Fred did not possess in association football were around in abundance when it came to cricket, so that with someone to translate his knowledge into popular journalese the *People* now found themselves sitting on a goldmine of information which many other papers did not enjoy. By calling up old friends and former colleagues, Fred could usually provide the *People* with a precise line-up of the Test squad in time for the paper to print it on the Sunday morning before the names were officially announced. During my time as BBC Cricket Correspondent there was a system (which still exists) that I was given the names of the Test squad on Saturday so that various pieces could be recorded for transmission after eleven o'clock on Sunday morning. It is a courtesy from the Selectors to the BBC – and a very deeply appreciated one – without which the Cricket Correspondent would have a few problems on five or six Sundays of the summer. The recordings were tagged, fore and aft, with a reminder that there was the strictest possible embargo on their transmission before 11 a.m. on Sunday.

Fred, of course, knew that I was given the information on

Saturdays and I am happy to put it on record that he never once embarrassed me by asking even for a hint of the names. I was certainly asked by *players*, men on the fringe of selection who were human enough to want to know, seventeen or eighteen hours in advance, and they, of course, got the same answer I would have been obliged to give FST if he had telephoned to ask. Never, I am happy to say, did he seek to breach the mutual confidence and respect which I like to think has always existed between us. But he was now a newspaperman, with a duty to get the information, if he could, before anyone else. He could, and he did. He provided more, and more accurate, information for the *People* than almost anyone else has ever done for any other newspaper. Undoubtedly his biggest exclusive, however, came in 1977 and it was a story which every national paper and scores of them overseas had to follow up.

Geoffrey Boycott, the best Test opening batsman in the world, had opted out of Test cricket after the first game of the series against India in 1974, beset by all sorts of problems, and he remained in self-imposed exile until June 1977, when the Australians were here. He then contacted the Selectors, before the Third Test, to say that he was ready to return. The fact was that they were delighted with the news; nevertheless, in view of Boycott's largely incomprehensible (to them) absence, the Selection Committee decided to 'let him stew' for a week or two before recalling him to England's ranks. But Fred had learned of the approach by Boycott, a man he cordially detested, in the course of a telephone call he (Fred) made to one of the Selectors. He broke the story in the *People* – 'Boycott Wants to Come Back' – to give himself the biggest scoop in that or many other cricketing seasons.

It gave him a curiously ambivalent feeling when the *People*, naturally, gave the story tremendous prominence. He takes great pride in his newspaper connection and recognised what a prime piece of beating-the-opposition he had pulled off. But his dislike of Boycott was so deep-seated that he was in some ways angry at the prospect of his recall: 'Any man who says he doesn't want to play for his country should never be asked again.' But with Geoffrey returning in glory with 107, 80 not out at Trent Bridge, 191 (his hundredth hundred) at Headingley and the Ashes regained he must have felt in his heart of hearts, that on balance, it was not a bad thing to have been associated, even in only a reportorial way, with the occasion. He would not admit it, though!

I have said that Fred takes pride in his newspaper connection and, no matter how peripheral this has been, it is absolutely true. At some stage of every Test Match Saturday while working for *Test Match Special* he will talk about what he is going to say on the morrow in 'my newspaper'. If the *Sunday People* (as it now is) is ever the subject of a gentle jibe from one of his commentary colleagues about a recent 'exposé', Fred will spring immediately to its defence. His loyalty is fierce and unswerving. Similarly with British Airways, against whom I have nursed a deeply-felt personal grievance for the last eleven or twelve years. One word of criticism is enough for Fred to swing round and intone, as if he has been programmed, 'The greatest airline in the world.'

I have been associated with FST in the production of a number of books, as has our colleague Trevor Bailey, who once asked me, 'How do you manage to pin Fred down when you need him for a specific bit of information or opinion?' Well might he ask. Writing a book with Fred is not easy. Once the idea is promoted and a contract signed he is genuinely enthusiastic, but he is far too restless a character to enjoy sitting down for two or three hours while one extracts some vital material. And he can be infuriatingly mercurial about changing things when they have been painstakingly turned into a chapter. When, in the 1977 BBC publication *Arlott and Trueman on Cricket* (which complemented a TV series), Fred was called upon to provide pen-portraits of twenty-five or twenty-six great players of his time, I received the summons: 'Now then, sunshine, I can put a bit o' brass your way.'

We adopted a system of my going to Fred's home, or his coming to mine, where I would make notes of his thoughts on, say, Compton, Bailey, Hutton, Statham and Evans and write up the tributes. At our next meeting Fred would then inquire, 'Who 'ave we done so far?', and on hearing the list he would, with absolute certainty, have at least one change of mind: 'Noooo, I never did like that four-letter-word. Take 'im out and we'll do somebody else.' (Let me hastily add that none of the five names mentioned above came into the hate category; it did, however, include some of the most distinguished cricketers the recent game had seen!) Consequently, the book took considerably longer to write than it need have done. Fortunately, I know my Fred; I knew what to expect.

The lack of attention to timekeeping detail which so disconcerted his *People* sports editors evoked a sympathetic response from me. In 1981, after a fairly industrious day's toil at the Benson and Hedges golf tournament at Fulford (York), I drove sixty miles to the Trueman residence for a pre-arranged session on a book we were doing called *My Most Memorable Matches*. As I arrived, FS and Veronica were coming out of the house on their way to dinner with friends! After Fred's confession – suitably concerned – that 'I'd forgotten all about it, sunshine,' it was Veronica who led him back inside with the firm admonition: 'We are not going *anywhere*, Fred, until you've done what Don came here to do.' That was a book which I finally completed by writing for two days and two nights before setting off on tour to India and Sri Lanka. Come to think of it, we still get a trickle of royalties on that one, so I suppose that in the end it was all worthwhile.

By far the most satisfying joint effort (for both of us) came when, in 1983, Fred asked me, 'Have you ever heard of a book called *James Herriot's Yorkshire*?' Of course I had. 'It's a beautiful book, Fred, and it's been a best-seller for ages.' 'Aye,' responded my friend with that small pause which acknowledges he has heard what has been said to him but proposes to pay no attention to the reply. 'Aye. Well, do you know that James Herriot is a Geordie from Sunderland [sic], who was brought up in Scotland. If *he* can write a book about Yorkshire that's a best-seller, what about "Fred Trueman's Yorkshire", eh? Now wouldn't that be a *better*-seller? We [!] can do it, can't we?'

The more I thought about it, the more I liked the idea. The only snag was that I was going off on tour to Fiji, New Zealand and Pakistan in the winter months, and during the following October I would retire from the staff of the BBC, a mandatory requirement on reaching the age of sixty. As a little personal eccentricity I was determined to work every minute of every day, right up to 5.30 p.m. on 3 October! So fitting in the writing was not easy. However, we set up first of all a series of interviews which were to be turned into six separate chapters of dialogue between FST and prominent Yorkshire personalities. And the first of these was James Herriot – or rather Alf Wight, who adopted that pen name to write his wholly delightful reminiscences of life as a Dales vet. A lovely man.

A delightful start had been made on the book and it continued as the most pleasant and satisfying literary effort with which we have been associated. But – having claimed that Fred's attention to detail is not what others, from his wife downwards would like it to be – let me now draw attention to what at first glance seems a contradiction of that contention. For one chapter of the book, designed to illustrate Fred's love of and interest in the bird-life around his home (for he is a very keen bird-watcher) a noted ornithologist, Peter Wright, furnished us with the results of a survey over a radius of ten miles from the bungalow. It was magnificently comprehensive, covering four pages of the book, listing the species under their natural habitat (fields and pastures, open moorland, lakes and streams, etc.) and providing the Latin name for each breed. It was, however, just one chapter in twenty-three which covered subject matter as far-ranging as Wensleydale cheese and an interview with Lord Wilson, Dales villages and brass bands, the Huddersfield Choral Society and racehorse training.

I have to say I was pleased with the book, damn pleased, perhaps *too* pleased. Consequently, it is possible that I saw Fred immediately after publication when I was in entirely the wrong state of mind. His greeting was not exactly what I had expected: 'That chapter on birds, sunshine. You've missed one out.' Startled, I reached for a copy. 'What bird have *we* missed out, Fred?' I inquired with a gentle emphasis which went, as far as I could gather, unnoticed. 'The lark,' he replied with what I felt, a trifle peevishly, was a touch of satisfaction.

Quickly I riffled through the pages, and now it was my turn to reflect satisfaction. 'Try page 55, line 15. It's listed as "skylark".'

'Oh aye?' replied my friend with that elaborate unconcern. And passed on to other conversational matters. Once again I had forgotten that no one – but no one – has the last word with F. S. Trueman. It might not be the *right* word but he always has the last one.

One literary endeavour in which I have long felt that Fred went a bit astray was with a book called *Ball of Fire*, published in 1976 by J. M. Dent and Sons Ltd. It was billed as 'an autobiography', but it was in fact ghosted by Barry Cockcroft, a television producer and director with Yorkshire TV. Barry is a most gifted film-maker who achieved fame with his brilliant record of life on a remote Swaledale farm run by the marvellous Hannah Hauxwell. It was a truly wonderful bit of television. Writing a first-person account of the life of a great cricketer, however, without a deep, personal knowledge of either the game or the man was, I feel, not quite his forte. Fred, it has to be said, was pleased with the book, which astonished me. True, it enabled him to get off his chest a lot of the anger and disappointment which had burned within him for many years, but I could not see that he had done himself any favours in doing so. Moreover, writing (ostensibly) about oneself – especially when one has been at the centre of so many mighty deeds – is virtually impossible without opening up oneself to allegations of immodesty. But worst of all, it seemed that Fred had recalled all the slights, the torments, the agonies and the resentments of his (then) forty-five years and poured them all out to his ghost in an unending torrent. It added up, as I saw it, to twenty years in first-class cricket in which Fred had experienced very little pleasure at all. It left a nasty taste in the mouth to think that this was the sum of an outstanding player's twenty years at the top.

This, I know, was Trevor Bailey's reaction as well – we both read the book over the weekend of a Test at Lord's. The irony of Brian Johnston's comment – 'I read it in one session between lunch and tea and thoroughly enjoyed every bumper hurled' – was clearly lost upon the publishers, who somewhat naively printed it on the dust-jacket of *Ball of Fire*. Any life-story which can be absorbed in a mere two hours of an afternoon is either a very thin volume indeed or a pretty superficial narrative. It did not show Fred in any sort of appealing light and, notwithstanding the gift of a copy with a most kind inscription, I wish Fred had not allowed it to be published.

Various attempts by a number of collaborators have been made to tap FST's enormous fund of 'stories', but none has been entirely successful. Many of the tales are better restricted to stag dinners, and attempts to combine some of the more seemly contents of his repertoire with anecdotes *about* Fred during his playing career have not quite come off. His literary efforts have been at their best when working in co-operation with someone like Trevor Bailey – two cricketing craftsmen able to combine their thoughts and their memories on a basis of mutual respect and personal liking. It is nevertheless true that, so enduring is Fred's fame as a player and so consistent has been the way he has remained in the public eye in one way and another for the past forty years, most publishers would still snatch his hand off if he offered to put his name to a book for them. Not many cricketers have been able to say *that* more than twenty years after retirement.

11

. . . and Broadcaster

By the time Fred retired from first-class cricket I was producing radio programmes for the BBC in the North of England, as well as sports commentating, and as soon as he was free of his contractual obligations to Yorkshire CCC I was anxious to get him involved in broadcasting as quickly as possible. Three years earlier I had recorded some marvellous reminiscences with Wilfred Rhodes and – without knowing at that time how much of a media person FST was to become in the future – it seemed a matter of vital importance to me that the memories of players like Fred, recalled in their own words, should be stored in BBC Archives as part of the history of the game. It very quickly emerged that Fred, in broadcasting terms, was a 'natural' given the right subject matter, encouragement and prompting. This is not always the case with those who, away from a microphone, are gifted raconteurs.

I tried (and failed) to set up a conversation-piece recording between Fred and the Bishop of Liverpool, partly to check the veracity of all those stories which had come back from Australian tours about 'getting hands together on Sunday', partly because it was a 'mix' of personalities which ought to lead to some excellent radio. Fred was ready, willing and able but unfortunately David Sheppard was too busy at the time I contacted him. I must add, however, that subsequently he was gracious and helpful on other matters. Then I heard a snatch of a broadcast by Raymond Brooks-Ward, the equestrian sports commentator, which contained the phrase, 'the Freddie Trueman of show-jumping'. Raymond was referring to Harvey Smith. I telephoned Fred: 'Have you ever met Harvey Smith?' 'No,' he replied, 'but I'd like to. They tell me he's my sort of feller.'

It took all of three weeks to trace and contact Harvey, but he immediately agreed to join us in a studio as soon as a convenient date could be found. Never having met Harvey myself, it was obviously necessary for the three of us to have an extended exchange of views before we ventured near a studio, so we met for lunch at the Harewood Arms three hours before the recording was due to take place in Broadcasting House, Leeds. There was an immediate and spectacular dinosaural confrontation between two archetypal Yorkshiremen who were both raging extroverts with reputations for calling spades bloody shovels.

There was no suggestion of animosity but there was a certain amount of determination on both sides that, conversationally, one was not going to be outshone by the other. There was an early, full and frank exchange of views in which Anglo-Saxon terminology was used with some freedom. This in itself was no great problem but for the fact that the head waiter, with an unparalleled lack of diplomacy, had placed the three of us at the next table to a couple of parsons in an otherwise empty dining-room! Fred's opening gambit – a nicely casual inquiry into a certain aspect of Harvey's sex-life – stopped one of the ecclesiastical gentlemen in his tracks, a spoonful of soup frozen in transit from plate to mouth. By the time Harvey had replied the priests had cut their losses and asked to be moved to another table. There were, fortunately, many available.

Lunch then continued in animated style while I reflected that it was not a bad idea to allow the two principals to get it all out of their respective systems before we reached the studio. Lunch concluded, I left Fred and Harvey to take coffee in the lounge while I settled the bill. As I followed them to the lounge my blood froze, because emerging from the room at that precise moment came the celebrated husband-and-wife acting partnership of Michael Denison and Dulcie Gray, who, it transpired, were appearing that week at the Grand Theatre, Leeds. Falteringly, I asked Mr Denison, 'Er, I hope you have not been driven out of the lounge by . . . er . . .' Ever the gentleman of the stage, he smilingly interrupted, 'Don't worry. I've known Fred a long time. Nothing to worry about at all.'

The recording went supremely well. There was scarcely any need for me to chair the discussion except, occasionally, to change the topic. Fred asked Harvey about show-jumping, talked of his father's and his own love of horses, spoke of his own admiration for Rubgy League players. This brought a warm and immediate response from Harvey, who went on to talk about how he had always fancied trying all-in wrestling! As in all good, not-too-heavily-rehearsed conversations it changed direction in unexpected fashion as the two of them warmed to each other and found much in common. When I had edited the tape we had forty mintues of fascinating chat between two outstanding sportsmen meeting for the first time. The BBC were able to sell copies, and transcriptions, of the recording all over the place.

From conversation-pieces we switched to other fields (my one subsequent disappointment was in failing to get Fred and the incoming Archbishop of Canterbury, Dr Runcie, together in a studio) and by the early 1970s, Fred was an experienced and highly competent radio broadcaster. He had, in the meantime, done a great deal of television work, particularly for Yorkshire TV in which he was very much at home with an audience. In the more remote atmosphere of a radio studio he learned quickly to adjust to the *absence* of an audience, which makes it an entirely different and, in some ways, more difficult medium. In radio programmes which we recorded before a live audience, such as *Sports Forum*, he could be quite brilliant, with his penchant for the odd outrageous remark and the graphic throw-away line. Like so many of his fellow countrymen there were no grey areas with Fred; he saw just about everything in terms of black or white, so we knew we were always on a winner in booking him for the *Forum* type of programme. The fees were small, especially in comparison with those he now commanded for TV appearances and speaking engagements (thanks to Veronica's businesslike handling of his affairs and then with John Maddock becoming his agent) but he never quibbled, never said he was unavailable. This is just one more example of Fred's loyalty which I have appreciated for so many years. There have never been any mawkish expressions of gratitude between us. We understand and, I think, appreciate each other.

The one thing which I had so far been unable to accomplish was to persuade my masters in London that Fred should be a member of the *Test Match Special* commentary team. I had advanced his name at every pre-season meeting where we discussed the composition of the *TMS* team. There was obviously a place for him since, year after year, we tried one ex-Test player after another – almost invariably of the 'amateur' persuasion – without achieving a settled partner-ship of inter-overs summarisers. Five of us – Head of Outside

Broadcasts (Robert Hudson) the Cricket Producer (Michael Tuke-Hastings) and the three English Regions OB producers, Richard Maddock (Midlands), Tony Smith (West) and myself – spent hours discussing the commentators, the summarisers and other cricketing matters before the start of every season, but in the event of any disagreement it was always London's word which was final.

There was an atmosphere which was uniquely BBC-ish about the reaction to my annual proposal of Fred as a member of the *TMS* team. No one ever said, 'No. Absolutely not,' because that would have meant giving a reason for the refusal, and if anyone *had* a reason it was one which he did not feel disposed to put into words. But when the lists were ultimately promulgated, Fred's name was always missing. I could never get an answer to the question 'Why?' It was, as in other aspects of working for the often admirable Corporation, like banging one's head against a wall of candy floss. Contentions were absorbed but never directly refuted.

Finally, Trevor Bailey emerged as the first *regular* inter-overs summariser of the modern era. He was immediately and unarguably brilliant in the role – succinct, authoritative, wickedly humorous and very easy to work with. The situation now screamed for a regular partner for Trevor, in my view, someone of comparable stature as a player but preferably a man with a contrasting style of thinking, and of verbal delivery. As I saw it, Fred had to be the answer, but was mine a truly objective view? I might insist that I was *thinking* like a producer in championing the Trueman cause, but I was also a commentator and so was my objectivity in question? And, even more to the point, I was a close friend of Fred, so impartiality (and objectivity once again) came into question. The situation remained unresolved until the winter of 1973–4, when, after a meeting to discuss the wider aspects of the Outside Broadcasts Department, the new Head, Cliff Morgan, asked me point-blank: 'What would you do to improve *Test Match Special*?'

'Two things,' I replied. 'First , I'd like to see Fred Trueman included as a summariser. Secondly, I would end the system by which we slavishly return to the studio for music the minute rain stops play.'

Cliff, a man for whom I have the most profound respect and liking, asked thoughtfully, 'Why has Fred never been tried?'

'Don't ask me,' I replied. 'I've been putting forward his name for years but got nowhere. I think it's perhaps a combination of fears that he might sound too ee-by-gum amongst so many public-school accents and that his language might be too spicy. That's daft. He's been broadcasting with me in the North, now, for seven or eight years and he's done some marvellous stuff. If he joined the team I could guarantee he would do a good job and apart from that, if we *talked cricket* whenever rain stopped play we would get some absolutely marvellous stuff. Just look at the vast accumulated knowledge of the game and of its folklore with John Arlott, Brian Johnston, Trevor and Fred – just chatting. It would be cricket broadcasting with a dimension we have never had before.'

I hope that loyal band of *TMS* listeners are forever grateful to Cliff Morgan for implementing both suggestions. From that moment in 1974 *Test Match Special* took off. Within the next decade the programme had been featured in magazines, supplements and most of the serious newspapers in the country. It had become cult broadcasting. Fred Trueman, together with Bailey, Johnston, Arlott and some of the visiting commentators from overseas, notably Alan McGilvray, played a major role in the transformation of *TMS* from a sound, serious and extemely competent area of sports broadcasting to one with an immensely wider popular appeal. Letters now came in shoals – previously a trickle – not only from the more erudite ranks of devoted cricket fans but now in increasing numbers from housewives who enjoyed a chorus of friendly voices in the house, discussing an enormous variety of topics, and they began to write: 'We like it best when rains stops play.' Well, that was, I suppose, a double-edged compliment but the essentially *cricket* listeners, too, were writing more kindly than critically.

Of course, it was not achieved with effortless ease. There were times when Fred needed help, just as we all need it from time to time. He talks best when fed the bait-ball, when given a specific aspect of a game to talk about and when he feels most at ease with whoever happens to be his commentary partner. He works wonderfully, for instance, with the utterly contrasting character of Brian Johnston (Eton, Oxford and the Guards!), who is probably the most superb natural broadcaster I have ever heard. I don't think Fred has always appreciated just how much he is indebted to Brian and (until his retirement in 1980) to John Arlott for the unobtrusive but ingenious way in which they have fed him opportunities to 'shine'. But there is no doubt that Fred has taken full advantage of those opportunities. And in the rain-stops-play period he has frequently been outstandingly good. As a purely personal view I have to say that whenever I am caught in the commentator's seat when a stoppage occurs the first sparring partner I look for is FST. He works better with some members of the team than others.

He has never realised – and he will not thank me at all for drawing attention to this – how uncomfortable he sounded when plucked from the bosom of his friends and colleagues on *TMS* to work for Kerry Packer's World Series in the Australian summer of 1977–8. It was the beginning of June when the news broke that most of the best players in the world had been bought up by Packer, and it was a considerable talking-point during the first One-Day International of the summer at Old Trafford. 'It can't work,' declared Fred. 'You can't put together teams of Test cricketers with no Test matches to play. There's no point to it.' That was during the game at Old Trafford. The second of the limited-overs internationals took place at Edgbaston two days later. I missed that game and rejoined my colleagues on 6 June at The Oval for the third match. Fred greeted me, 'He's a great feller, this Kerry Packer, you know, sunshine. He's going to put on some marvellous stuff this winter.'

To be scrupulously fair about the matter, Mrs Veronica Trueman, that shrewd lady, was extremely impressed by the organisation of the World Series, too, and particularly by the way Kerry Packer looked after his mercenaries, and their families. However, this is not the place to debate the rights and wrongs of the staging of the World Series. It is an inescapable fact that in international cricket terms the matches were meaningless, and so the entire strength of the Packer marketing organisation was devoted to attempting to 'sell' the series to spectators in the grounds and to television viewers. An essential ingredient of this was for the commentators to display artificial excitement, admiration, apprehension and any other ersatz emotion which could be conjured up. This was not Fred's strong suit, by any stretch of imagination. As a visitor to Australia during the series I listened to his brave but quite unsuccessful efforts to join the party. That he was willing enough to do what was required by the man who was paying him rather well to be there was clear enough; but Fred just could not convince himself that any part of the nonsense conjured up excitement, admiration or apprehension. And it showed.

With one or two notable exceptions he was working with amateur commentators, and pretty poor amateurs, too. No one provided the sort of professional broadcasting back-up to which he was accustomed with *Test Match Special*. Most of his colleagues were busy enough trying to keep their own heads above water by giving the 'cricket' a semblance of credibility. All Fred's efforts – and he approached his duties with a rather grand air of the experienced BBC broadcaster in a group made up largely of ex-players with little or no broadcasting experience – were submerged in an ocean of advertisements and implausibility. He will argue that he did a very good job for Kerry Packer. So he did – by lending his name and reputation to the series.

In 1984 he struck problems of a different nature – his disillusionment with what was happening inside Yorkshire cricket. Like everyone else who cared deeply for the county club, its history, traditions and great record, he had become heartily sick of the internal feuding between the established authority of the club (the Committee, of which he was a member) and the supporters of Geoffrey Boycott. Fred was implacably, and most vocally, opposed to the Boycott support group, who, however, made most of the headlines because they stirred up most of the trouble on which headline-writers feed. He was one of the men seeking re-election in the 1984 hustings for Committee places, but he did no campaigning. Fred relied upon his reputation as the county's greatest-ever fast bowler to sustain his candidature, but from Veronica we learn that he feared the worst.

'We had been in Australia and took a break in Hong Kong on the way home. Fred bought a lovely necklace in the design of a Yorkshire rose and I was delighted with it. I told him, "I'll wear this the next time we are in the Yorkshire Committee-Room." I remember his words all too clearly. Fred said, "You won't be there. I won't be voted back." "Why do you say that?" I asked, and very, very sadly he said, "They don't like me in Yorkshire." '

His words proved to be prophetic. Sixty-five Yorkshire members of the Craven district voted for him; 128 voted for his opponent, a complete unknown, but a Boycott supporter. One of the outstanding personalities in the history of the game was toppled by a man whose only connection with cricket had hitherto been at an utterly insignificant level. Notwithstanding his premonition, his forecast to Veronica, Fred was nevertheless devastated by that result and the figures. His pride was shattered, his anguish was terrible to see – though few outside his family and a circle of close friends were allowed to see it. It was an inward rage which fired him now to swear oaths never again to watch Yorkshire play cricket, never again to wear his player's tie, never again to lift one finger to help in any way the Club which he felt had wronged him so terribly. He vowed to burn his blazers and sweaters and his caps. The anguish and the fury are as keenly felt today as they were in March 1984. Above all – and this, I submit, is the most important factor to be considered – Fred was HURT. It is easy enough for those who know him but slightly, or not at all, to think only in terms of Fred's anger, his resentment. But by far the most potent emotional shock he suffered at that time was in being deeply and painfully hurt.

Eighteen years earlier every Yorkshire boy had been Freddie Trueman when playing his own imaginative cricket against the school wall or on the local recreation ground. Fred strode the Broad Acres like a god. He was the most instantly recognisable sporting personality in Britain. He was fêted and lionised in all strata of society. At home, in the north-west corner of the county he had, he felt, integrated with the county membership as closely as could be expected of him. He had helped the local (Craven) cricket league in a number of ways, done his bit for local charities. And a paltry sixty-five Yorkshire members had said they wanted him to represent their interests at Headingley. It was a body blow which left him sick and sour, and it was the sourness which, almost tragically, now began to seep into other aspects of his life. It took a tremendous effort of will-power for Fred to walk through the gates of Headingley for that summer's Test against the West Indies. If he had not been on duty for *Test Match Special* nothing on earth would have persuaded him into the ground. He felt that the eyes of every Yorkshire member were on him – not in the way which had meant so much to him for so many years but now looking at him as the man who had been rejected. It went deep down into Fred's most sensitive areas in a way which very few of our *TMS* colleagues could understand. It took a Yorkshire mind to understand that tortured Yorkshire soul, as the bitterness now overflowed into his broadcast comments.

It shouldn't have happened, of course, because it sounded an alien note in *Test Match Special*. Over a decade the programme had come to mean 'fun' broadcasting in the sense that, while we treated the cricket with the dignity it merited, we never lost sight of the fact that it was a game we were talking about and not a form of warfare or international political dispute. Laughter, or a smile, was rarely more than a sentence or two away. But all that was changed for Fred in the summer of 1984, and nowhere more so than at Headingley, where his anger, disappointment and frustration overflowed. We hoped he would be able to get over it, in time.

12

Fred at Home

On a summer day there are few more pleasant places to sit in the sun than Fred's garden. His home is splendidly remote from busy roads or large centres of population; it faces south-east so that it enjoys sunshine for a substantial part of the day. It is heavily populated with tits and finches at any time but is visited by an impressive variety of other birds. It is enclosed by a high brick wall which provides nesting areas for some species; the shrubs and low trees accommodate others. Beyond the bottom wall are higher trees, a stream where the kingfisher and the dipper skim the water, and beyond that are the slopes of the Pennines where pines march side by side with heather and bracken. This is one of the two places where Fred is able to relax – even though the phone rings incessantly and his answering-machine must be the most over-worked in Britain. His punishing routine is one which demands as a matter of sheer physical necessity an occasional day of rest and relaxation.

Consider his schedule of engagements taken at random from four or five pages of his diary. 8 May: Benson and Hedges gold award adjudication at Old Trafford, 9th: an opening ceremony with 'Noddy' Pullar in Lancashire; 10th: a lunch in Blackpool with Brian Statham; 11th: lunch, 'Talk of London'; 14th: dinner in Manchester; 15th: dinner in Chester; 16th dinner in Stoke-on-Trent; 17th: lunch in City of London; 19th golf day and dinner (Variety Club of Great Britain), Royal Liverpool Golf Club; 21st: dinner in Birmingham; 22nd: TV programme at Masham (Wensleydale); 23rd: One-Day International, Headingley; 24th: dinner, Leeds; 25th: dinner, Amsterdam. Now, that is an absolutely typical two or three weeks in the life of Freddie Trueman. It is not a period which has been particularly singled out. Even when he joins close friends in Spain for a winter holiday he flies back to England on two, three and sometimes half a dozen occasions to carry out speaking engagements or opening ceremonies or adjudications. The merry-go-round simply never stops.

Fred has a genuine and deep-seated love of the countryside and of the Yorkshire Dales in particular. Long before he made his home there he made his first discovery of the Dales when driving from York to a pre-season practice match with Yorkshire in the old market town of Settle. Previously he had never been so far west in his native county, and as his car climbed over a summit between Nidderdale and Wharfedale he was startled by the sheer beauty of the scene stretching before and below him. He made himself a promise that one day he would live in this glorious country.

His bungalow, though well off the beaten track, is not isolated because others have been quick to appreciate the attractions of the area. But his walled garden gives him all the seclusion he needs without shutting out the scenery about him. His dining-room is dominated by that onyx table delivered from Mexico via a skateboard, and his bookshelves are lined with books recording the facts and records of more than 150 years of cricket. I doubt if there are many he has not memorised. The showcase filled with memorabilia, each one a bit of cricket history in itself, made identification not-too-difficult when the house was featured in the TV programme *Through the Keyhole*.

In the window of his lounge stands a bust by the sculptress Betty Miller and in the dining-room hangs a portrait in oils by John Blakey. On the walls hang prints of Northern industrial scenes by Lowry which contrast splendidly with a selection of David Shepherd's brilliant wildlife studies. Fred is a great admirer of Shepherd both as an artist (who insists 'I have no talent; I was *taught* to paint') and a conservationist. As if life was not full enough already for both men they arranged last year a programme of mutual co-operation – David to help Fred with his scanner project for the Airedale Hospital, Fred to give his support to the David Shepherd Conservation Foundation.

His first old English sheepdog, William, achieved a certain fame when introduced to Radio 3 listeners by Brian Johnston (who, I have always insisted, can conduct an intelligible interview with anyone or *anything*) and cricket-lovers still write to inquire about succeeding generations of Trueman dogs. The second was Tara and the present incumbent is Digby. All have had characters of their own, all have enjoyed the gruff affection of the master of the house, whose arsenal of pipes is housed to the right of the fireplace. When he is not tearing about the country or jetting about the world he is not an early riser. Just as in his playing days, the opportunity for an extra hour in bed is a luxury to be savoured. A day at home with no timetable to be kept, no schedule of engagements to be followed, is the greatest luxury of all. Fred has a beautiful home and is at peace in it.

Bird-watching, which he undertakes quite simply for the pleasure of watching and identifying the various species, delights him. He is knowledgeable without involving himself in scientific research which might tend to make it a bit of a chore. He encourages wildlife without recourse to undue artificiality beyond a couple of bird-boxes and a few bags of nuts in winter; the garden provides a wealth of natural habitats in itself. Nevertheless, even in such a gentle context, the competitive element is present and our personal relationship is not without a touch of one-upmanship. Fred is visited by a nuthatch, a bird I have never seen. When I call upon him the nuthatch is never seen; when I am absent the bird duly returns. Thus, when we were once involved in a Radio 3 broadcast while I was on tour in India and Fred was at home, he cheerfully tossed into the cricket conversation (chaired by Brian Johnston in London) the splendidly irrelevant information that 'the nuthatch you have never seen, sunshine. He was here this morning.' The opportunity was too good to miss. 'From where I am sitting, Fred, I can see twenty or more hoopoes hopping about the outfield,' I replied. Naturally, I could not expect to get away with that, even if it did take him several months to hit back. Back home in England, I had a phone call from Fred, newly returned from a speaking engagement in South Africa: 'I've been admiring a golden oriole.' Chagrined, I rushed off to the Leighton Moss bird sanctuary near my home on Morecambe Bay, in search of a bittern. Alas, I heard one but did not see it, so that particular game had to be scored thirty-fifteen to Fred.

His visits to the Marbella area of Spain, where a number of the Truemans' closest friends escape from the English winters, enable him to relax in a different way. He plays a lot of golf (some element of competition in his life is still necessary), enjoys dining out in an area where celebrities are the rule rather than the exception and so he is unlikely to be singled out for special, intrusive attention, and is happy enough just lounging in the sun beside someone's swimming pool. On these occasions he is likely to be found in the company of Desmond and Betty Bailey, Bob and Sue Platt, Bill and Valerie Sutcliffe, or perhaps financial consultant Claude Brownlow and his wife Morag or hoteliers John and Maureen Smith – all these a part of the inner circle. But FST at large in a foreign, non-cricketing land?

It would probably be unjust to describe Fred as a xenophobe. Let us just say he is less at ease with those who do not speak the Queen's English than those who do. It is reliably reported – and in the context of Spain, Desmond Bailey is our Boswell to Fred's Johnson – that after well over a decade of visiting the country, FST has so far mastered just one word of the Hispanic tongue. Evidence of this, which startled a house-party, came when they were experiencing flooding problems in a thunderstorm. As water cascaded from the roof, could find no access to over-burdened drains and lapped ankle-deep around the garden, and an army of workmen looked on in shoulder-shrugging impotence, Fred embarked upon a frenzied, mimed indication of the problem as he saw it, gesticulating wildly towards the roof, the drainpipes, the torrents. Finally, when his frustration reached breaking-point, he was driven to break the habit of a lifetime. Choking with fury at the inactivity of the workmen, the first word of any foreign language to be uttered by F. S. Trueman now echoed across his waterlogged garden: 'Agua.' The workmen gazed at each other with further shrugging of shoulders. They scarcely needed to be told that the problem was 'water' – too much of it – in any language. Obviously they did not realise it was an historic moment.

If that was no laughing matter to Fred, it is nevertheless true that his laughter is heard more frequently in Spain than probably anywhere else. He is not a man who laughs easily. He is happier making others roll in the aisles with that inexhaustible supply of after-dinner stories than listening to jokes himself. That, of course, is one of the snags of being a dispenser of bawdy tales – the odds are that a percentage of the listeners have heard them before, though one has to say that FST comes up with more original material than most professional stand-up comics one has heard. It is very difficult indeed to tell Fred one that *he* hasn't heard. He enjoys holding court, performing for an audience, no matter whether he is on stage or simply amongst a group of friends. Exhibitionism is never far beneath the surface and it is, in general, fairly necessary for him to be the centre of attention. On the other hand, take him away from what constitutes an audience and it becomes a different matter altogether.

One particularly pleasant day I remember was when my wife and I were staying with Fred and Veronica for a Test Match at Lord's and on the rest day (Sunday) FST was involved in a charity match at Arundel with the Courage Eleven. We went by train to Sussex on one of those lovely summer's days when England always seems the best place in the world to live – two pairs of old friends embarking on a day out together. Fred had no 'audience' to impress, so there was no requirement for him to assume an artificial personality. He was just himself. We had a perfectly pleasant conversation all the way there and all the way back, and we laughed for most of the time. It was an utterly delightful day, not least of all for a supper in the garden of Arundel's MP, Michael Marshall (a mutual friend and fellow Lord's Taverner) which included freshly picked straw-berries. It was not the only time the four of us have spent together, but I have rarely seen Fred so completely relaxed as he was on that occasion. There was no window-dressing, no artificiality, no monologue, no pretentiousness, no striving for effect. It was a Freddie Trueman so few people have ever seen, and that is an enormous pity. He would have an entirely different public image if he could be like that more frequently. But then, perhaps, he wouldn't have quite such an eye- and ear-catching personality – and that is important to him. Who is to say which is right and which is wrong?

He does, I am assured, relax in Spain and he laughs a lot when he is there. He particularly enjoys barbecues, with over-cooked sausages as his favourite dish (sausages taken out from England, of course). Fred likes to preside over the preparation of the food, which causes a certain disquiet amongst the guests since he usually cooks with a large cigar in his mouth. He is apt to laugh *at* his friends as often as he laughs *with* them, and has a tendency – not exclusive to Yorkshiremen but certainly prevalent amongst them – to find humour in the misfortunes of others. Thus, in 1988, when he and Desmond Bailey set out on a search for a site for a new villa which Desmond was planning to build, it was Cap'n Bailey who was elected to drive his Renault 5 (known widely in the Marbella area as the Yellow Peril) on the exploratory expedition. Fred urged Desmond ever onwards into the foothills of the Sierra Blanca until they ran out of road. 'Go on,' ordered FST, as the Renault bounced off rocks and skidded wildly on shale. When they finally ground to a halt, male chauvinism emerged in all its glory as the two wives got out and pushed while Desmond remained at the wheel. Fred, it scarcely needs to be reported, held the supervisory and organisational role. The car had to be abandoned and the foursome returned, weary and footsore, but with Fred enjoying hugely the fact that the Yellow Peril had had to be left behind. He enjoyed even more learning the following day that it took a crane and a Landrover (and a lot of pesetas) to recover it. 'But,' recalls Bailey, 'I had the last laugh when Fred had a bit of trouble with several hire cars.'

Now, that is a story which will be noted with more than passing interest by his distinguished contemporary and captain, D. B. Close. Fred is generally a confident driver who is far from reckless. He is far too conscious of how much his cars cost to treat them in a cavalier fashion. His first, acquired during his National Service days in the RAF, was a 1932 MG midget and it was his pride and joy – even though he could scarcely be described as an experienced driver. Since those days he has never been without a car and it's a safe bet that he could tell, to the penny, what each one cost.

Consequently, and with the utmost delight, Fred has for more than thirty years 'collected' stories of Brian Close's driving misadventures. If he merely used that collection as an after-dinner speaking routine he could absolutely guarantee to bring the house down every time. They are magnificent stories and FST tells them magnificently. The two of them were once invited to take part in a race on the Oulton Park circuit in Cheshire, in which all the cars were driven by personalities from other sporting fields, and Fred announced a pragmatic policy even as the cars waited on the starting-grid. 'I'm going to make sure I keep behind that mad pillock,' he declared with a nod in Close's direction. And so he did. That was one occasion when winning glory was a matter of personal indifference to FST. But that is the merest drop in the ocean of Fred's repertoire. Anyone who can persuade him to go through the list of anecdotes is set for at least half an hour of the highest-quality entertainment. Occasionally, and irritably, Close threatens, 'I am going to bloody well sue Fred one of these days. And you, too, for encouraging him,' he adds with a sideswipe at myself.

Politically, Fred stands firmly to the right, which seems a trifle anachronistic to many people, especially those from the more southerly areas of England, given his birthright, his birthplace and his background. There is, in some quarters, a rather foolish tendency to look upon working-class Northerners as inevitably and irredeemably socialist in principle. It is a facile manifestation of the North–South divide. Fred is a firm believer in the Monarchy and has a greater regard for the hereditary peerage than for the *nouveau riche* promotions from the ranks of industry to the Upper House. Yet he is far from a forelock-touching member of the proletariat. The surest way for anyone regarding himself as socially superior to provoke an explosion is to address FST as 'Trueman'. Brian Sellers, when Yorkshire's cricket chairman, made the mistake on a couple of occasions. A few others, daring, provocative or merely misguided, have been equally foolish. Preserving his personal dignity is important to him. By and large he dislikes people of the Left (loony, or relatively rational), yet he can be won over, personally if not politically, by those who take the trouble to be courteous, helpful and intelligent – Ken Livingstone and Harold Wilson, for instance, as we have seen. In short, Fred's attitude to his fellow creatures is, like his bowling was, unpredictable. Few batsmen could ever forecast what delivery was coming next; so it is with people. His reactions can startle even those who know him best.

One point on which he has shown complete consistency, however, is his care and concern for children. He has been a superbly generous father to his own three children, and to Veronica's two as well. He has done a tremendous job of fund-raising for orphans and handicapped youngsters, almost all of it unpublicised. Dear old Maurice Leyland – a wonderful Yorkshire cricketer in pre-war days and a much-loved coach afterwards – used to set targets for the young Trueman to encourage his development (Ray Illingworth came to do something similar in later years with his son-in-law, Ashley Metcalfe), and on one occasion was obliged to deliver a stone (i.e. 14 lbs) of humbugs to the

Yorkshire dressing-room at Harrogate when FST took six wickets and hit 50 runs. This, naturally enough, *was* publicised and it seemed that every boiled-sweet manufacturer in the North of England decided to get in on the act. Fred was swamped by a deluge of confectionery so great that even after players and staff had taken their fill there was still a huge amount of the stuff left over. So he took the goodies along to a home for handicapped kids outside the town and there, amongst a tragic complement of spastic cases he met a small boy who could walk only with the help of a tubular steel frame. 'Are you getting on all right?' asked Fred and the youngster replied, with a bright smile, 'Yes, thanks, Mr Trueman. I'll win the Brighton road race next year.' It was a heart-rending moment for the iron-hard man of cricket. The terrible pathos of that little boy's courage caused him to break down completely and he had to leave before he had talked to all the children. But he promised himself, there and then, that his future charity work would be for the very young. And he has kept that promise. This is the chapter of the Trueman story which has never reached the headlines.

Occasionally he springs upon his friends the news that they will be assisting in some of his endeavours, which usually takes them by surprise. When two North Yorkshire policemen were shot trying to arrest a criminal on the run Fred decided to put on a huge banquet and cabaret in Harrogate to raise money for the officers' families and dependents. Veronica (as ever) was promptly pressed into service and so was Jack Mewies, but the first that two others knew of the event was when Fred blithely, in the middle of *Test Match Special* at Headingley, announced his intentions along with the news that his old mates, Brian Johnston and Don Mosey, would be the speakers. Brian and I looked at each other, smiled and silently accepted the invitation. This caused a certain amount of amusement amongst our colleagues until they learned that *they* would be on parade as well, sitting as guest celebrities at tables which had been 'bought' for £1,000 a time by companies, clubs and organisations of all kinds who had been persuaded, coaxed or bludgeoned into supporting the occasion. Emissaries were despatched in all directions – Fred is not a reluctant delegator – to ensure that the maximum amount of money was extracted from every possible source. If the actual, physical work of setting up the banquet was largely undertaken by others the real point is this: if Fred had not dreamed up the idea, the event would not have taken place; if he had not called upon a huge pool of friends and contacts it would not have been supported as it was; if he had not called in a great reserve of favours, there would have been no raffle prizes or auction lots. And the families of those dead police officers would not have received thousands of pounds. So it was when the Statham-support dinners came along, and in dozens of other similar cases. Each time we are left to marvel at the restless energy of the man.

The Fred Trueman Golf Classic, staged each June in Harrogate, raises thousands of pounds towards a Scanner Appeal for the Airedale Hospital, near Keighley. The advance planning is largely done by step-daughter Sheena, who spends up to seven months sorting out a mass of administrative details and is joined on the day of the tournament by her mother, as both of them go through a tireless non-stop routine of making sure everything goes smoothly. Imagine the nightmare of finding a last-minute replacement celebrity for a team who have been looking forward for weeks to playing with one particular personality. In the 1990 Classic Veronica and Sheena had scarcely reached Harrogate Golf Club when a plaintive phone call came from Farokh Engineer (former Lancs and India wicketkeeper-batsman):'Could he be excused? The BBC had just phoned to ask him to provide expert comments for Radio 3 in the Benson and Hedges semi-final between Lancs and Somerset at Old Trafford.' What had happened was that Clive Lloyd had been booked to do that particular broadcast and then had accepted an invitation to carry out the Gold Award adjudication at the *other* semi-final between Notts and Worcestershire at Trent Bridge. He duly turned up in the commentary box in Nottingham (where Mike Hendrick was the summariser), leaving Peter Baxter, the BBC Radio cricket producer with no one to provide expert comments at Old Trafford. Hence the panic-stricken late phone call to 'Rooky' Engineer. And as the chain-reaction clattered on, Sheena and Veronica were left at the end of the line. They sorted out the mess with unflappable serenity.

In the evening came Fred's turn to toil. After the Golf Classic dinner at the Crown Hotel he stood with sweat streaming down his face as he coaxed ever more money out of the audience for his appeal fund, drawing £10 notes out of a top hat to determine raffle-prize winners, auctioning memorabilia, introducing cabaret acts (showbiz friends he had coaxed into 'doing a turn') and interspersing the whole breathless performance with merry quip and jest of his own. It was a tour-de-force of heroic proportions.

The publicity which helped to create his image in the early fifties has in no way diminished in the nineties. Some of it comes in different forms and some for varying reasons, but the very name of Fred Trueman in a headline still attracts fascinated attention. His twin daughter Rebecca projected him back into the limelight in June 1990 in a way which neither he, nor anyone else, could ever have anticipated. Several weeks earlier, she had secretly married in Los Angeles the son of film star Raquel Welch. It took the British press a couple of months to become aware of the fact, but once the news became public the cricket world was entranced by the idea that Fiery Fred was now related, albeit tenuously and by marriage only, to the Sex Goddess of Hollywood. FS could have coped with that aspect of things; after all, he had been enduring it for two or three decades. But what the public in general did not perhaps realise was that as a father – and a loving and caring one – he was deeply hurt that 'Becky' had not involved him, not told him, not given him the opportunity to give her the sort of magnificent wedding he had given to her elder sister Karen and her step-sister, Sheena.

It was the *Daily Mirror* which broke the story in England at the beginning of June, just as Becky flew back from California to explain matters to her father, who was by now getting unwelcome phone calls from every other newspaper in the country. The *Sunday People*, to which Fred had been contributing his words for more than thirty years, now saw itself in an advantageous position to get the full story only forty-eight hours after the *Mirror*, rather sketchily, had announced the wedding. Fred and Rebecca agreed, and this is the story she gave to the *Sunday People*:

> I was in Los Angeles last December with Coral Stringfellow [ex-wife of London nightclub-owner Peter Stringfellow] and we met Damon (Welch) at a reception. It was a pleasant evening; a group of us went for dinner together afterwards and Damon invited us to a charity event the following evening. I liked this young man and what particularly impressed me was the way he refused to use his mother's name to push himself or even to help with the charity work. He was simply himself, doing a job. Raquel's name

was never mentioned. We continued to see each other until I came home for Christmas. There was no doubt by this time that we were attracted to each other, but we were both conscious of the fact that we each had things we wanted to do with our lives. Damon was involved in sports medicine administration and physical-fitness training; I was looking for some sponsorship as a sports-car driver.

However, we realised we had become quite close during those weeks before Christmas and we kept in touch by telephone. The more we talked, the more we realised we wanted to spend more time together, so when my efforts to get backing for my ideas of a career in sports-car driving came to nothing I decided to fly back to the USA. It was my intention to spend three months there while Damon and I saw whether we had a really worthwhile relationship. We felt a spiritual bond had been formed; now was the time to see how strong it was.

Damon was wonderful when I reached Los Angeles, and we quickly realised how close we had become. About ten days before my birthday (27 March) he proposed and I was delighted. I was not so much concerned with a formal engagement as I was that we had made a firm commitment to each other, and I immediately telephoned to England. My family were as delighted as I was, and after Damon and I had talked it over we decided that it would be best to be married in England, probably in about a year's time. It was only later we realised that I could not stay in the USA simply as a fiancée if I wanted to work, as I did. That would require a work permit. We had, we felt, given our hearts to each other but legal technicalities were still in the way. The only thing to do was to get married now. We had both wanted to do this in our own time and with our families properly involved, but that would have taken a long time to arrange. So we went ahead with a small ceremony, with just a couple of witnesses, resolving to have a service later, in England, so that the marriage was solemnised in the eyes of God.

It was difficult for both of us. I hadn't met Damon's parents and he did not know mine, so we hoped to keep the marriage secret until we had the chance to expain it all in our own way. We should have known it's difficult to keep that sort of secret when the bridegroom is Raquel Welch's son and the bride is the daughter of Freddie Trueman.

But I have to say that when I flew back to England in June there was no anger or rejection from Dad. He was disappointed, a little sad that he had not been able to give me the sort of wedding he would have liked. Then he said, 'Well, you've done it now. You're twenty-five and you have your own life to lead.' And quickly he added, 'Are you both all right?' He was happy for me and that made *me* happy. So was Veronica. I had the support of the family, Sheena and her husband David. . . . I had always wanted to get married in church but you can't always control the way things work out. I still want to have my marriage blessed in church and I look forward to the day when Damon and I can see that happen.

That was Rebecca's own story. It wasn't quite the style of usual *Sunday People* stories. They didn't print it. They printed another one altogether. The lovely blonde, bubbly Becky (she calls Dad and Veronica the Flintstones, Fred and Wilma, with their neighbour Peter Parfitt as Barney Rubble!) flew back to Los Angeles after a week, feeling relieved that the situation had been explained. Fred, however, was left to deal with a further stream of press inquiries and a fair amount of good-natured leg-pulling from his friends. From Hollywood, on the other hand, it was reported that Ms Welch was somewhat less than pleased by telephone calls from British newspapers who regarded the personality at their end of the story as more important than hers. Nevertheless, some of the more optimistic of Fred's friends hope it will be possible in due course to meet at a Dales garden party the lady described in Leslie Halliwell's filmgoer's 'bible' as 'the dynamic curvaceous sex symbol of the late sixties'. Merely to witness the meeting between father-of-the-bride and mother-of-the-groom should be an experience not to be missed.

13

Last Word – or is it?

Once, in an unguarded moment, Fred wrote that 'some of the old-timers don't understand the way the game has changed', and if he had been a politician instead of a professional sportsman there is no doubt that someone would have dragged that comment out of the archives and damned him with it in his later, critical years. His modern lament – the subject of parody in many quarters – that 'I just don't know what's going off out theer', brings the immediate riposte from present-day cricketers that (you've guessed it) old-timers like Fred don't understand how the game has changed. When he expresses this mystification during Test commentary – and it has to be said that he does it quite often – I am always the one asked to 'have a word with Fred about it'. And when I gently venture the suggestion to him that 'it is our job to tell the listeners what *is* happening out there' his reply is almost tortured in its frustration, 'But I *can't*, sunshine, because I *don't* know what they're trying to do.'

This view has evoked a considerable sympathy from Fred's contemporaries in recent years, when batsmen in Tests have been seen to ignore simple basics of the game like playing *through* the line of the ball, and bowlers are so frequently seen to be unable to bowl a consistent line. But the most dangerous philosophy for a professional critic to adopt is that nothing today is as good as it was in the old days. Not only have we a new generation of players, but there is a new generation of spectators as well – men and women who did not see Trueman and Statham bowl or Hutton and Washbrook open the innings. Fred's problem has become one of how to achieve a balance between his honest, realistic view of cricket in his time and an acceptance that not all is complete dross in the present era.

He has found it difficult to accept with equanimity the overtaking of some of the records he set, most notably the figure of 307 Test wickets. It was possible for him to shrug off the fact that Lance

Gibbs 'crawled past my record in 1976' because he was a slow bowler and '*they* can go on until they qualify for the old-age pension'. Gibbs was, in fact, a most respected off-spinner and it was perhaps less than tactful of Fred, in *Ball of Fire*, to comment tartly, 'His wickets cost him more runs than mine. I *took* my wickets; he *bought* his.' This, to some extent, ignores the necessary expertise of the slow bowler, though in terms of sweated labour, one can understand Fred's point of view. It has, however, been less easy to accept the progress made in the 1980s by fast bowlers from various countries. Fred had a high regard for Dennis Lillee's fast bowling, though he has remained unconvinced that any Australian has been better than Ray Lindwall. In Richard Hadlee, particularly during the second half of his outstanding career, I think Fred has seen the bowler he might have become if he had decided to play on for an extra year or two. Fred had the knowledge and the experience to cut down his run, slacken the pace a little and still be an effective practitioner of the art of swing and seam bowling. Whether he had the temperament to do so is another matter. Hadlee is an altogether more phlegmatic character than Fred ever was. To use a card-playing analogy, RJH would be the expert at poker, FST more at home with pontoon or three-card brag.

Botham and Willis are the two Englishmen who have overtaken Fred's 307, and that leaves him resentful – of the greater number of Tests they have been given, and more consistently grouped together, plus (especially in Willis's case) an infinitely less taxing stint of county championship bowling when not engaged in Test cricket. He has groaned aloud in the commentary box at the expense of some of Botham's Test bowling because he (and his contemporaries) know with absolute certainty that no captain under whom Fred played would have permitted anything like the same latitude. It is equally certain that twenty-five years earlier Botham would have not been picked for Test after Test, as he was, irrespective of his figures with bat and ball, not for what he *had* done in the previous half-dozen or even dozen games but for what he *might* do in the next one. Looking at things from that point of view it is entirely possible to understand Fred's resentment, while still wishing he would express it less volubly.

On the other hand, it is undoubtedly true that memory is fallible occasionally and that distance lends enchantment when looking back on career highlights. When Trevor Bailey tells us (and Radio 3 listeners) that someone's batting is inexcusably slow it evokes a hundred thousand smiles amongst those who saw him frustrate so many fielding sides on so many occasions. In Australia more than anywhere else it evokes explosions of: 'My oath, listen to that flyming barnacle talking about *slow* batting.' But Trevor invariably slips in such provocative asides with a twinkle in his eye and his tongue in his cheek. Fred, in contrast, induces near-apoplexy amongst those who batted against him, and those who adjudicated, when he claims never to have bowled deliberately to hurt a batsman and never to have caused an umpire to scurry away in search of proof that he was of genuinely legitimate birth. The difference is that Fred proffers these outrageous propositions with the conviction that he is telling the absolute truth. He now firmly believes that he never set out to make a batsman wince or grimace as a ball trapped his knuckles against the handle or thumped into his rib-cage. Gone are Fred's fondest memories of those grim smiles of satisfaction, unremembered are the threats to 'pin him to t'bloody sight screen', dissolved into the mists of time are those terrible recriminations flung over his shoulder at umpires as he stomped back to his distant mark with hair flopping, sleeve flapping, sweat dripping, dark threats of retribution spilling from his lips. He now believes absolutely that for twenty storm-tossed years he combined the fast-bowling talents of a demon with the manners of Little Lord Fauntleroy, the threat of a ravenous lion with the gentleness of Bambi. He would not be Fred if he didn't; the marvellous contradictions of his character have achieved their full flowering.

What his friends now work so hard to impress upon him is that it is pointless to mourn the lost opportunities, futile to dwell upon hypotheses of what his total of Test wickets might have been if he had played in the number of matches he should have played in. Rather should he reflect, with satisfaction and contentment, on what he did and was.

Could he have possibly contemplated, on that May morning at Fenners, even one tiny part of the life which stretched ahead of him? Could he have imagined that he would dine with princes and potentates, re-write the existing record books, bring thousands of cricket spectators to the edge of their seats and send thousands in his audiences rolling in the aisles? Could the boy on his first trip to

London have foreseen the day when he would jet, first-class, round the world dozens of times and be entertained like visiting royalty when he landed? Could he have envisaged the endless toil it would all entail, or that when most people are thinking of retirement he would be working as hard as ever? And if he had been able to look into the future, would he have wanted to change anything? If, for instance, he could have been a devil on the field and a diplomat off it he would almost certainly have been fast bowling's first knight. But would it have been possible for him to achieve that combination? Probably not. He was a hostile fast bowler with every breath he drew, every threat he uttered, every ball he bowled. He could not compromise. He made enemies at times with almost the same regularity that he took wickets, and those in a position to do so took their revenge – not on the field of play but in the committee rooms and selection sessions. They savaged him and they wounded him. But in the end they never beat him. Frederick Sewards Trueman is still there, his name ranked with the greatest, his striking-rate very nearly the best of all time from the bowlers of all cricket-playing nations.

It is difficult to believe there will ever be another like him, another who at sixty years of age, twenty-two years after retirement as a player, is immediately recognisable by the utterance of the first syllable of his first name: Fred.

Index

A Selected List of Biography Available from Mandarin

☐	7493 0155 4	**Milligan: The Life and Times of Spike Milligan**	Dominic Behan £3.99
☐	7493 0113 9	**Peggy Ashcroft**	Michael Billington £3.99
☐	7493 0093 0	**Agnelli**	Alan Friedman £3.99
☐	7493 9021 2	**Finest Hour**	Martin Gilbert £7.50
☐	7493 9020 4	**The Road to Victory**	Martin Gilbert £7.50
☐	7493 9005 0	**The Orton Diaries**	John Lahr £4.99
☐	7493 0258 5	**What Fresh Hell is This? Biography of Dorothy Parker**	Marion Meade £4.99
☐	413 18060 3	**Vivien: The Life of Vivien Leigh**	Alexander Walker £3.95

All these books are available at your bookshop or newsagent, or can be ordered direct from the publisher. Just tick the titles you want and fill in the form below.

Mandarin Paperbacks, Cash Sales Department, PO Box 11, Falmouth, Cornwall TR10 9EN.

Please send cheque or postal order, no currency, for purchase price quoted and allow the following for postage and packing:

UK	80p for the first book, 20p for each additional book ordered to a maximum charge of £2.00.
BFPO	80p for the first book, 20p for each additional book.
Overseas including Eire	£1.50 for the first book, £1.00 for the second and 30p for each additional book thereafter.

NAME (Block letters) ....

ADDRESS ....

....

....